HANNAH ARENDT
AND THE NEGRO QUESTION

HANNAH ARENDT
AND THE NEGRO QUESTION

Kathryn T. Gines

Indiana University Press

Bloomington and Indianapolis

This book is a publication of

Indiana University Press
Office of Scholarly Publishing
Herman B Wells Library 350
1320 East 10th Street
Bloomington, Indiana 47405 USA

iupress.indiana.edu

Telephone   800-842-6796
Fax   812-855-7931

⊖ The paper used in this publication meets the minimum re-
quirements of the American National Standard for Information
Sciences—Permanence of Paper for Printed Library Materials,
ANSI Z39.48–1992.

Manufactured in the United States of America

Cataloging information is available from the Library of Congress.

ISBN 978-0-253-01167-1 (cloth)
ISBN 978-0-253-01171-8 (paperback)
ISBN 978-0-253-01175-6 (ebook)

1 2 3 4 5 19 18 17 16 15 14

To my mother, Kathleen Smallwood Johnson,
whom I watched go to law school while caring for
six children and four adults. You taught me about
the implications of Supreme Court decisions and
their impact on constructions of race and systems
of racism.

To my partner, Jason, and our children,
Jason II, Kyra, Jaden, and Kalia, for your patience
and support through it all.

And to my dearest "sisters in writing"
for our weekly writing retreats and for the precious
gifts of encouragement and enthusiasm.

What is important for me is to understand. For me, writing is
a matter of seeking this understanding, part of the process of
understanding. . . . Men always want to be terribly influential,
but I see that as somewhat external. . . . I want to understand.
And if others understand—in the sense that I have understood—
that gives me a sense of satisfaction, like feeling at home.

—Hannah Arendt,
interview with Günter Gaus (October 28, 1964)

The very process of opinion formation is determined by those
in whose places somebody thinks and uses his own mind,
and the only condition for this exertion of the imagination
is disinterestedness, the liberation from one's own private
interests. . . . I remain in this world of universal interdependence,
where I can make myself the representative of everybody else.

—Hannah Arendt,
Between Past and Future

Contents

Preface

PHILOSOPHER AND POLITICAL theorist Hannah Arendt is among the most insightful and influential intellectuals of the second half of the twentieth century, and her work remains relevant to the global political landscape of the twenty-first century.[1] The ongoing publication and multiple reprints of Arendt's books attest to the continued importance of her scholarship. Her correspondence with teachers, mentors, and friends has also been collected and published, attracting additional attention. As Arendt's classic writings along with earlier scholarship and personal letters have become increasingly more accessible, her works are being reread and reinterpreted in light of her Jewish identity and what have been described as her Jewish writings. Furthermore, in spite of her distance from feminism, significant feminist interpretations, appropriations, and critiques of Arendt have also brought new perspectives to her work.

One of Arendt's great contributions to philosophical and political thought is her mastery of distinction making. She takes familiar philosophical and political terms (like public/political, private, and social; race thinking and racism; imperialism and colonialism; antisemitism and Jew hatred—all relevant concepts for my project here) and locates them in an unfamiliar historical framework that encourages a different understanding of the concepts in question. Even if the reader ultimately disagrees with or rejects the distinctions drawn by Arendt, as I often do, she still has the opportunity to think with Arendt about these terms and their connections to one another in provocative ways that result in more acuity—as for example when Arendt shows the relationship between imperialism and totalitarianism. Unfortunately, in spite of her insight and influence, Arendt's writings about anti-Black racial oppression (or the Negro question) in particular often reflect poor judgment and profound misunderstandings. In her sincere attempts to critique, confront, and even save the Western philosophical tradition, she too becomes entangled within it. In that regard, Hannah Arendt might be seen as a case study for the limitations of the Western philosophical tradition.

I was introduced to Arendt's scholarship when I read *The Human Condition* in a graduate course titled "Democracy and Difference." After that, I went on to read and analyze numerous essays, from "What Is Authority?" to "Reflections on Little Rock," and several of Arendt's books, from *The Origins of Totalitarianism* to *On Violence*. Although I respect Arendt's brilliant writing style, her insight, her influence, and her mastery of distinction making, I do not see myself and my experiences as a Black woman adequately represented in her writings about the political in general, or anti-Black racial oppression in particular. Consider the following examples.

In *The Human Condition*, Arendt distinguishes between the public and the private realms, stressing that excellence achieved in the public sphere surpasses any achievement possible in private. In reading this, I think about all the forms of excellence that are excluded from this model of measuring achievement. Perhaps this model is not problematic for a white, property-owning male whose women, children, and slaves in the private sphere create the conditions for the possibility of him entering the public sphere (as was the case in the model Arendt describes). However this model, which renders invisible that which is done in private space and celebrates that which is done in public space, poses numerous problems for women and people of color, especially those who are activists and intellectuals. When reading "Reflections on Little Rock," I am shocked, not by Arendt's prioritization of the marriage issue, but rather by her casual relegation of racial discrimination in public education, housing, and employment to social issues. My shock is exacerbated by her suggestion that Black parents who allowed their children to integrate schools were merely seeking upward social mobility. In *The Origins of Totalitarianism*, I am initially impressed at the connections Arendt makes between racism, imperialism, and totalitarianism, only to become outraged at her condescending and stereotypical characterizations of people of African descent. The frustration continues with her very generous recounting of the conditions under which American slavery is preserved with the founding of freedom in *On Revolution*, and then her less open-minded reading of Black student protesters and of Frantz Fanon in *On Violence*.

Although there is no shortage of feminist critiques of Hannah Arendt, I have searched in vain for a comprehensive racial critique of Arendt's major writings since I took that graduate course many years ago. Essays have been published on Arendt's controversial "Reflections on Little Rock" and her portrayals of Africans and African Americans in her other writings. Yet there is still no sustained analysis of Arendt's treatment of the Black experience in the United States and elsewhere. Toni Morrison has noted, "If there's a book you really want to read, but it hasn't been written yet, then you must write it." To this Alice Walker adds, "I write not only what I want to read—understanding fully and indelibly that if I don't do it no one else is so vitally interested, or capable of doing it to my satisfaction—I write the things that *I should have been able to read*."[2] Until now, no book has focused primarily or exclusively on "Hannah Arendt and the Negro question" in the specific contexts of anti-Black racism and civil rights in the United States; the American, French, and Haitian Revolutions and institutionalized slavery; French and British imperialism and colonialism; and racial violence. Following the advice of Morrison and Walker, this is the book about Hannah Arendt that I wanted to read and should have been able to read.

Acknowledgments

Fɪʀsᴛ ᴀɴᴅ ғᴏʀᴇᴍᴏsᴛ, I want to acknowledge and thank my partner, Jason, who made sure that our four beautiful and brilliant children were lovingly engaged so that I could have the space and time to think and write. My heart is also filled with gratitude for the many scholars and friends who offered fruitful feedback and critical commentary at various stages of this book. Robert Bernasconi offered invaluable insight throughout the entire process and reminded me along the way that this book needed to be written and I was the one to write it.

Sara Beardsworth, Mary Beth Mader, and Ronald R. Sundstrom read this work in its earliest stages. Charles S. Johnson, Bill Lawson, Paul C. Taylor, Tommie Shelby, Naomi Zack, Lewis Gordon, Michael Straudigl, and many others offered suggestions at various conferences, including the Gesichter der Gewalt/Faces of Violence Conference in Vienna, Austria; the Global Anti-Black Racism Conference in Paris, France; the Spindel Conference in Memphis, Tennessee; and the Lewis University Philosophy Conference in Romeoville, Illinois. Dan Stone and Richard King provided comments that helped to shape several chapters of the manuscript. I gave talks on Hannah Arendt in the philosophy departments at Morgan State University, De Paul University, and Miami University—all of which brought new perspectives to the project. Gabeba Baderoon, Solsiree del Morale, Shirley Moody Turner, and Leticia Oseguera offered love and encouragement as writing and workout partners. My research assistants Kimberly Harris and Shaeedah Mensah helped with citations and quotations. Dee Mortensen is an amazing editor with an outstanding team at Indiana University Press. Many thanks to all of the eyes and hands that read and touched this manuscript from start to finish.

Portions of chapters 1 and 7 were previously published in "Hannah Arendt, Liberalism, and Racism: Controversies concerning Violence, Segregation, and Education," *Southern Journal of Philosophy* (*Special Issue: Spindel Supplement: Race, Racism, and Liberalism in the 21st Century*) 47(S1) (2009). Portions of chapters 4 and 5 were previously published in "Race Thinking and Racism in Hannah Arendt's *The Origins of Totalitarianism*," in *Hannah Arendt and the Uses of History: Imperialism, Nation, Race, and Genocide*, edited by Dan Stone and Richard King (New York: Berghahn, 2007). Portions of chapter 6 were previously published in "Arendt's Violence/Power Distinction and Sartre's Violence/Counter-Violence Distinction: The Phenomenology of Violence in Colonial and Post-Colonial Contexts," in *Faces of Violence: Explorations and Explications from the Phenomenological Viewpoint*, edited by Michael Straudigl (Leiden, Netherlands: Brill, 2013).

Abbreviations

AB	Arendt to Baldwin, November 21, 1962, Library of Congress, no. 005041, General, 1938–1976, n.d.—"Bac–Barr" miscellaneous—1955–1971, series: Correspondence File, 1938–1976, n.d., box 9
AE	Arendt to Ellison, July 29, 1965, Library of Congress, no. 005820, General, 1938–1976, n.d.—"E" miscellaneous—1963–1975, series: Correspondence File, 1938–1976, n.d., box 10
BPF	*Between Past and Future: Eight Exercises in Political Thought* (New York: Penguin, 1993)
BOT	*The Burden of Our Time* (London: Secker and Warburg, 1951)
CE	"The Crisis in Education," in *BPF*
CR	*Crises of the Republic:* (San Diego, CA: Harcourt Brace, 1972)
EJ	*Eichmann in Jerusalem,* edited by Amos Elon (London: Penguin, 2006)
EJQ	"The Enlightenment and the Jewish Question," in *JW*
EU	*Essays in Understanding, 1930–1954: Formation, Exile, and Totalitarianism,* edited by Jerome Kohn (New York: Schocken, 2005)
HC	*The Human Condition* (Chicago: University of Chicago Press, 1998)
JP	"The Jew as Pariah," in *JW*
JW	*The Jewish Writings,* edited by Jerome Kohn and Ron H. Feldman (New York: Schocken, 2007)
LKPP	*Lectures on Kant's Political Philosophy,* edited by Ronald Beiner (Chicago: University of Chicago Press, 1992)
OA	"Original Assimilation: An Epilogue to the One Hundredth Anniversary of Rahel Varnhagen's Death," in *JW*
OR	*On Revolution* (London: Penguin, 1990)
OT	*The Origins of Totalitarianism* (New York: Harcourt Brace, 1966)
OV	*On Violence,* in *CR*
Pie	Melvin Tumin, "Pie in the Sky," *Dissent* 6(1) (Winter 1959):71
PRB	David Spitz, "Politics and the Realm of Being," *Dissent* 6(1) (Winter 1959)

Reply   "A Reply to Critics," *Dissent* 1(2) (Spring 1959)

RLR   "Reflections on Little Rock," *Dissent* 6(1) (Winter 1959)

RV   *Rahel Varnhagen: The Life of a Jewish Woman,* edited by Liliane Weissberg and translated by Richard Winston and Clara Winston (1957; rpt., Baltimore, MD: Johns Hopkins University Press, 1997)

WIF   "What Is Freedom?," in *BPF*

WR   "We Refugees," in *JW*

HANNAH ARENDT
AND THE NEGRO QUESTION

Introduction

THIS BOOK'S TITLE echoes Richard Bernstein's *Hannah Arendt and the Jewish Question* in which he asserts that the Jewish question and Arendt's wrestling with it left an impression on her thinking and writing.[1] Bernstein's title is quite provocative and he is careful to explain, "'The Jewish question' never referred to a single, well-defined, determinate issue or question. On the contrary, it was used to designate a whole series of shifting, loosely related, historical, cultural, religious, economic, political, and social issues, ranging from what rights were due to the Jews as citizens of nation-states to whether the Jews constituted a distinctive people, race, or nation."[2] The concept of the Jewish question, which is thought to have emerged in the middle of the eighteenth century, has European origins and is connected to naturalization, landholding, and fears of Jewish influence through money and the dissemination of ideas.[3] There are controversies surrounding the phrase, including how it has been used for the purposes of antisemitism and Jew hatred, as well as whether Jews themselves have uncritically accepted it.

My title is also intended as a provocation, using the phrase "the Negro question" to evoke what is alternately referred to as "the Negro problem." The question is enveloped in a myriad of controversies in the Americas, Europe, Africa, and Asia that have resulted in large part from the persistent and, some would say, permanent problem of anti-Black racism coupled with long-standing institutions like slavery and colonialism/imperialism throughout these regions.[4] Like the Jewish question, the Negro question is neither singular nor monolithic, and it too is interwoven with Arendt's thinking about race, slavery, imperialism, totalitarianism, violence, and other dominant themes in her writings.[5]

The purpose of this book is to acknowledge Arendt's keen philosophical and political insights without ignoring or bracketing her problematic assertions, assumptions, and oversights regarding the Negro question. I make the following main arguments: (1) A fundamental flaw in Arendt's orientation toward and claims concerning the Negro question is that she sees the Negro question as a Negro problem rather than a white problem; (2) Arendt's analysis of the Jewish question has implications for her analysis of the Negro question, but Arendt does not readily connect the two; (3) Arendt's commitment to rigidly distinguishing what is properly political from the private and the social influences her analysis of the Negro question in a way that undermines her understanding of and judgments about it. More specifically, Arendt's delineation of the Negro question as a social issue prevents her from recognizing that anti-Black racism (like Jew hatred) is a political phenomenon; (4) Arendt's representational thinking and judgment are flawed and further inhibit her understanding of the Negro question.

"There Isn't Any Negro Problem; There Is Only a White Problem"

The Negro question is multifaceted. Historically, it has been connected to the emergence of racialized slavery with the transatlantic slave trade and the ensuing debates about abolition and emancipation; the development of race hierarchies and scientific racism used to establish the inferiority of Blacks; contentions about segregation versus integration; efforts at gaining civil and political rights; and debates about full citizenship. It has also entailed questions about access to public transportation, lodging, education, employment, the court system, and political office. A shortcoming in Arendt's approach to analyzing and interpreting the Negro question is that she sees the Negro question as a Negro problem rather than as a white problem. Unlike Richard Wright—who when asked by a French reporter about the Negro problem in the 1940s responded, "There isn't any Negro problem; there is only a white problem"—Arendt consistently frames the Negro *question* as a Negro *problem*.[6]

The "Negro question" and the "Negro problem" are phrases that have often been used interchangeably. The Negro question as it pertains to slavery, segregation, colonialism/imperialism, citizenship, equal rights, and so on (or to anti-Black racial oppression more generally, and the means available to identify, confront, and overcome that oppression) has frequently been referred to and thought of as a Negro problem. The use of "problem" here can be interpreted in two ways. First, Black people are being conceptualized as the problem. That is, we pose a problem or a burden for whites—and even for ourselves. Or, second, anti-Black racism is basically Black people's problem. That is, anti-Black racism is a problem that concerns only Black people and not whites or others. What I find appealing about Wright's reply to the French reporter is that he articulates both a paradigmatic and an epistemological shift. THERE ISN'T ANY NEGRO PROBLEM; THERE IS ONLY A WHITE PROBLEM. This claim goes against the two interpretations of the "Negro problem" just offered. It negates the conceptualization of Black people as a problem *and* the notion that anti-Black racism is Black people's problem. Wright does this while simultaneously situating white people—or, more specifically, white people's anti-Black racism—as the problem.

Although Arendt describes her writing as a process of seeking understanding (*EU* 3), her writings about the Negro question frequently reveal a failure to understand that what she judges to be a Negro problem is actually a white problem. The problem of anti-Black racism in its social, political, and even psychological manifestations and consequences is fundamentally a white problem. However, since Arendt does not adopt this framework, for her the problem in Little Rock has to do with the Black parents who put their children in harm's way, not with the white parents and politicians exerting the harm ("Reflections on Little Rock"). The problem with integrating schools and neighborhoods is that Black students cause the schools to break down and that the very presence of Black families turns previously good—code for white—neighborhoods into slums ("Crisis in Education"). The problem with protesting on college campuses has to do with violent, irrational, and unqualified Black students, not with the systematic racism in higher education against which these students are protesting (*On Violence*). The problem with violence is not the original or constitutive violence of America's founding fathers and Europe's imperialists, but rather the anticolonial violence and resistance of the colonized in Africa (*On Revolution, The Origins of Totalitarianism, On Violence*).

One might contend that as a German Jewish intellectual and an immigrant to the United States, Arendt should not be expected to have the insight of a Black American intellectual like Wright who is well versed in the anti-Black racism precipitated by the white problem. But this line of thinking would not account for the insights of other European intellectuals (e.g., Gunnar Myrdal from Sweden or Alfred Schutz, who immigrated to the United States after he fled to France from the Austrian *Anschluss*) newly introduced to the U.S. brand of anti-Black racism. It is worth noting that like Wright, Myrdal identifies the Negro problem as a white problem in his encyclopedic study *An American Dilemma: The Negro Problem and Modern Democracy* (1944). Myrdal asserts, "We have been brought to view the caste order as fundamentally a system of disabilities forced by whites upon the Negroes, and our discussion of the Negro problem up to this point has, therefore, been mainly a study of whites' attitudes and behavior. . . . *The Negro problem is primarily a white man's problem.*"[7] Schutz takes up Myrdal's analysis in the essay "Equality and the Meaning of the Structure of the World," where he also examines the white problem.[8]

The notion that Arendt was not in a position to know better also does not take into consideration the opportunities Arendt had to engage with Black intellectuals about the Negro question. Arendt interacted with Richard Wright, James Baldwin, and Ralph Ellison, with seemingly little impact on her judgments concerning the Negro question. For example, Arendt and Paul Tillich were introduced to Wright at the home of Dorothy Norman during his first visit to France in early 1946.[9] Furthermore, Arendt wrote to both Baldwin and Ellison about the Negro question in response to their writings and interviews on the topic.

Arendt reads, but does not sufficiently engage, the multilayered arguments concerning the white problem in Baldwin's "Letter from a Region in My Mind," which was first published in the *New Yorker* on November 17, 1962.[10] This piece was published again as "Down at the Cross: Letter from a Region in My Mind" in *The Fire Next Time* (1963).[11] We know that Arendt read the article in the *New*

Yorker because she sent Baldwin a personal letter (dated November 21, 1962) referencing and responding to it. Her acquaintance with Baldwin is highlighted in the closing line: "In sincere admiration, cordially (that is, in case you remember that we know each other slightly) yours, Hannah Arendt" (AB).

In her letter to Baldwin Arendt describes the publication of his article as "a political event of a very high order" that impacted her "understanding of what is involved in the Negro question" (AB). She adds, "Since this is a question which concerns us all, I feel I am entitled to raise objections" (AB). Her objections pertain to Baldwin's discussion of love. Arendt says that she is "frightened" by the "gospel of love" he offers because love is a stranger in politics, and the intrusion of love into politics results in hypocrisy. Arendt claims that Baldwin's article is an event in her understanding of the Negro question only to add that she is "entitled" to raise objections to the article (since the Negro question "concerns us all"), and then she neglects to engage Baldwin on his own terms. Far from articulating exactly how Baldwin's article has helped her to understand the Negro question differently, Arendt largely ignores the terms of the question as outlined in the very article to which she is objecting.

Baldwin's reflections can hardly be reduced to a "gospel of love" (or hatred). He speaks at length about Christianity, his own conversion and salvation experience, as well as his disillusionment with religion in the first part of the essay. Baldwin does mention love intermittently throughout the piece, noting for example, "I do not know many Negroes who are eager to be 'accepted' by white people, still less to be loved by them."[12] He also speaks about hatred, namely how difficult it is to be Black in an anti-Black environment and the spiritual resilience required *not* to hate (or to teach one's child not to hate) under such overwhelming conditions.[13] But his general argument is not about bringing love or hatred into politics. Rather, Baldwin is articulating the specificity of being Black in the American context—the violence of everyday life, police brutality, unequal power relations, and the advantages of rejecting the myth of whiteness.[14]

Arendt fails to respond to Baldwin's in-depth examination of white power and his emphasis on political freedom for Blacks. He writes pointedly about the white problem, "White people in this country have quite enough to do in learning how to accept and love themselves and each other, and when they have achieved this—which will not be tomorrow and may very well be never—the Negro problem will no longer exist, for it will no longer be needed."[15] He continues, "White Americans find it as difficult as white people elsewhere to divest themselves of the notion that they are in possession of some intrinsic value that black people need, or want. And this assumption—which, for example, makes the solution to the Negro problem depend on the speed with which Negroes accept and adopt white standards—is revealed in all kinds of striking ways."[16] Baldwin disrupts the common framing of so-called race relations as improving either when white people are

able to "accept" and "tolerate" people of color, or when people of color have sufficiently assimilated to the myth of whiteness. He also negates the prevalent notion that people of color have a pathological aspiration to white values and standards.

The tone of Arendt's letter to Baldwin is consistent with what Ralph Ellison
negatively describes as "the Olympian authority that characterized Hannah Arendt's
'Reflections on Little Rock' in the winter 1959 *Dissent* (a dark foreshadowing of
the Eichmann blowup)."[17] Arendt commits an error that is common among those
with white privilege, namely, recentering whiteness as a source of entitlement and
a position from which one can raise objections—all the while erasing whiteness
as a source of the very problem in question. With a paternalistic pen, Arendt con-
gratulates Baldwin for being published in the *New Yorker* (would she also describe
her publications in the *New Yorker* as "political events"?), only to assert that he
does not understand politics. Arendt rejects Baldwin's analysis but expects him to
acknowledge her entitlement to reframe the debate on her own terms. The letter
is also an example of Arendt imposing her theoretical framework for the public-
private distinction and what is to be included or excluded from each realm.

Arendt's resistance to love and politics along with her analysis of the public
and private spheres are articulated together in *The Human Condition*. There she
asserts that the public realm is the realm of appearances where "the presence of
others who see what we see and hear what we hear assures us of the reality of the
world and ourselves" (*HC* 50). The public realm is the world itself, what is common to us all—unlike our privately owned place in the world (52). Accordingly,
the public realm can only tolerate what is relevant and worthy of being seen and
heard. Love is relevant, but it should not be seen or heard in public and it can
only survive in the private realm. Arendt states, "For instance, love, in distinction
from friendship, is killed, or rather extinguished, the moment it is displayed in
public" (51).[18] She continues, "Because of its inherent worldlessness, love can only
become false and perverted when it is used for political purposes such as change
or salvation of the world" (52).

Later, in her discussion of forgiveness and love, Arendt asserts, "Love, by its
very nature, is unworldly, and it is for this reason rather than its rarity that it is
not only apolitical but antipolitical, perhaps the most powerful of all antipolitical
human forces" (*HC* 242).[19] Arendt is consistent on this point; in her letter to Baldwin she asserts, "Hatred and love belong together, and they are both destructive;
you can afford them only in the private and, as a people, only so long as you are
not free" (AB).[20] Love has no place in politics. Love and hatred belong together,
but only in the private realm.

Given the disconnect between Baldwin's essay and Arendt's reply, we might
ask: where is the seeking of understanding in this corrective to Baldwin's "preaching"? Arendt's commitment to a particular vision of the public realm leads her to

reject love as intolerable, apolitical, and even antipolitical—a perverted way to attempt to change the world. This is just one of many instances in which Arendt's seeking of understanding in her writing reads like an external framework imposed on a problem by someone with white biases. To be fair, in her letter to Baldwin Arendt does, perhaps for the first time, offer an explicit connection between the Negro and the pariah, noting, "All of the characteristics that you stress in the Negro people: their beauty, their capacity for joy, their warmth, and their humanity, are well-known characteristics of all oppressed people. They grow out of suffering and they are the proudest possession of all pariahs" (AB). But she ignores Baldwin's overall thesis. She misses the point that the Negro question is tied to the white problem. Not only does this approach equate the Negro question with a Negro problem, but this perspective also negates the agency of Blacks as intellectuals and political subjects grappling with the white problem.

In addition to Wright and Baldwin, Arendt also had interactions with Ralph Ellison. According to Elisabeth Young-Bruehl, "One evening in October 1968 she and other editorial board members of the *American Scholar* listened, stunned, to two hours of Ralph Ellison's anger. . . . Ellison had taken exception to an editorial decision, claiming that an article should have been shown to him before it was published."[21] But Arendt became acquainted with Ellison long before this incident, when he offered a strong critique of her "Reflections on Little Rock." While I have not found any reply from Arendt to Ellison's aforementioned reference to her "Olympian authority" in "The World and the Jug," she does reply to the more nuanced critique he offered in a later interview.

Arendt read Ellison's interview with Robert Penn Warren (published in 1965 in *Who Speaks for the Negro?*) in which he elucidates where Arendt goes wrong in "Reflections on Little Rock."[22] In a letter, Arendt concedes to Ellison, "your remarks seem to me so entirely right, that I now see that I simply didn't understand the complexities of the situation" (AE). But Arendt's concession does not prevent a repetition of her error in judgment in "Crisis in Education" and *On Violence*. Although Arendt's correspondence with Baldwin and Ellison have different tones (she is offering a corrective to Baldwin, but acknowledges that Ellison is right), both examples point to the different situated knowledge of Baldwin and Ellison compared to Arendt. They have different knowledge concerning the Negro question and profoundly different perspectives. Ellison's interview and Arendt's responding letter will be examined in more detail in chapter 1.

The Jewish Question Revisited: From Abstract Humanism and Assimilationism to the Parvenu and the Pariah

On November 14, 1941, in "The Jewish Army—The Beginning of Jewish Politics?," Arendt writes, "One truth that is unfamiliar to the Jewish people, though they are beginning to learn it, is that *you can only defend yourself as the person you are at-*

tacked as. A person attacked as a Jew cannot defend himself as an Englishman or Frenchman. The world would only conclude that he is simply not defending himself."[23] Over twenty years later, in a 1964 interview in Germany, Arendt states, "If one is attacked as a Jew, one must defend oneself as a Jew. Not as a German, not as a world citizen, not as an upholder of the Rights of Man, or whatever" (*EU* 12). The claim that Jews must defend themselves as Jews seems to be motivated by at least two factors: Arendt's doubtfulness about abstract humanism in formulations such as the rights of man; and her critique of assimilationism. These quotations might be read as a rejection of the demand to assimilate or adjust to the dominant oppressive system in its social and political manifestations. I underscore Arendt's suspicion of humanism, her anti-assimilationism, the distinctions she draws between the parvenu and the pariah, and the corresponding differentiation between the social and the political as themes that we find in the so-called Jewish writings in an effort to analyze how her positions sometimes seem to shift when she moves from the Jewish question to the Negro question.

Arendt's "We Refugees" highlights the challenges of being a displaced and stateless Jewish refugee with no legal status, rights, or protection. She correlates being Jewish with being merely human, stating, "If we should start telling the truth that we are nothing but Jews, it would mean that we expose ourselves to the fate of being human beings who, unprotected by any specific laws or convention, are nothing but human beings" (WR 272–273). While some might embrace being acknowledged as at least human (many groups, particularly members of the African diaspora, have been denied even their bare humanity), Arendt warns of the perils of being nothing but human: "I can hardly imagine an attitude more dangerous, since we live in a world in which human beings as such have ceased to exist for quite a while; since society has discovered discrimination as the great social weapon by which one may kill without any bloodshed" (273). Arendt continues to develop this idea of the abstract nakedness of humanity and what she calls "The Perplexities of the Rights of Man" in *The Origins of Totalitarianism*.

Richard Bernstein describes Arendt as deeply skeptical of "the type of abstract humanism and defense of abstract rights which claimed that all human beings possess inalienable rights even outside a viable political community."[24] He elaborates, "The dark underside of the Enlightenment conception of a human being as someone who possesses rights simply by virtue of being an 'abstract human being' is to leave human beings completely defenseless and powerless in the face of totalitarian terror."[25] Of course, Arendt is not the only skeptic. For another critique of the emptiness of humanism, we can turn to Aimé Césaire's *Discourse on Colonialism* (1955). Césaire offers the following indictment against what he calls "pseudo-humanism": "For too long humanism has diminished the rights of man, its concept of those rights has been—and still is—narrow and fragmentary, incomplete, biased . . . and sordidly racist."[26]

For Arendt, the Enlightenment is not only associated with abstract humanism as noted by Bernstein, but also with assimilationism. Arendt situates the Jewish question as beginning in the age of the Enlightenment, a time (one of many) during which Jews were pressured to assimilate. She posits, "The modern Jewish Question dates from the Enlightenment; it was the Enlightenment—that is, the non-Jewish world—that posed it. Its formulations and its answers have defined the behavior and assimilation of Jews" (EJQ 3). For Arendt, "Assimilation always meant assimilation to the Enlightenment" (OA 22). She continues, "Enlightenment promised the Jews emancipation and above all provided them with arguments for demanding equal human rights, hence almost all of them became Enlightenment advocates. But the *problem* of Jewish assimilation begins only *after* [the] Enlightenment" (OA 22–23, emphasis in original).

Given the connection Arendt makes between the Jewish question, assimilation, and the Enlightenment, it is not surprising that Arendt's attitude in these essays seems staunchly anti-assimilationist. She seems disappointed with Jews who seek to deny their Jewish identity, separate from other Jewish people, and assimilate into society. The price of assimilation is too high and in the end it offers no guarantees of protection against antisemitism. One of the ironies of assimilation is that the more a Jew attempts to deny her Jewishness, the more firmly her Jewishness is externally confirmed (or overdetermined from the outside). That is to say, the attempted assimilation of Jews and their emphatic denial of this aspect of their identity become a kind of social marker of their being Jewish.

In "We Refugees" Arendt explains how in their attempts to adjust and assimilate to a new environment after being displaced, Jewish refugees do not mingle with the already present native Jewish society. This behavior of avoiding native Jews in a country in which one is a Jewish immigrant or newcomer is rooted in unwritten and never publicly spoken social laws backed by public opinion (WR 271). "Whatever we do, whatever we pretend to be, we reveal nothing but our insane desire to be changed, not to be Jews" (ibid.). But the desired benefits, real or imagined, of assimilation remain elusive. Arendt warns, "We don't succeed and we can't succeed; under the cover of our 'optimism' you can easily detect the hopeless sadness of assimilationists" (272). The assimilated Jews worked at "proving all the time their non-Jewishness" and yet "they succeeded in remaining Jews all the same" (273).

Arendt describes the pressure to assimilate as a social pressure with political implications: "Man is a social animal and life is not easy for him when social ties are cut off. Moral standards are much easier kept in the texture of a society. Very few individuals have the strength to conserve their own integrity if their social, political, and legal status is completely confused" (WR 271). Rather than fighting to make changes in their social or legal status, Arendt explains, "we decided instead, so many of us, to try a change in identity" (ibid.). She laments, "It is true that most of us depend entirely on social standards; we lose confidence in our-selves if society does not approve us; we are—and always were—ready to pay any price in order to be accepted by society" (273). Thus, assimilation also has per-sonal and psychological consequences. Bernstein notes that for Arendt, in the German Jewish context, "assimilation was aggressively active, requiring the sac-rifice of 'every natural impulse' and the suppression of passion."[27] Arendt even goes so far as to describe assimilation, especially when examined in relationship to the Jewish parvenu, as a form of self-annihilation (RV 186).

According to Bernstein, the parvenu "desperately seeks to escape his pariah status and to be accepted by, and assimilated to, a society that treats the Jew as an outcast."[28] In *Rahel Varnhagen*, Arendt describes the parvenu as one who uses fraud for social gains: "This fraud . . . is of the greatest value for social success and positions in society" (RV 237). Arendt explains, "Nineteenth-century Jews, if they wanted to play a part in society, had no choice but to become parvenus par excel-lence, and certainly in those decades of reaction they were the choicest examples of parvenus" (238–239). The parvenu is aware of her pariah status and seeks to es-cape it through assimilation into a society that will never fully embrace or accept her. She is constantly conscious of her Jewishness even in her attempted abandon-ment of her Jewish identity. The parvenu is also always conscious of the expec-tations of society, and she tries desperately to meet these expectations, to make their desires her desires.[29] The deceptive, self-annihilating life of the parvenu—who sacrifices everything for social acceptance, and in the end gains nothing—is contrasted with the pariah, who is characterized by Arendt as free.

The pariah is a social outcast, but the conscious pariah accepts this outcast status and uses it to her advantage. In "The Jew as Pariah," Arendt expounds on this point: "the status of the Jews in Europe has been not only that of an oppressed people but also of what Max Weber has called a 'pariah people'" (JP 276). Arendt describes the pariahs as the social outcasts, the Jewish poets, writers, and artists who "out of their personal experiences . . . have been able to evolve the concept of pariah as a human type" (ibid.).[30] Looking to the work of Heinrich Heine, she as-sociates with this pariah group the common people, social ostracism, the songs of the oppressed, and those who seek refuge in nature (278–279).[31] Unlike the par-venu, the pariah rebels against society rather than assimilating to society. The pa-riah is "outside of the real world and attacks it from without" (280).

I present Arendt's analysis of the parvenu and pariah in what have been iden-tified as her Jewish writings because it has implications for some of her conten-tions concerning the Negro question. For example, in "Reflections on Little Rock" when Arendt presents Black parents as social climbers, we might hear echoes of her account of assimilating parvenus and ask why she chooses to portray Black par-ents as parvenus rather than as conscious pariahs. Elisabeth Young-Bruehl men-tions that these categories "though never mentioned, governed her approach" in the Little Rock essay.[32] Young-Bruehl also asserts, "Arendt saw in black people's struggles for integration all the dilemmas of Jewish assimilation."[33]

Limitations of Arendt's Conception of the Political

While the case can be made that the dominant concepts and terms in Arendt's classic writings are already being gestured at in her earlier Jewish writings, there is also a disruption between the concreteness (and the more radical tone) of the Jewish writings and the abstractness (and perhaps more conservative tone) that permeates the later political writings. Analyzing these writings side by side, there are clear connections between them, but there are also glaring disjunctions. As she moves away from the Jewish question and toward the question of the political in general (and the problem of anti-Black racism in particular) there are some incongruities.

Arendt's analysis contrasting the social parvenu with the political pariah foreshadows the distinction between the social and the political that she develops in more detail in her other writings. Bernstein notes that this parvenu-pariah distinction "is intimately intertwined with Arendt's first gropings toward formulating the distinction between society and politics—or 'the social' and 'the political' as she later describes it."[34] And Hanna Pitkin agrees, stating that *Rahel Varnhagen* "already contains, in embryonic form, what will become the basic distinction of *The Human Condition,* that between the social and free political action."[35] In *The Human Condition,* Hannah Arendt presents a notion of the political that relies heavily on the public-private distinction and a strong critique of the rise of the social, which she asserts has distorted this distinction. The impact of the rise of the social on the separation of public and private space is a central aspect of Arendt's project, not only in *The Human Condition,* but also before that in *The Origins of Totalitarianism* and afterward in *Between Past and Future* and *On Revolution.* This perspective also informs her problematic analysis of anti-Black racial discrimination in "Reflections on Little Rock" and *On Violence.*

Given Arendt's notoriety for maintaining a rigid division between what is properly political and that which is merely social or private, we should not take it lightly when she discloses that in 1933 "belonging to Judaism had become my own problem, and my own problem was political. Purely political!" (*EU* 12). Arendt lays claim here to an aspect of her identity (her Jewishness) that she is expected to deny, renounce, or ignore altogether. Furthermore, she insists that her problem, the problem of belonging to Judaism (which entails antisemitism, Jew hatred, statelessness, a lack of rights, and so on), is political. It is not social, not private, not personal, not emotional, not a figment of her imagination. It is purely political.

Arendt does not elaborate on why her problem is purely political. What qualifies belonging to Judaism as a political problem? I ask this question not to deny or undermine her claim that it is in fact a political problem, but rather to call into question how she constructs and applies the criteria for what constitutes a political problem. Her exclamation is made in a 1964 interview, after the publication of *The Origins of Totalitarianism, The Human Condition, Between Past and Future, On Revolution,* and "Reflections on Little Rock"—all writings in which she argues for a clear division between the political, the private, and the social. And the claim is made about her experience of belonging to Judaism in 1933, before the publication of these same texts.

To what can we attribute this apparent disconnect between her 1933 experience, the publication of her classic political writings, and her assertion in 1964 that her problem was purely political? If Judaism and the Jewish question are political problems, can we conclude that the Negro question and anti-Black racism are also political problems? And if they are not, is Arendt being inconsistent? Arendt's attitudes and ideals about politics and what counts as political in the explicitly Jewish context are not always consonant with her broader theoretical framework concerning what is political, especially when it comes to Africans and African Americans. Arendt frames the Jewish question as a political question, yet she frames the Negro question (for her, a Negro problem and not a white problem) as a social question.

Understanding and Judging

In addition to the political, the private, and the social, two additional concepts that permeate Hannah Arendt's writings are understanding and judging. Arendt explains that it is more important for her to understand than to be influential: "For me, writing is a matter of seeking this understanding, part of the process of understanding. . . . I want to understand. And if others understand—in the sense that I have understood—that gives me a sense of satisfaction, like feeling at home" (*EU* 3). If understanding is more internal for Arendt, we might describe judging as a more external process. She presents judging in terms of representative thinking, enlarged mentality, and disinterestedness. Arendt claims, "The more people's standpoints I have present in my mind while I am pondering a given issue, and the better I can imagine how I would feel and think if I were in their place, the stronger will be my capacity for representative thinking and the more valid my final conclusions, my opinion" (*BPF* 241–242). According to Arendt, this description captures what she calls the enlarged capacity that enables people to judge and form opinions. Arendt continues, "The only condition for this exertion of the imagination is disinterestedness, the liberation from one's own private interests" (ibid.).

The significance of these two concepts (understanding and judging) in her work is signaled in the titles of edited collections of her essays, such as *Essays in Understanding: 1930–1954* (2005) and *Responsibility and Judgment* (2003). I am interested in how these two ideas function as motivations for her thinking and writing about the Negro question. Arendt claims disinterestedness and representational thinking in formulating her opinions, but her positions are frequently partial and her strongly articulated judgments too often represent the oppressors and not the oppressed. Arendt's "sense of satisfaction" and "feeling at home" juxtaposed with her "representative thinking" and "disinterestedness" concerning anti-Black racism leave many readers disappointed with her analyses and conclusions. This disappointment is not about Arendt's lack of tact or what might be considered political incorrectness, but rather about her failure to utilize some of the tools at her disposal (not only her ideas, but also her lived experience). Arendt claims to have sympathy for "the Negroes" and other oppressed groups, but whether the problem is slavery, integration, higher education, imperialism, or violent resistance—her arguments and theoretical framework reveal that her sympathies are elsewhere. Despite Arendt's critiques of the Western philosophical tradition, in the end her sympathies are with that tradition in spite of all of its hierarchies and inadequacies.

Overview of the Chapters

The first three chapters of this book focus primarily on the short but exceedingly controversial essay "Reflections on Little Rock." Chapter 1, "The Girl, Obviously, Was Asked to Be a Hero," takes as its focal point Arendt's errors and assumptions about the photo that she asserts prompted her to write her reflections. I argue that Arendt wrongly frames the desegregation crisis in public education as a Negro problem rather than as a white problem, and she assumes that the Black parents who allowed their children to integrate previously all-white schools were motivated by the prospects of upward social mobility (like the parvenu). Arendt does not consider the possibility that these parents, who were exercising their legally gained rights to equal educational opportunities for their children, could be rebelling against their outsider status (like the conscious pariah). Chapter 2, "The Most Outrageous Law of Southern States—the Law Which Makes Mixed Marriage a Criminal Offense," explores the close relationship between segregation laws in education and mixed-marriage laws. I argue that the case Arendt makes against miscegenation laws is also applicable to the discrimination laws in education that she defends. Chapter 3, "The Three Realms of Human Life: The Political, the Social, and the Private," examines how Arendt's three categories are operating in the Little Rock essay and *The Human Condition*. Contra Elisabeth Young-Bruehl, I argue that Arendt's theoretical framework itself is the issue, not the lack of space in the Little Rock essay to make these distinctions and their complex histories clear.

I shift away from the Little Rock essay to *On Revolution* in chapter 4, "The End of Revolution Is the Foundation of Freedom," where I examine Arendt's analysis of the American and French Revolutions. I highlight the relationship between institutionalized slavery and the foundation of freedom in Arendt's analysis of the American Revolution. Additionally, I examine her critique of the social question in the French Revolution and the issue of slavery in the French and Haitian

Revolutions, which is ignored by Arendt. Chapter 5, "A Preparatory Stage for the Coming Catastrophes," focuses on Arendt's analysis of race thinking, racism, and imperialism. I argue that the groundwork for race thinking and racism was laid before the age of imperialism as she describes it. Furthermore, although Arendt attempts to take a position against racism, there are elements of racism in her analysis and in her descriptions of persons of African descent.

Next, I explore the unbalanced response to violence in several of Arendt's writings. In chapter 6, "Only Violence and Rule over Others Could Make Some Men Free," I begin with an analysis of the theme of violence in the political realm as presented by Arendt in *The Human Condition* and *On Revolution*. I argue that while Arendt is uncritical of violence there, in other writings she gives a sharp criticism of violence and those she labels as violent. I show how Arendt's representation and critiques of Sartre and Fanon in *On Violence* are inaccurate. Using the analyses of Sartre and Fanon, I take the position that revolutionary violence is a legitimate and justified component of the decolonization process. In chapter 7, "A Much Greater Threat to Our Institutions of Higher Learning than the Student Riots," I examine Arendt's discussion of the Black Power movement and student protests at colleges and universities. I argue that Arendt's understanding of the Negro question in the ten years between "Reflections on Little Rock" and *On Violence* did not improve and in fact worsened, as evidenced by her blanket description of Black students as academically unqualified to attend institutions of higher learning and her claims that they sought to lower academic standards through violence and threats of violence. The conclusion, "The Role of Judgment in Arendt's Approach to the Negro Question" provides an overview of the theme of the Negro question as taken up by Arendt in the various contexts already discussed with special attention to Arendt's conceptualization of judgment. I argue that rather than enlarging her understanding, Arendt's concept of judgment, which she derives from Kant, actually inhibits her understanding of the Negro question.[36]

A Note on Language

Throughout this book I capitalize the terms "Negro" and "Jew." I capitalize "Black" and "Blackness," and I use Black rather than African American in many cases because it is a more inclusive term. I keep "white" in lowercase as an intended disruption of the norm (i.e., the convention of either capitalizing or lowercasing both terms). Additionally, I hyphenate anti-Black racism, keeping Black capitalized. But I do not hyphenate or capitalize antisemitism, following Arendt in some cases and also Schmuel Almog's "What's in a Hyphen?," *SICSA Report: Newsletter of the Vidal Sassoon International Center for the Study of Antisemitism* (Summer 1989). These preferences are applied throughout the text, but not to direct quotations from other works.

1 "The Girl, Obviously, Was Asked to Be a Hero"

THE OPENING LINES of Hannah Arendt's "Reflections on Little Rock" essay read: "It is unfortunate and even unjust (though hardly unjustified) that the events at Little Rock should have such an enormous echo in public opinion throughout the world" (RLR 46). Arendt goes on to situate these events *inside* the context of American slave history and *outside* the world politics of imperialism and colonialism. In her view, the one great crime that created a color problem in America was slavery, while the color problem in Europe was created by colonialism and imperialism.[1] She asserts, "The country's attitude toward the Negro population is rooted in American tradition and nothing else. The color question was created by the one great crime of American history and is soluble only within the political and historical framework of the Republic" (ibid.). It is fascinating to see Arendt casually describe discrimination toward African Americans here as an attitude rooted in tradition. But even more interesting is her acknowledgment that the color question was created by slavery and requires a solution within the political and historical framework of the United States. This suggests that a political solution is needed.

Despite opening the essay with the weight of the historical realities of slavery, race, racism, and the political consequences of these realities in the U.S. context, Arendt does not situate and analyze the color question in a "political and historical framework." She chooses instead to characterize segregation, especially in education, as a social issue. Arendt presents the desegregation crisis in public education as a Negro problem (namely, a problem of Black parents seeking upward social mobility, like parvenus) rather than a white problem (specifically, the problem of white supremacy and anti-Black racism in the form of legally sanctioned racial segregation).

The Publication of "Reflections on Little Rock"

Written for *Commentary* in 1957, Hannah Arendt's "Reflections on Little Rock" was steeped in controversy from the very beginning. Arendt explains that this essay did not get published at that time because her contentious viewpoint "was at variance with the magazine's stand on matters of discrimination and segregation" (RLR 45).[2] The gossip and consternation swirling around Arendt's "Reflections on Little Rock" cannot be overstated. According to Norman Podhoretz,

Arendt's essay was deemed so controversial that *Commentary* did not want to publish it. The editors eventually offered a compromise that *Commentary* would publish her piece alongside a reply by Sidney Hook in the same issue. This was not typical, since replies were usually published in the issue that followed the essay of interest. After several delays, which in Arendt's estimation allowed the proliferation of rumors about her position before it was even published, Arendt withdrew her article from *Commentary*.

Both Hook and Arendt published their essays elsewhere. Hook published his in the *New Leader* (April 21, 1958) under the title "Democracy and Desegregation." Arendt's somewhat tendentious reflections did not appear in print until 1959, when she agreed to allow *Dissent* to publish the original essay without revisions. Arendt explains that she did so in an effort to challenge "the routine repetition of liberal *clichés* [which] may be even more dangerous" than she initially thought (RLR 45). But Arendt's often contested stance in "Reflections on Little Rock" proves to be as pernicious, if not more so, than the liberal clichés against which she wants to position herself. In addition to the "Preliminary Remarks" and the original essay, *Dissent* also included two critical replies to "Reflections" in the same issue. Arendt's reply to her critics was published separately in a later issue of the magazine along with an angry letter from Hook, critiquing Arendt again, and a fiery response to Hook from Arendt.

"If You Look at the Picture the Right Way, You See What I See"

In "A Reply to Critics,"[3] Arendt explains that a newspaper photograph of a "Negro girl" persecuted by white children while attempting to integrate a school prompted the writing of "Reflections on Little Rock." She adds that her reflections unfolded around three questions: "What would I do if I were a Negro mother?," "What would I do if I were a white mother in the South?," and "What exactly distinguished the so-called Southern way of life from the American way of life with respect to the color question?" (Reply 179–181). When "Reflections on Little Rock" is read together with the "Preliminary Remarks" added to the original essay and her later "A Reply to Critics," we find Arendt making several errors in judgment, coupled with factual errors. All of these mistakes have implications beyond the Little Rock crisis in particular and the intervention of the federal government in public school integration at the local level more generally.

Let us begin with Arendt's errors and assumptions about the photograph that is a primary point of interest in "Reflections." Arendt describes it in the following way: "I think no one will find it easy to forget the photograph reproduced in newspapers and magazines throughout the country, showing a Negro girl, accompanied by a white friend of her father, walking away from school, persecuted and followed into bodily proximity by a jeering and grimacing mob of youngsters. The girl, obviously, was asked to be a hero—that is something neither her absent father nor the equally absent representatives of the NAACP felt called upon to be" (RLR 50). But Arendt is mistaken about the image, the friend, the father, and the NAACP representatives. Her point of departure for seeking to understand the situation is already steeped in multiple misunderstandings.

Danielle S. Allen notes in *Talking to Strangers: Anxieties of Citizenship since Brown v. Board of Education* that Arendt is referring to a front-page photograph in the *New York Times* on September 5, 1957.[4] The newspaper's front page on this date actually features two photographs pertaining to school desegregation. Each photograph includes a fifteen-year-old Black female student, and the young ladies are wearing similarly patterned dresses. The top image depicts the National Guard creating a barrier preventing Elizabeth Eckford from gaining access to Central High School in Little Rock, Arkansas, while a white female student is allowed to bypass the barrier.[5] The bottom image shows Dorothy Counts and Dr. Edwin Thompkins surrounded by "jeering" white students while walking toward (not away from) Harding High School in Charlotte, North Carolina.[6] Arendt mistakenly describes the photo of Counts in Charlotte rather than the one of Eckford in Little Rock. And her interpretation of the photograph and assessment of the scene are wrong in both cases.

Elizabeth Eckford, arriving at Central High School, initially thought that the National Guard was there to protect her. Eckford soon realized the soldiers were there (under orders from Arkansas governor Orval E. Faubus) to keep her out of the school rather than to protect her from the crowd. Unfortunately, Eckford did confront the angry, white, racist mob on her own in Little Rock. But this was due to a breakdown in communication, not neglect on the part of her parents or the NAACP, as suggested by Arendt. It should be stressed that NAACP representatives and the parents of the Little Rock Nine wanted to accompany their children to Central High School, but were explicitly instructed not to do so by Little Rock's school superintendent, Virgil Blossom.[7] Blossom's rationale was that "if violence breaks out . . . it will be easier to protect the children if the adults aren't there."[8] In spite of Blossom's instructions, Daisy Bates, the president of the NAACP in the state of Arkansas, wanted some adult protection for the children. Bates asked a white minister, Rev. Dunbar Ogden, if he and other ministers would accompany the children and thereby prevent an attack from the expected angry white mob. Ogden told Bates that the white ministers were hesitant to do this. But Ogden and his twenty-one-year-old son, David, along with one other white minister (Rev. Will Campbell) and two Black ministers (Rev. Z. Z. Driver and Rev. Harry Bass) agreed to accompany the students.[9]

With this arrangement in place, the students were advised of a new plan to meet at a designated location before going together to the school by a late-night phone call from Bates. But Elizabeth Eckford and her parents were not aware of the change in plans because they did not have a telephone. This unfortunate break-

down in communication led to Eckford's fate: facing alone a racist white mob calling for her to be lynched, on one side, and National Guards pointing bayonets at
her as she attempted to enter the school, on the other. Eckford later told Bates,
"Somebody started yelling, 'Lynch her! Lynch her!' . . . They came closer, shout-
ing, 'No nigger bitch is going to get into our school. Get out of here.' I turned back
to the guards but their faces told me I wouldn't get help from them."[10]

When Eckford finally made it back through the mob and to a bus stop, Dr.
Benjamin Fine, the education editor of the *New York Times,* sat beside her and put
his arm around her. Fine is the author of the article "Arkansas Troops Bar Negro
Pupils; Governor Defiant" that accompanies the photograph of Eckford in the
New York Times. Fine does not mention his own consolation of Eckford, but does
name Grace Lorch, described as "a white woman" who "walked over to comfort
her." Lorch is quoted in the article as saying to the angry mob, "She's just a little
girl. . . . Why don't you calm down? . . . Six months from now you'll be ashamed of
what you're doing." Fine would later share his experience in the crowd with Bates:
"Daisy, they spat in my face. They called me a 'dirty Jew.' I've been a marked man
ever since the day Elizabeth tried to enter Central."[11] He continued, "A girl I had
seen hustling in one of the local bars screamed, 'A dirty New York Jew! Get him!'
A man asked me, 'Are you a Jew?' I said, 'Yes.' He then said to the mob, 'Let him
be! We'll take care of him later.'"[12]

While Elizabeth Eckford was one of nine students to integrate Central High
School in Little Rock, Dorothy Counts (the girl in the photograph Arendt actually
describes) was the only Black student allowed to integrate Harding High School
in Charlotte. Every other request by Black families to integrate this high school
was denied by the school board. Dorothy's father, Dr. Herbert Counts, and family
friend Dr. Edwin Thompkins, both professors at John C. Smith University—a Presbyterian theological seminary—took Dorothy to school on the first day. Upon
their arrival they found the roadway in front of the school, a path that was usually
open, had been blocked off. Consequently, Dr. Thompkins walked with Dorothy
to the school while Dr. Counts, very much present for his daughter, parked the
car. Contrary to Arendt's description, Dorothy's father was not absent and Dr.
Thompkins was not "a white friend of her father"—he is Black.

After school, Dr. R. A. Hawkins, a local dentist, NAACP activist, and another African American friend of Dr. Counts, walked Dorothy from the school
to the car, where her father was again present and waiting. This scene after school
is not depicted in the photograph, but is described in the accompanying article,
"School Integration Begins in Charlotte with Near-Rioting" written by Clarence
Dean. According to Dean, as Dorothy and Dr. Hawkins walked from Harding
High School to the car, the white crowd threw water, paper cups, and sticks at
them. At this, the local police "did not intervene," but when the crowd tried to
rock the car as Dorothy and Dr. Hawkins got in, "the police closed in firmly and

cleared the crowd away."[13] Dean also mentions two other Black students integrating schools in Charlotte on that day, both accompanied by a parent: "Gustavas Allen Roberts, 16, was admitted to Central High School. His younger sister, Girvaud Lilly Roberts, 12, was enrolled at Piedmont Junior High School. The boy was accompanied by his father, a construction worker, and the girl by her mother."[14]

Parts of this background information were not available to Arendt because some of the details provided here would not become available until decades after the events of 1957. However, other information was readily accessible, not only in the photographs themselves but also in the captions and articles printed with the photographs. In the specific example of Dorothy Counts, there is never a description of Dr. Thompkins as a white friend of her father. Arendt assumes that Thompkins is white.[15] Also, Dean states in the same article that Dr. Hawkins (identified as a Negro dentist, but he was also a member of the NAACP) met Dorothy after school and they walked together to her father, who was waiting for her in a car. The article makes it clear that neither the NAACP nor the father were absent from the scene as Arendt claims.

It seems that the facts about the Counts family and their friends do not line up with Black families as they apparently existed in Arendt's imagination. It did not occur to Arendt that Dr. Counts was valedictorian of his high school class before earning several degrees with honors.[16] She did not imagine that Dorothy, who spent several weeks in summer camp in another state with a white roommate to prepare to attend Harding High School, felt pity rather than fear walking through the crowds of angry white students. In *The Dream Long Deferred: The Landmark Struggle for Desegregation in Charlotte, North Carolina*, Frye Gaillard notes that Dorothy "walked through them calmly, feeling, she remembered later, a strange mix of emotions, though oddly enough, fear was not among them. . . . She felt pity for them . . . that they would not do these things if they had grown up in a family as loving as her own."[17] Dorothy later looked back on the situation with journalist Tommy Tomilson: "People say, 'How did you let somebody spit on you? How did all those people say those things?' I always say, *if you look at the picture the right way, you see what I see.* What I see is that all of those people are behind me. They did not have the courage to get up in my face."[18]

How is it that Arendt's interpretation of the photograph(s), the starting point for her reflections, is so wrong? Arendt does not see what Dorothy sees in the photograph. Arendt is not seeking understanding; rather, she thinks that she already understands. Arendt looks upon the photographs with already formed assumptions that adversely impact how she sees and judges them. Arendt has already made up her mind about the Black parents and the NAACP: they are neglectful and opportunistic, seeking upward social mobility through the federally forced integration of public schools. The photograph and the crisis in Little Rock serve as confirmations of Arendt's already formed judgment, not as a starting point for seeking understanding.

Lessons from Martha Arendt: "One Must Defend Oneself!"

Let us contrast Arendt's critical stance toward Black parents with her own experience as a child living in a community and attending a school where she had to deal with antisemitism. In a 1964 interview in Germany with Günter Gaus, Arendt offers the following reflections:

> You see, all Jewish children encountered anti-Semitism. And it poisoned the souls of many children. The difference with us was that my mother always insisted that we never humble ourselves. That one must defend oneself! When my teachers made anti-Semitic remarks . . . I was instructed to stand up immediately, to leave the class and to go home, and to report everything. Then my mother would write one of her many certified letters, and with that, my involvement in the affair ended completely. . . . But if such remarks were made by children, I was not allowed to report it at home. This did not count. Whatever is said by children, one can respond to oneself. In this way, these things have never been a problem for me. There existed rules of behavior by which my dignity was, so to speak, protected, absolutely protected, at home. (*EU* 8)[19]

Arendt discloses that she and all Jewish children experienced antisemitism. She attended a school with students and teachers who made antisemitic remarks. Rather than shelter Arendt from this antisemitic environment, her mother taught her not to humble herself or yield to it.

From this perspective, Elisabeth Young-Bruehl reads the Little Rock essay as a reflection of Arendt's "Jewishness more than any conservatism" and adds, "This child was not given the 'absolute protection of dignity' Martha Arendt had once so conscientiously given her daughter, who had been instructed to leave social situations where she was not wanted and go home."[20] But let us reconsider the instructions Arendt received from her mother. Martha Arendt told her daughter to leave a class when the teacher made an antisemitic remark, but young Hannah was not allowed to report remarks made by other children because "whatever is said by children, one can respond to oneself" (*EU* 8). I would like to make two additional points here. First, there is no indication in the Gaus interview (or in Young-Bruehl's biography) that Hannah Arendt was ever withdrawn from school altogether. In this regard, the parents of Dorothy Counts went a step further: Counts ultimately left the school that she integrated. Second, we might contrast Arendt's claim that "whatever is said by children, one can respond to oneself" in this interview with her concerns about the tyranny of the majority among children in "Crisis in Education," where she seems to take a different position. In the latter essay Arendt asserts that children cannot rebel against other children because of the numerical superiority of the majority, the lack of reason among children, and the fact that they cannot flee the world of children because the adult world is barred to them (CE 181–182).

Beyond these points I challenge the assumption—made by Arendt and repeated by Young-Bruehl—that Black parents were denying their children protection and dignity. Many Black parents did in fact instill dignity and self-respect in their children, helping them to confront the racist and white supremacist situation in which they lived. But Hannah Arendt does not consider the possibility that Black parents could or would teach their children lessons similar to those taught by her own mother. She does not consider the possibility that Dr. Counts, as described by Gaillard, "was a family man first of all. But he believed, as he often told his children, that they could be what they wanted to be and go where they wanted to go and the chains of prejudice did not have to bind them."[21] Dorothy Counts recalls the lessons she learned from her father: "We always thought that we were as good as anybody. . . . My dad used to tell us . . . You don't slump your shoulders."[22] The night before her first day of school at Harding, Dr. Counts told his daughter, "Remember the things that you have been taught. Hold your head up. You're the same as they are. You can do whatever you want to do."[23] And when Dorothy got out of the car with Dr. Thompkins to go into the school, Dr. Counts told his daughter again, "Hold your head high."[24]

Arendt's inability, or unwillingness, to connect the lessons she received from her mother to similar lessons taught by Black parents is revealed by her reply to the question, "What would I do if I were a Negro mother?" Arendt does *not* say that if she were a Negro mother she would teach her children to defend themselves and not to humble themselves.[25] Rather, she says, "under no circumstances would I expose my child to conditions which made it appear as though it wanted to push its way into a group where it was not wanted. Psychologically, the situation of being unwanted (a typically *social* predicament) is more difficult to bear than outright persecution (a *political* predicament) because personal pride is involved" (Reply 179, my emphasis). Arendt implies that Black parents are sacrificing their children's pride, which is "indispensible for personal integrity," by forcing their children to push their way "out of one group and into another" (ibid.). And again, this is described as a social and not a political issue. She adds, "If I were a Negro mother in the South, I would feel that the Supreme Court ruling, unwillingly but unavoidably, has put my child into a more humiliating position than it has been in before" (ibid.).[26]

"Involved in an Affair of Social Climbing": Black Parents as Social Parvenus, not Conscious Pariahs

Part of the problem here is Arendt's oversimplification of the Black community concerning the issue of school integration. Arendt does not acknowledge that there

were members of the Black community who spoke out against the *Brown* decision, including Zora Neale Hurston. In 1955 Hurston wrote a letter to the editor
of the *Orlando Sentinel* stating, "I regard the ruling of the U.S. Supreme Court
as insulting rather than honoring my race. Since the days of the never-to-be-
sufficiently-deplored Reconstruction, there has been current the belief that there
is no greater delight to Negroes than the physical association with whites." She
explained, "The whole matter revolves around the self-respect of my people. How
much satisfaction can I get from a court order for somebody to associate with me
who does not wish me near them?"[27] Some might read Hurston as agreeing with
Arendt on this point. But I would suggest that Hurston is rejecting the assumption among whites (and shared by Arendt) that all Black people want nothing
more than to socialize with white people. Even if the case is made that Hurston
agrees with Arendt's position, one could argue that Hurston, like Arendt, is incorrect about the motivations for integration. The goal was not merely association with whites. Following Kwame Ture (formerly Stokely Carmichael), I think
there is a need to see beyond integration as defined by white Americans. Ture asserts, "To many of them, it means black men wanting to marry white daughters;
it means 'race mixing'—implying bed or dance partners. To black people it has
meant a way to improve their lives—economically and politically."[28] Put another
way, integration is a thoroughly political, not simply a social, issue.

As already mentioned, Arendt assumes that Black parents are not protecting
their children's dignity. Beyond this, she also assumes that all Black parents readily
sent their children into white schools in order to socialize with white students who
did not want them around. But for every Black family that allowed their children
to integrate a previously white-only school, there were countless more who were
either not allowed, or simply refused, to integrate. Furthermore, some Black parents who allowed their children to integrate previously white schools later opted
to remove their children from those schools. For instance, only three of the Little
Rock Nine went on to graduate from Central High School.[29] And in Charlotte,
Dorothy Counts withdrew from Harding after the windshield to her brother's car
got shattered when he picked her up from school one day. In a public statement
Dr. Counts explained, "In enrolling Dorothy at Harding High School, we sought
for her the highest educational experience that this tax supported school had to
offer a young American. . . . Needless to say we regret the necessity which makes
the withdrawal expedient."[30] Dr. Counts's statement makes no mention of a desire to assimilate, to associate with white people, or to achieve upward social mobility. He does, however, describe enrolling his daughter at Harding High School
as an effort to "enjoy full citizenship."[31]

Ralph Waldo Ellison gave a direct and critical response to Arendt's negative
judgment of Black parents for "exploiting their children" in the Little Rock essay.[32]
In an interview with Robert Penn Warren, Ellison asserted that Arendt "has ab-

solutely no conception of what goes on in the minds of Negro parents when they send their kids through those lines of hostile people. Yet they are aware of the hostile overtones of a rite of initiation which such events actually constitute for the child, a confrontation of the terrors of social life with all the mysteries stripped away."[33] For Ellison, such an initiation is required for Black youth because racism is not reserved for adults. Black parents have to equip their children with the tools to endure racism even in childhood. Ellison continued, "And in the outlook of many of these parents (who wish that the problem didn't exist), the child is expected to face the terror and contain his fear and anger *precisely* because he is a Negro American. Thus, he is required to master the inner tensions created by his racial situation, and if he gets hurt—then his is one more sacrifice. It is a harsh requirement, but if he fails the basic test, his life will be even harsher."[34] Ellison stresses that heroism and the ideal of sacrifice are an integral part of the social *and* political Black American experience. Managing and controlling fear and anger in the face of racist hostility is a method of survival in a white supremacist society that is intertwined with a white supremacist political system. It is one of the ways that Black parents prepare their children to contend with the white problem.

Arendt wrote Ellison several years later (July 29, 1965) and claimed to understand his point about the ideal of sacrifice: "You are entirely right: it is precisely 'ideal of sacrifice' which I didn't understand; and since my starting point was a consideration of the situation of Negro kids in forcibly integrated schools, this failure to understand caused me indeed to go into an entirely wrong direction" (AE). According to James Bohman, this admission does not really change her argument: "Arendt grants only that she may not have understood the situation culturally, but all that she explicitly changes is her understanding of the role of children in the front lines of desegregation and nothing else in her analysis."[35] And Elisabeth Young-Bruehl comments, "Even though Ellison argued in terms she could appreciate and moved her to amend her views, Hannah Arendt remained convinced that education should not be the sole or even the most important source of social or political change."[36] I would add that although Arendt told Ellison that he was entirely right in this 1965 letter, she did not alter her judgment of Black parents as social climbers.[37]

Arendt suspects that Black families want to assimilate and socialize with white people so much that they are willing to rely on government intervention (in this case, the legally enforced integration of public schools) to be able to mingle with them. She states, "Instead of being called upon to fight a clear-cut battle for my indisputable rights—my right to vote and be protected in it, to marry whom I please . . . or my right to equal opportunity—I would feel I had become involved in an affair of social climbing; and if I chose this way of bettering myself, I certainly would prefer to do it myself, unaided by any government agencies" (Reply

180). It is clear that she believes that the Black parents who allowed their children to integrate white schools did so for the purpose of what she calls social climbing. In her view, the political rights to be fought for pertain to voting, marriage, and equal opportunity, but not to education, which Arendt assumes is irrelevant to equal opportunity.

Arendt explicitly articulates her doubts about equal educational opportunities being a central issue for Black parents when she claims, "If it were only a matter of equally good education for my children, an effort to grant them equal opportunity, why was I not asked to fight for an improvement of schools for Negro children and for the establishment of special classes for those children whose scholastic record now makes them acceptable to white schools" (Reply 180). Arendt asks these questions rhetorically, suggesting, first, that Black parents were not fighting to improve their children's schools, and, second, that outstanding scholastic records might make Black students more "acceptable" to white schools—though still in separate "special classes."[38] Is it possible that Black parents' right to have an equal educational opportunity for their children does not constitute an indisputable right to equal opportunity for Arendt because she does not imagine that this is what the parents are actually seeking? Arendt interprets the Supreme Court decision outlawing segregation in public schools as a form of government aid for social climbing because she imagines that social climbing is the main goal for Black families.

Looking at racial integration in public schools through the lens of Jewish assimilation, Arendt misreads the motivations of Black parents as deriving from a desire for acceptance and upward social mobility (like the parvenu) rather than as conscious efforts to get legally gained rights enforced by political institutions (like the pariah). Young-Bruehl states, "The 'absent father' had done what no parent ought to do: he asked his child to go where she was not wanted, to behave like a parvenu, to treat education as a means of social advancement."[39] This is also a point made by Seyla Benhabib: "Arendt likened the demands of black parents, upheld by the US Supreme Court decision in *Brown v. Board,* to have their children admitted into previously all-white schools, to the desire of the social parvenu to gain recognition in a society that did not care to admit her."[40] Arendt adopts the parvenu-pariah distinction from Bernard Lazare and employs it in *Rahel Varnhagen: The Life of a Jewish Woman.*[41] Lazare was the author of *L'Antisémitisme, son historie et ses causes* and also provided legal counsel for the Dreyfus family during the Dreyfus Affair.[42]

Richard Bernstein explains that the Jewish parvenu "desperately seeks to escape his pariah status and to be accepted by, and assimilated to, a society that treats the Jew as an outcast."[43] In contrast to the parvenu, the conscious pariah "rebels and transforms the outcast status thrust upon the Jew into a challenge to fight for one's rights."[44] Arendt does not view Black parents or the NAACP activists as conscious pariahs fighting for their rights and the rights of their children. For her, access to equal educational opportunities does not constitute an indisputable right, and she does not imagine the NAACP activists and Black parents as rebels trying to transform their outcast status by fighting for their constitutional rights.

"Caution and Moderation": The Gradualism of *Brown I* and *II*

The Supreme Court handed down the *Brown v. Board of Education of Topeka* decision (also known as *Brown I*) on May 17, 1954. And although *Brown I* was interpreted as outlawing the segregation of public schools, *Brown II* (May 31, 1955, about three months before the murder of Emmett Till in Mississippi) offered the ambiguous caveat that school integration should be carried out with "all deliberate speed." But the integration of schools would be slow and incremental, at best. The Charlotte and Little Rock situations occurred in 1957, three years after *Brown I* and two years after *Brown II*. Some, including Arendt, have assumed that after the *Brown* decision masses of Black students were integrating white schools across the nation. But that simply was not happening. For example, in North Carolina, Davidson M. Douglass explains, "By engaging in well-publicized, but decidedly token, integration, North Carolina managed to maintain an almost completely segregated school system for the first decade after *Brown*."[45]

The slow and gradual process of symbolic school integration calls into question Arendt's advocating "caution and moderation" and opposing "impatience and ill advised measures" in integrating public schools (RLR 48). Several of these facts about gradualism were mentioned in critical responses to "Reflections" from Sidney Hook and David Spitz, which means this information was readily available to Arendt. For example, Hook rejects Arendt's call for gradualism as beside the point because the issue is not when or how the law would be enforced, but rather that the law be enforced in the end. At some point the law would be tested by Black families exercising their legal right to send their children to schools in their districts and neighborhoods. Whenever this happened, whether sooner or later, "once it is tested, the law cannot abdicate before the interference of mob violence without making a mockery of *the Negro child's constitutional right* to the equal protection of the laws."[46] For Hook this is no different and no less important than the right to vote. David Spitz recognizes the importance of caution and moderation but also identifies the danger of not doing enough.[47] Highlighting the more obvious point that Arendt ignores, Spitz explains, "We must move, no doubt, with all deliberate speed. But what is frightening, in the years since *Brown v. Board of Education*, let alone the century since the Civil War, is that in seeking to be deliberate we have made very little speed."[48] These facts are not reflected in

Arendt's prefatory remarks nor in her "Reply to Critics." Rather than reevaluate or adjust her position, she held it all the more firmly.

In Defense of White Mothers and White Rights in the South

Aside from Arendt's critical misjudgment of Black parents, something that gets overlooked in "Reflections on Little Rock" is her strong advocacy for white parents and their rights. To the question, "What would I do if I were a white mother in the South?," Arendt replies, "I would deny that the government has any right to tell me in whose company my child receives its instruction. The rights of parents to decide such matters for their children until they are grown ups are challenged only by dictatorships" (Reply 180). She is defending the choices of white parents for their children without regard for the lack of choices afforded to Black parents for their children.

Arendt also rejects arguments that segregation ought to be limited to private schools (while public schools are integrated) on the basis that it is unfair to poor white families. Private schools "would make the safeguarding of certain private rights depend upon economic status and consequently underprivilege those who were forced to send their children to public schools" (RLR 55). Thus, Arendt places the private right of whites to racism above the right to equal educational opportunities for Black families. It is even more astounding that Arendt presents private segregated schools as providing opportunities that would underprivilege poor white families, yet she does not reflect on the numerous ways that underfunded segregated public schools underprivilege Black families. Tumin asks, "What then of Negro children and *their* parents and *their* rights? Where in the fabric of Miss A.'s minimum government do these rights get respected and protected?"[49] Along the same lines, Hook asserts, "If it is wrong to force white parents to send their children to an integrated school because of their private right over their children, it is wrong to force Negro parents to send their children to segregated schools, and wrong to force white parents who do not object to their children associating with Negro children to do the same."[50]

Arendt does not seem to consider Black parents' and students' rights as comparably important to those of white parents and students. She takes a stand against efforts at forced or legalized desegregation except in extreme or rare circumstances. In her response to critics, Arendt gives an example of such a circumstance. She insists that if she were a white mother and thought "the South could be materially helped by integrated education, I would try . . . to organize a new school for white and colored children" (Reply 180). If the school had consenting parents and children, and southern citizens still organized to get the state to interfere in the opening and functioning of the school, then "this would be the precise moment when, in my opinion, the federal government should be called upon to intervene. For here we would have again a clear case of segregation enforced by governmental authority" (181). What Arendt overlooks in this last comment is a fact that she noted in the original Little Rock essay, namely, that state and local governmental authorities already enforced segregation in public schools and many other public venues.

One additional issue to take into consideration here is Arendt's outspoken defense of states' rights against federal interference without regard for the trampling of local rights by state interference. Arendt argues against federal enforcement of school desegregation laws on the basis that it upsets the balance of power between the federal and state governments, but she does not explore the issue of authority in state versus local governments (RLR 54). For example, in Little Rock the school board and the mayor approved school integration at the local level. It was Governor Faubus who overrode their local authority and used his state authority to stop school integration in Little Rock. Spitz describes Arendt's states' rights argument as a "superficial notion of federalism . . . that would gladden the heart of John C. Calhoun" (PRB 58). He also points out her lack of concern about local rights: "while the leaders of the Southern states do not want the national government to interfere in their activities, they do not themselves hesitate to interfere in the activities of local communities" (59). Once again, we see Arendt advocate for white rights (in this case, states' rights) while simultaneously ignoring Black rights (and local rights).

But Was Arendt Right?

Let us consider the possibility that in spite of her misjudgments and false assumptions, Arendt may have been correct about segregation and education. Looking at the conditions of the public school system in the United States since the 1954 *Brown* decision, there are certainly members of the African American community who muse that schools were better when they were separate. For example, in *Teaching to Transgress: Education as the Practice of Freedom*, bell hooks explains, "School changed utterly with racial integration. . . . When we entered racist, desegregated white schools we left a world where teachers believed that to educate black children rightly would require a political commitment. Now, we were mainly taught by white teachers whose lessons reinforced racist stereotypes."[51] Having said that, we should not be revisionist about the conditions of many Black schools, especially in the South, in the first half of the twentieth century. Charles Houston documented disparities between Black schools and white-only schools in the 1930s, when southern states spent five to ten times more on white pupils than on Black pupils. In a documentary titled *Examples of Educational Discrimination among Rural Negros in South Carolina*, Houston "contrasted the unheated cabins and tarpaper shacks that served as schools for black children with the tidy brick and stone structures where white children learned."[52]

Still, in "Does the Negro Need Separate Schools?" (1935) W. E. B. Du Bois discusses the harms of school integration in the 1930s, which bear some similarity to Arendt's claims in the 1950s.[53] He explains that the reality of the racial attitudes of white America toward Black America coupled with the need to defend against the growing animosity of whites necessitates separate Black schools.[54] Taking a position against school integration on this basis, he insists, "we must give greater value and greater emphasis to the rights of the child's own soul . . . by putting children in schools where they are wanted, and where they are happy and inspired, than in thrusting them into hells where they are ridiculed and hated."[55] Du Bois asserts, "I know that race prejudice in the United States today is such that most Negroes cannot receive proper education in white institutions."[56] Rather than be admitted to white schools to be at best tolerated or at worst crucified—but in either case to be denied a proper education—Du Bois declares, "there is no room for argument as to whether the Negro needs separate schools or not. The plain fact faces us, that either he will have separate schools or he will not be educated."[57] Here Du Bois underscores the harms of integrated schools (like Arendt does) while he also emphasizes the importance of caring Black teachers (like hooks does) and the need for separate Black schools at that time.[58]

Du Bois's article raises questions for my analysis of Arendt. Would Du Bois agree with Arendt's positions in "Reflections on Little Rock"? Was Arendt right about segregation in education? While the arguments by Du Bois point to similarities with Arendt (for example, both are concerned about the harms of pushing children into a group or an environment in which they are unwanted), there are some key differences. Unlike Arendt, Du Bois understands that regardless of which side one takes on school segregation or integration, the primary goal for Black parents is the education of their children, not socializing with white families. He is clear that Black children need a quality education and for him the issue is not whether they have a scholastic record that makes them acceptable to white schools, but rather that they are likely to be tormented in white schools regardless of their academic abilities.

To further contrast Du Bois and Arendt, he understands that the lack of faith in Black schools results from the larger system of anti-Black racism in which Black families are entangled, not from disinterest in educational equality. Consequently, he is clear that when American Negroes do not fight for adequate support of or increased efficiency in Black schools, this inaction is based in (1) fear that supporting segregation (i.e., supporting separate Black schools) "is a fatal surrender of principle, which in the end will rebound and bring more evils on the Negro than he suffers today," and (2) the misperception that as a race Black people are "constitutionally and permanently inferior to white people."[59] Du Bois describes this self-doubt and seeking of external validation for self-worth as "the logical consequence of the 'white' propaganda which has swept civilization for the last thousand years, and which is now bolstered and defended by brave words, high wages, and monopoly of opportunities."[60] So while Du Bois may agree with Arendt about the potential harm to the Black children who integrate white schools, I do not think he would agree with her claims that segregation in education is strictly a social issue tied to upward social mobility. Rather, he frames education as a public and political issue connected to larger issues of racial injustice and inequality.

Let me emphasize that the question for Arendt is not whether it would have been better for Blacks to maintain our own schools. She does not express any concern about unequal schools for Black children and she claims that Black parents are ultimately uninterested in equal educational opportunities. In defending the right to discriminate in the private realm, Arendt makes no attempt to defend the right of Black families to equal public schools. The rights of white parents and southern states to maintain segregated public schools are among the main concerns articulated in Arendt's reflections. Furthermore, when considering Arendt's defense of whites' right to discriminate, we should also remember that the *Brown* decisions turned out to be more form than substance. While the laws about segregated schools changed with *Brown I*, the caveat of "all deliberate speed" in *Brown II* and the lack of enforcement that resulted often left segregation in education unchanged.

On this point, it is worth noting how Du Bois's position evolved from the 1935 article "Does the Negro Need Separate Schools?" to the later "What Is the Meaning of 'All Deliberate Speed'?" (1957), where he takes up the *Brown II* decision explicitly.[61] Underscoring the disconnect between the stated principles of U.S. democracy and the actual practices of racial injustice, Du Bois points to the repeated failure of the nation and the courts to uphold the ideals of equality and unalienable rights. He states, "Several decisions had raised serious questions as to the judicial honesty in this nation. The critical decision came in 1954 when the Supreme Court declared unanimously that race separation in public schools was unconstitutional."[62] But in the face of mobs in the South and the championing of states' rights, "finally even the Supreme Court took a step backward and said the enforcement of the law need not be immediate but could be achieved with all deliberate speed."[63] For Du Bois, the *Brown I* decision resulted from Black people organizing and fighting back. Unfortunately, the *Brown II* decision followed the historical pattern of racial injustice in the United States—a failure to "face and settle today the accumulated problems of the last 338 years."[64] There is not a call for separate Black schools in this article, only an indictment against U.S. racial policies and a concluding rhetorical question as to "whether the United States is a democracy or the last center of 'white supremacy' and colonial imperialism."[65] So while Du Bois in 1935 might have agreed with Arendt's concerns about the harms of putting Black children in white schools, in 1957 his position did not line up with Arendt's claims about Black parents, white rights, and states' rights in "Reflections on Little Rock."

In the half-century since *Brown I* and *II*, the Supreme Court decisions have remained more symbolic than substantive. As legal scholar and civil rights attorney Derrick Bell notes, "The *Brown* decision recreated the nineteenth century's post–Civil War Reconstruction/Redemption pattern of progress followed by retrogression."[66] In *Silent Covenants* Bell explains, "The eleven states of the former Confederacy had a mere 1.17 percent of their black students attending school with white students by the 1963–1964 school year. In the following year, the percentage [rose] to 2.25 percent."[67] There were more school desegregation attempts through busing and other programs, but by the 1980s the Reagan era began and the *Brown* era seemed to approach its demise.[68] Even in the twenty-first century, many public schools are as segregated or in some cases more segregated than they were at the time of the *Brown* decisions. According to Bell, statistically "many black and Hispanic children are enrolled in schools as separate and probably more unequal than those their parents and grandparents attended under the era of 'separate but equal.'"[69] Public school systems in many impoverished and minority communities continue to contend with the systematic inequities that began long before 1954. Again emphasizing the goal of equal education, Bell notes, "With an advocate's hindsight, Robert Carter suggested that while *Brown* was fashioned on the theory that equal education and integrated education are one and the same thing, the goal was not integration but equal educational opportunity."[70] But now, in the second decade of the twenty-first century, equal educational opportunities remain out of reach for many.[71]

To conclude, Arendt's factual errors regarding the photograph she describes in "Reflections," along with her errors in judgment—especially her claim that Black parents subjected their children to racist mobs for the purpose of social climbing—should not be overlooked. In addition to rejecting her misjudgments of Black parents and her oversimplified representation of the Black community, we must also pay attention to the ways Arendt prioritizes whites' right to discriminate over Blacks' right to equal educational opportunities. When Arendt questions the government's decision to "enforce civil rights where no basic human and no basic political right is at stake" (RLR 56), she fails to understand the ways in which access to a quality public education (and higher education) impact other areas that she sees as properly political. Her misclassifications allow her to categorize public schools as social institutions rather than as public and political institutions. It turns out that even if Arendt does not understand, she does in many ways share, the common prejudices of (white) Americans toward Blacks.

2 "The Most Outrageous Law of Southern States—the Law Which Makes Mixed Marriage a Criminal Offense"

In "REFLECTIONS ON Little Rock," Arendt is adamant that the fundamental human rights and civil rights issue was not equal educational opportunities, but rather anti-miscegenation laws. This position is emblematic of Arendt's double-edged scholarship, which often offers innovative insights alongside outrageous oversights. On the one hand, she is right to characterize the egregiously offensive anti-miscegenation laws in the United States as a violation of rights. On the other, Arendt completely misses how intimately interconnected the marriage issue is to racial discrimination in education, housing, employment, and places of amusement, which she dismisses as social rights. In order to provide some context for the interrelationship between segregation, education, and miscegenation, my starting point will be the many decades of legal strategizing and the systematic litigation that led up to the *Brown* decision. Arendt's insights are undermined not only by her oversights, but also by the fact that she speaks out against Black families and political organizations with an offensive and paternalistic tone, all the while making unwarranted claims about their priorities and positioning herself in alignment with what Gunnar Myrdal has described as the white man's rank order of discrimination.

Unequal Education, the NAACP, and Getting to *Brown*

While it is not possible to offer here an in-depth legal analysis of all the Supreme Court cases that have impacted constructions of race and systems of racism in the United States, it is important to identify some of these cases and the work of the NAACP's legal campaign in the fight against unequal education in segregated schools. Long before *Brown v. Board of Education*, several race, slavery, and segregation cases were brought before the U.S. Supreme Court. Two key decisions not mentioned by Arendt in the Little Rock essay are *Dred Scott v. Sandford* (1857) and *Plessy v. Ferguson* (1896). The *Dred Scott* decision declared that both enslaved and free Blacks were not and could never be citizens and furthermore that Blacks had no rights that had to be recognized by whites.[1] And while the Fourteenth Amendment (one of the Reconstruction amendments adopted in 1868) includes clauses for citizenship (state and national), due process, and equal protection before the law on paper, that protection has not always been experienced in practice.[2] The *Plessy* decision, reached after the adoption of the Fourteenth Amendment, sanctioned racial segregation of the railroads but had implications beyond railroad cars. The decision symbolized (if not concretized) the ongoing lack of equal protection for Blacks under the law despite their recently established citizenship. The plaintiff, Homer Plessy, argued that the segregation law violated the Fourteenth Amendment (i.e., denied him equal protection before the law) and asserted that segregation was a badge of inferiority for the colored races.[3] Ruling against Plessy, the Supreme Court upheld the separate-but-equal accommodations in railroad transportation as constitutional.[4] Along with America's crime of slavery these are two significant cases Arendt ignores in the Little Rock essay, though they too contributed to what she calls the color question in the United States.[5]

Looking specifically at the education issue, Michael Klarman notes in *From Jim Crow to Civil Rights: The Supreme Court and the Struggle for Racial Equality* that during the antebellum period in the United States Black people in the South were excluded from public schools. During Reconstruction more educational opportunities were provided (a condition for states to be readmitted into the Union), but for the most part racial segregation in public education existed in fact (replacing exclusion) before Reconstruction and then continued by law after Reconstruction. He states that while at the time "many southern blacks supported integration in principle, *they generally pursued equal funding of segregated schools* instead, capitulating to staunch white resistance."[6] Furthermore, at times there has been as much white resistance to *equality* in education as to *integration* in education. Klarman explains, "Southern whites had always been hostile to school integration, and by 1900 they were even less supportive than they had formerly been of providing equal education funding for blacks."[7] And when funding for education in the South increased in the early twentieth century (1900–1915), those funds were disproportionately allocated to white schools.[8] This has been just a brief glimpse into the ongoing fight for basic rights and for basic educational opportunities, not to mention equal educational opportunities, in the century before *Brown*.

One of the major contributors to the legal work that resulted in the *Brown* case is Charles Houston. After earning his law degree from Harvard Law School, Houston worked tirelessly in his father's private practice and at Howard University, where he helped to establish a law program emphasizing constitutional law.[9] He eventually took a leave from Howard University Law School to work for the NAACP's national legal campaign.[10] The NAACP followed a legal strategy derived from what is commonly referred to as the Margold Report to attack the separate-but-equal doctrine of *Plessy*.[11] Nathan Margold had researched civil rights, including "equal protection case law . . . jury exclusion, jim crow transportation, residential segregation, disfranchisement and equal apportionment of school funds."[12]

He asserted that there should be an attack on the constitutionality of segregation, rather than attempting to try the overwhelming number of cases that would be needed to make a difference in these areas: "It would be a great mistake to fritter away our limited funds on sporadic attempts to force the making of equal divisions of school funds in the few instances where such attempts might be expected to succeed.... On the other hand, if we boldly challenge the constitutional validity of segregation if and when accompanied irremediably by discrimination, we can strike directly at the most prolific source of discrimination."[13] After finishing the report, Margold accepted a position elsewhere and was not able to lead the legal campaign to implement it. Though not the organization's first choice (Karl Llewellyn was also considered), Houston was selected by the NAACP as Margold's successor.

Advocating a variation of the Margold strategy, Houston proposed that the entire budget of the Garland Fund granted to the NAACP be used to campaign against discrimination in education (including unequal apportionment of school funds).[14] He sought to expose the ills of segregation and to achieve equal educational opportunities. In *Groundwork: Charles Hamilton Houston and the Struggle for Civil Rights*, Genna Rae McNeil asserts, "What was of importance to Houston ... was a planned legal program that laid a 'foundation' with respect to research, cases and community involvement in struggle against racial discrimination and for equal rights."[15] Consider the following aims outlined by Houston in "Educational Inequalities Must Go":

(a) equality of school terms;
(b) equality of pay for Negro teachers having the same qualifications and doing the same work as white teachers;
(c) equality of transportation for Negro school children at public expense;
(d) equality of buildings and equipment;
(e) equality of per capita expenditure for education of Negroes; [and]
(f) equality in graduate and professional training.[16]

The repeated emphasis is on equality, not assimilation or social climbing. Eventually, the NAACP identified cases of segregation in education, starting with graduate schools and professional schools to establish precedents before working on colleges and then the public school system.[17] This legal work was being done in the 1930s, two decades before *Brown*, and it refutes Arendt's assumption that the NAACP did not fight for equal educational opportunities. Even though Arendt claims that "the most startling part of this whole business was the Federal decision to start integration in, of all places, the public schools" (RLR 50), we must remember that in the NAACP strategy, the struggle against segregation in public schools came *after* fighting for educational equality and challenging several separate-and-unequal professional schools and colleges.

Houston's health began to decline, and after surviving a heart attack in 1949 he died of acute coronary thrombosis in 1950.[18] Before his untimely death, Thurgood Marshall, James M. Nabrit Jr., and others were already assisting with the NAACP legal work.[19] Rather than fighting for the equality to be real in the separate-but-equal doctrine, Marshall and Nabrit eventually sought to challenge the doctrine itself. Nabrit asserted, "We had nothing to lose by an outright assault on segregation."[20] During this time, the Supreme Court gave decisions in two particular cases on which Houston, Marshall, and Nabrit had worked, *Sweatt v. Painter* (1950) and *McLaurin v. Oklahoma State Regents* (1950). Both of these decisions reiterated the idea that for separate to be constitutional, equality had to be genuine, but also went on to suggest that "the existence of segregated schools, no matter how good they were, implied inferiority—that separate could never be equal."[21]

After the *Sweatt* and *McLaurin* cases, the NAACP held a policy session during which they explored the best means to end segregation altogether. Kluger notes, "And while no one in the NAACP camp questioned the desirability of that goal, feeling was by no means unanimous that the straight route to it was the wisest one."[22] Marshall did not want to argue before the same judges that *Plessy* was unconstitutional, only to lose and then try to argue for equal facilities. After seeking feedback and advice, Marshall moved forward with a two-pronged approach: arguing that facilities were unequal and therefore unconstitutional, but also that equality could not be achieved as long as facilities were separate.[23]

These cases, along with numerous others accumulated over earlier decades, created precedents that laid the groundwork for arguments against the constitutionality of segregation, leading to what we know now as the *Brown* decision.[24] Arendt either did not know or was unwilling to acknowledge the political implications of the legal work that went into the *Brown* case. Furthermore, Arendt did not perceive the overlaps between the marriage issue that she prioritizes and the racial discrimination in education, housing, employment, and places of amusement that she dismisses as social rights.

A Hierarchy of Rights: Marriage as an Inalienable Human Right

Arendt claims that although the government's civil rights program dealt with the franchise (a political issue) and segregation (a social, but at times public, issue), it "did not go far enough, for it left untouched the most outrageous law of Southern states—the law which makes mixed marriage a criminal offense" (RLR 49). Once again, we see Arendt's distinctions at work, this time resulting in a hierarchy of rights with marriage laws at the top and other forms of racial discrimination down below. Arendt establishes this hierarchy of rights when she declares, "The right to marry whomever one wishes is an elementary human right compared to which 'the right to attend an integrated school, the right to sit where one pleases on a bus, the right to go into any hotel or recreation area, or place of amusement, regardless of one's skin or color or race' are minor indeed" (ibid.). The right to marry is an inalienable right in accordance with the right to "life, liberty, and the pursuit of happiness."[25] For Arendt, in the social realm discrimination is expected and even necessary, but mixed marriages, a private realm issue for her, constitute "a challenge to society" (RLR 53). Partners in a mixed marriage prefer "personal happiness to social adjustment" and this is their "private business" (ibid.). Arendt continues, "The scandal begins only when their challenge to society and prevailing customs, to which every citizen has a right, is interpreted as a criminal offense so that by stepping outside the social realm they find themselves in conflict with the laws as well" (ibid.).

It has been speculated that Arendt prioritized the marriage issue because of her own choice of partner. Elisabeth Young-Bruehl asserts, "Arendt, whose marriage to a Gentile could never have taken place in her homeland while the Nuremberg Laws were in force, felt that the laws against racial intermarriage . . . ought to be the first front for action."[26] Parallels can certainly be drawn between the anti-miscegenation laws in the United States and the Nuremberg Laws in Germany. But I am not convinced that this was Arendt's primary concern. I do not think that she made this particular connection between her experience and the Black experience—in the same way that she did not see how her own upbringing (the lessons about antisemitism she learned from her mother) might be compared to the lessons taught by Black parents (raising their children to handle anti-Black racism in the United States). If Arendt had offered an analysis that rejected the marriage laws as an attempt to protect white purity and white supremacy, I might be more convinced that she was going in the direction mentioned by Young-Bruehl.

"Minorities Were Never the Best Judges on the Order of Priorities"

Aware that she had taken a controversial position (in part because of the issues preventing her from publishing the essay in *Commentary* in the first place), Arendt felt compelled to add "Preliminary Remarks" to the Little Rock essay in which she attempts to explain (and insists on maintaining) her position on marriage laws. She acknowledges that two points were brought to her attention after she wrote her article (the first concerned marriage laws and the second education). However, she does not adjust her position in either case—on marriage laws or education. Arendt contends that "the marriage laws in 29 of the 49 states constitute a much more flagrant breach of [the] letter and spirit of the Constitution than segregation of schools" and mentions, "to this, Sidney Hook (*New Leader*, April 13 [*sic*]), replied that Negroes were 'profoundly uninterested' in these laws; in their eyes, 'the discriminatory ban against intermarriages and miscegenation is last in the order of priorities'" (RLR 45).

Arendt is quoting here from galleys of the essay that Hook originally wrote as a rebuttal to her essay when the two pieces were to be published together in *Com-*

mentary. From the standpoint of the *Commentary* editors, Arendt's position was wrong and her essay was deemed too dangerous to publish in their magazine. The arrangement to publish Arendt's essay with Hook's reply was considered a compromise solution to the alternative—rejecting Arendt's article altogether. When Arendt withdrew her essay from *Commentary,* Hook suggested it was because she could not handle his critique.[27] Hook later published his essay (which now contains no explicit reference to Arendt or to the issue of interracial marriage) in the *New Leader* under the title "Democracy and Desegregation."[28]

On the issue of marriage laws and priorities as quoted by Arendt from Hook's unpublished galleys, Arendt retorts, "I have my doubts about this, especially with respect to the educated strata in the Negro population" (RLR 45). But Arendt grants, "it is of course perfectly true that Negro public opinion and the policies of the NAACP are almost exclusively concerned with discrimination in employment, housing and education" (45–46). Disapproving of the focus on these particular areas of discrimination, Arendt goes on to make a flagrantly paternalistic declaration: "This is understandable; oppressed minorities were never the best judges on the order of priorities in such matters and there are many instances when they preferred to fight for social opportunity rather than for basic human or political rights" (46).[29]

Melvin Tumin takes a sarcastic tone in his critique of Arendt's claim about the order of priorities, demonstrating how ridiculous he thinks Arendt's position sounds:

> Poor, unenlightened Negros, for whom Arendt feels so much sympathy! How misguided of them to press for equality of opportunity on jobs, housing, health, voting, and all these other trivia, instead of wising up to their own best interests and demanding the repeal of the laws against intermarriage! . . . The NAACP clearly has an immediate and urgent responsibility to call meetings of Negroes all over the United States so that Miss Arendt could explain to them why they ought to stop fighting for equality, in general, and why, if they are going to work on anything, it ought to be on intermarriage. (Pie 68)

By framing Arendt's position in this way, Tumin problematizes the condescending manner with which Arendt expressed her position, while also questioning the soundness of her prescribed order of priorities, which places the marriage laws above discrimination in education, housing, and employment.

Arendt positions herself against Hook and the apparently misdirected minorities (or "unenlightened Negros," to borrow Tumin's phrase) in the original essay and the "Preliminary Remarks." Reasserting her position on marriage laws all the more vehemently, Arendt states, "But this [wrong order of priorities pursued by oppressed minorities] does not make the marriage laws any more constitutional or any less shameful; the order of priorities in the question of rights is to be determined by the Constitution, and not by public opinion or by majorities" (RLR 46). Although Arendt claims to be taking her cues from the Constitution, she is presenting her own view, not a constitutional view. As her critic David Spitz points out, "Now, as one who has occasionally to read the Constitution, I am not aware of any provision in that document concerning marriage, and certainly none that proclaims as a paramount right the freedom to marry whom one pleases" (PRB 63). He continues, "If, then, there is an order of priority in rights, it must come from a source other than the Constitution, in this case from Miss Arendt herself" (ibid.).

Arendt and "the White Man's Rank Order of Discrimination"

Arendt's prioritization of marriage ignores the opposite analysis offered not only by Hook, whom she quotes, but also by her New School for Social Research colleague Alfred Schutz, a phenomenologist and sociologist who wrote "Equality and the Meaning of the Structure of the World" in 1955 (soon after *Brown*, though it was not published until 1957). Schutz's essay examines the structure of the system of relevance, the commonsense notion of equality as relational, and the ways that concepts like in-group and out-group, and subjective and objective, influence our understanding of equality. One example analyzed by Schutz is the distance between equality as a political ideal in the United States and actual practices. He states, "A good example is the change in the meaning of the notion of equality in the political ideals of the United States from the Declaration of Independence ('We hold these truths to be self-evident, that all men are created equal') to the wording of the Fifth and Fourteenth Amendments and the various interpretations given by the United States Supreme Court to these amendments, leading to the 'separate but equal' doctrine and the latter's recent abolishment."[30]

Schutz was influenced by Gunnar Myrdal's *An American Dilemma: The Negro Problem and Modern Democracy*.[31] Myrdal takes up the issue of priorities and outlines both the "white man's theory of color caste" and the "white man's rank order of discrimination."[32] Beginning with the theory of color caste, Myrdal explains that "almost unanimously" white Americans are concerned about preserving racial purity, rejecting social equality, and maintaining segregation as a defense against both social equality and the danger of miscegenation.[33] Myrdal is clear that the caste mechanism described is tied to what he calls the "anti-amalgamation maxim." This maxim also influences the white man's order of discrimination, described as an elaboration of the theory of color caste. Accordingly, the top priority for whites is to prevent intermarriage or, more specifically, sexual intercourse between Black men and white women.[34] The next priority is to maintain discrimination around social interactions more generally (dancing, bathing, eating, drinking, and so on); then discrimination in public facilities (schools, churches); then political disfranchisement; discrimination in law courts; and, finally, discrimination in securing land, credit, jobs, and so on.[35] Although Arendt is taking a position against mixed-marriage laws, it is both puzzling and troubling that her ordering of priorities in the Little Rock essay is actually aligned with the "white man's rank order of discrimination" that Myrdal describes.

To claim that Arendt aligns herself with southern white racist segregationists is not an exaggeration. The main difference between Arendt and white segregationists is that she endorses interracial marriage as a fundamental human right while they reject it. Aside from this admittedly significant point of disagreement, Arendt, like many white racists, defends racial discrimination as a social custom and rejects the legal enforcement of desegregation. Arendt belittles discrimination in employment, housing, and education as issues of social opportunity rather than basic human or political rights (RLR 46). Rejecting the very idea of social equality—"without discrimination of some sort, society would simply cease to exist" (51)—Arendt portrays African Americans as social opportunists seeking upward mobility. Myrdal describes this position (when taken by whites) as the "theory of no social equality" and asserts that it is a rationalization that is even more dominant than the aversion to intermarriage.[36] The marriage argument becomes "an irrational escape on the part of Whites from voicing an open demand for difference in social status between the two groups for its own sake."[37]

Myrdal goes on to assert, "The Negro's own rank order is just about parallel, but inverse, to that of the white man. The Negro resists least the discrimination on the ranks placed highest in the white man's evaluation and resents most any discrimination on the lowest level."[38] He adds that the issue of marriage "is of rather distant and doubtful interest."[39] Unlike Arendt, Myrdal does not interpret this as a failure to properly judge the order of priorities. Myrdal understands what Arendt's critics attempted to explain to her, namely, "this inverse relationship between the Negro's and the white man's rank orders becomes of strategical [sic] importance in the practical and political sphere."[40]

The case could be made that overtly linking miscegenation laws with other segregation laws might have undermined the entire civil rights program. It would have confirmed whites' fears that Black people wanted to integrate the schools in order to achieve social equality (a suspicion that Arendt shares with white segregationists) and race mixing. Or more specifically, it would have confirmed whites' fears that Black males would have sexual access to white females. Like Myrdal, Spitz highlights the strategic significance of avoiding miscegenation laws. He asserts that in political conflicts, we have to identify what we can fight and gain support for now: "To fight *now*, as a matter of first principle, for the repeal of anti-miscegenation laws is, I believe, to give strength to the very contention that is most frequently, and by all accounts most tellingly, employed by those who resist the repeal of segregation laws—namely, the contention that this is but a device to promote sexual intercourse among the races" (PRB 64). Spitz is sure that a fight against miscegenation laws would not only confirm such suspicions, but would also undermine the battle against other forms of racism. He claims, "There is, consequently, no surer way to prevent acceptance of the principle of equal opportunity for the Negro in the South than to push the issue of miscegenation into the forefront at this time. The Negroes, if not Miss Arendt, know this" (PRB 64).

Both Myrdal and Spitz raise important (even if somewhat problematic) points. Avoiding miscegenation laws did help Black political organizations' efforts in other areas of the civil rights campaign, including the NAACP strategy in building up to the *Brown* case. One example of this intentional avoidance of miscegenation and emphasis on education is *McLaurin v. Oklahoma State Regents* (1950), a case for graduate school integration. George McLaurin held a master's degree but was denied admission to the University of Oklahoma's doctoral program in education because he was Black. He won admittance through the state court but was not allowed to attend classes with white students. In describing his legal strategy for desegregation, Thurgood Marshall confirmed that the *McLaurin* case was selected as a test case for the Supreme Court because McLaurin's age helped to refute claims that he was seeking intermarriage. Marshall explained, "The Dixiecrats and the others said it was horrible. The only thing that the Negroes were trying to do, they said, was to get social equality. As a matter of fact, there would be intermarriage, they said. The latter theory is the reason we deliberately chose Professor McLaurin. . . . He was sixty-eight years old and we didn't think he was going to marry or intermarry—they could not bring this one on us, anyhow."[41]

But even if this was the general strategy, it does not mean that the miscegenation laws were altogether ignored by "oppressed minorities." The most obvious Supreme Court cases to demonstrate this point are *McLaughlin v. Florida* (1964), in which the Court ruled Florida's anti-miscegenation laws unconstitutional, and *Loving v. Virginia* (1967), in which Virginia's anti-miscegenation law, called An Act to Preserve Racial Integrity (1924), was also ruled unconstitutional.[42] The *McLaughlin* and *Loving* rulings overturned *Pace v. Alabama* (1883), a case in which the Supreme Court unanimously upheld anti-miscegenation laws as constitutional.[43]

Reluctance on Marriage Laws and Reluctance to Abolish Slavery

To the strategy of avoiding the issue of miscegenation for practical reasons, highlighted by Spitz, Arendt responds by comparing the reluctance to take on marriage laws to the reluctance of the founding fathers to abolish slavery. In "A Reply to Critics" she argues, "The reluctance of American liberals to touch the issue of the marriage laws, their readiness to invoke practicality and shift the ground of the argument by insisting that the Negroes themselves have no interest in the matter, their embarrassment when they are reminded of what the whole world knows to be the most outrageous piece of legislation in the whole western hemisphere, all this recalls to mind the earlier reluctance of the founders of the Republic to follow Jefferson's advice and abolish the crime of slavery" (181).

Here is a stunning example of Arendt's simultaneous insight and oversight concerning segregation. Arendt understands that practicality is not a sufficient excuse for ignoring the unjust anti-miscegenation laws.[44] This is a key insight by Arendt, but she does not apply it to her own analysis of the various types of segregation laws. Arendt fails to understand that her framework dividing the public, the private, and the social, which she uses to privilege marriage laws above other racist laws, is also not a sufficient excuse for ignoring the unjust laws in education, housing, and employment. Unfortunately, her ordering of priorities imposes an artificial hierarchy on the types of racial oppression that result from various segregation laws. As a result, Arendt is oblivious to the fact that many of the arguments that she makes against marriage laws are also applicable to the discrimination laws in education that she defends.

An additional insight by Arendt here, just as in the opening lines of "Reflections," is the comparison that she makes between the segregation issue and the color problem created by slavery (America's "great crime"). Her insight is that a reluctance to take on segregation now is tantamount to the reluctance to take on the issue of slavery at the time the country was founded. But what she overlooks is just how interconnected are the histories of racialized slavery and anti-miscegenation laws in the United States. Segregation was a continuation of the color problem created by institutionalized and racialized slavery. Put another way, the Jim Crow laws were a white supremacist solution to the problems of emancipation and the abolition of slavery.

Connecting Anti-Miscegenation Laws to School Segregation

It has been argued that the term "miscegenation" was coined in an 1863 pamphlet, *Miscegenation: The Theory of the Blending of the Races Applied to the American White Man and Negro.*[45] The pamphlet defines miscegenation as "the blending of the various races of men—the practical recognition of the brotherhood of all the children of the common father."[46] Although this term did not appear until the second half of the nineteenth century, the criminalization of interracial sex and interracial marriage in America goes back to seventeenth-century colonial times. According to Winthrop Jordan, "As early as the 1660s the Maryland and Virginia assemblies had begun to lash out at miscegenation in language dripping with distaste and indignation. By the turn of the century it was clear in many continental colonies that the English settlers felt genuine revulsion for interracial sexual union, at least in principle."[47] But even before then, the 1630 case of Hugh Davis is often cited as an early example of anti-miscegenation sentiment. Davis, a white man, was sentenced to receive public corporal punishment "before an assembly of Negroes and others for abusing himself to the dishonor of God and shame of Christians, by defiling his body in lying with a negro."[48] In *American Slavery, American Freedom*, Edmund Morgan asserts, "It was in the area of sexual relations that the authorities were most assiduous to separate the races."[49] He cites later acts, from 1691 and 1705, that sought to prevent relationships between the English and Negroes, mulattoes, or Indians, noting that both acts "gave less attention to intermarriage than to the illicit relations of white women with black or mulatto men."[50]

Violations of these laws were punishable by fines, banishment, extended sentences of servitude (for white indentured servants), and servitude for the child produced by the sexual relations. According to Morgan, unions between white women and Black men that resulted in children had harsher penalties because "the result of such unions could be a blurring of the distinction between slave and free, black and white."[51] Thus, the two central concerns with regard to miscegenation were not only limiting Black men's access to white women's bodies, but also preserving racial distinctions and corresponding political distinctions between those enslaved and those free. The children born to Black mothers did not pose the same issue because in Virginia by 1662 children took on the status of their mother—meaning, the children of Black mothers were born into slavery. Morgan explains, "The laws said nothing about black women who had illegitimate children by white fathers. . . . Since the mother was a slave, the child, in spite of his intermediate color, would be a slave. . . . And the assembly took pains in all its laws to identify them with blacks and to deny them any benefit from a free paternity."[52]

Also significant to this discussion is the status of free Blacks, mulattoes, and American Indians in colonial Virginia. Their color "rendered freedom inappropriate for them," and Morgan asserts, "they were denied the right to vote or hold office or to testify in court proceedings."[53] Similar laws continued into the eighteenth and nineteenth centuries, including the 1753 Act for the Better Government of Servants and Slaves. Codes in 1819, 1849, and 1860 included provisions against miscegenation, and these provisions continued after emancipation and into the twentieth century with such laws as the aforementioned Act to Preserve Racial Integrity (1924). Miscegenation, color, slavery, freedom, and social and political rights are all intertwined and have been for centuries. Arendt's clear-cut divisions between the public, the private, and the social do not accommodate these interconnections.

There are pertinent overlaps and intersections between the miscegenation issue and the school integration issue that Arendt misses. When the *Brown* decision was announced, it was feared that the language used might affect marriage laws as well, making it difficult to enforce anti-miscegenation laws.[54] Southern whites insisted that integrating schools would be a slippery slope to intermarriage. Georgia governor Herman Talmadge's position on ending segregation was described by *Newsweek* in this way: it would "'create chaos not seen since Reconstruction days.' . . . The school decision, he believes, will lead to a breakdown in segregation, and that inevitably will result in intermarriage and the 'mongrelization' of the races."[55] Similar sentiments can be found in the hate mail sent to Little Rock school superintendent Virgil Blossom in the aftermath of the integration of Central High School. The racist mail is filled with fear and anger about the possibility of race mixing. One note (postmarked February 11, 1958) states, "THERE ARE TWO THINGS GOD DID NOT CREATE A MULE AND A MULLATOO."[56]

White segregationists resisted integration in education precisely because the segregation of schools was a tool by which they sought to prevent social equality and race mixing, on the one hand, and equity in education, on the other. Remembering these motives, it should not be surprising that two of the prominent iconic figures for school integration, Elizabeth Eckford and Dorothy Counts, are young women and not young men. This is significant because while the young women might be thought of as contaminating the white space more generally, the young men represented a specific threat to white purity and stoked fears about their access to white female bodies.

The young men who did integrate the high schools in Charlotte and Little Rock had to confront issues around social co-educational events like plays and the prom. There was fear that the Black male students would be allowed to play romantic roles opposite white female students, or have an opportunity to attend dances with white female students. In the case of Gustavas Allen Roberts, who integrated Central High School in Charlotte, the school principal received threats warning that Roberts would be hurt if he attended the prom. When the prom was canceled altogether, there were more threats that the prom better go on, only segregated. Ernest Green, who integrated Central High School in Little Rock, explains that he continued to participate in social activities with Black students at Horace Mann High School in part because "I wasn't going to Central High School's prom, and I wasn't going to be invited to be in the school play at Central."[57]

The fears of race mixing were explicitly articulated in an NBC radio broadcast that included four white students and three of the Little Rock Nine. When asked why they wanted to go to Central High School (when Black kids had their own schools), Ernest Green replied:

> The reason that I went over to Central is not because I have a school of my own. I, being a citizen of the U.S., have just as much rights as the other [white] person. So why can't I go to the school that's closest to me or the school that's in my neighborhood? . . . I mean it's not that I want to socialize or mix with other [white] people. But it's just that I want to get an education, just like everyone else. Really, I mean the purpose of going to school is not for socialization [with whites]. . . . I don't know how people get that idea. We're going there for education. Education only.[58]

Green was articulating a political argument, appealing to his rights as a citizen, rather than a social argument for school integration.

When the white students were asked why they did not want to go to school with Black students (interestingly, the interviewer used "Negroes" to name/race the Black children but "these children" when describing the white children, leaving whiteness unnamed/unraced), a student named Sammie, expressing a social anxiety within the white community, replied: "Well, I think it's mostly *race mixing... marrying each other.*" A white girl named Robin (described as a moderate) then interjected, "May I say that, as a whole, there has been some intermarriage and I think there is a low class that will go ahead and do it and then there is a very highly educated class—and to them it doesn't matter. But the middle class... they are just there for education. They are not going to intermarry."

By now it should be clear that school segregation laws and laws banning interracial marriage are different means to achieve similar ends: the prevention of race mixing. In this regard, Arendt is right about the scandalous nature of the marriage laws. Arendt makes a strong point and indeed has put her finger on something significant. Where she goes wrong is in her insistence on a hierarchy with regard to the multifaceted dimensions of anti-Black racism. Arendt fails to recognize that marriage laws and segregation laws in education, housing, employment, and public spaces are not mutually exclusive issues. On the contrary, they actually reinforce one another.

When we examine Arendt's attempt to dictate the proper order of priorities for oppressed minorities along with her privileging of marriage laws over education and other forms of racial discrimination, it is evident that Arendt's theoretical framework dividing the political, the social, and the private informs her hierarchical ordering of rights and priorities in the Little Rock essay. In her privileging of marriage laws above other forms of anti-Black racial oppression, Arendt neglects to see how intimately interconnected the former issue is to the latter. Adamantly committed to her own ordering of priorities, Arendt does not see how these issues are interrelated. Her hierarchy informs her stand against interracial marriage laws while simultaneously supporting segregation in education. Arendt's position concerning marriage laws is far more potent when we consider its implications beyond this dubious artificial hierarchy. It is not the case that we should confront marriage laws *instead of* other discrimination laws. The latter are not less important than the former. Rather, we should remain mindful that the laws prohibiting interracial marriage and the other Jim Crow laws in education and elsewhere were all ultimately motivated by white supremacy and the fear of race mixing and racial equality (in the political, social, and private realms).

3 "The Three Realms of Human Life
The Political, the Social, and the Private"

Hannah Arendt's "reflections on Little Rock" is only tangentially about the school desegregation crises that occurred in Arkansas. While this may seem like an odd claim to make, a closer look at the essay shows that the key themes taken up broadly address the division between the public, the private, and the social, as well as questions about social versus political rights; state versus federal rights (or the division of power); plurality; and the appropriate location of equality. There are obvious overlaps between Arendt's arguments in the Little Rock essay and other writings considered more central to her political thought. Elisabeth Young-Bruehl asserts, "The theoretical framework of Arendt's 'Reflections on Little Rock' was the one she had developed at length in *The Human Condition,* which was not widely known until after her article appeared in a 1959 issue of *Dissent.*"[1] Margaret Canovan has argued that Arendt's positions in "Reflections" are quite consistent with many of her other major political writings, including not only *The Human Condition* but also *The Origins of Totalitarianism, On Revolution,* and *On Violence.*

Having said that, my aim here is to examine Arendt's delineations between the political, the private, and the social by focusing on the Little Rock essay and *The Human Condition* in particular. I am responding to Young-Bruehl's claim that "when Hannah Arendt wrote topical essays like 'Reflections on Little Rock' and 'The Crisis in Education,' she employed the complex schematism elaborated in *The Human Condition,* but she seldom paused to recapitulate its main elements."[2] In contrast to Young-Bruehl, I take issue with the framework itself, not the lack of space (or complex history) available for Arendt to make her distinctions clear in the Little Rock and "Crisis in Education" essays.

Arendt's Distinctions in "Reflections on Little Rock"

In "Reflections," Hannah Arendt identifies the three realms of human life as the political, the social, and the private. She examines two "altogether different" points that the civil rights program addresses: (1) the right to vote and (2) the issue of segregation. The first issue—the right to vote, along with the right to run for office— are proper political issues. Arendt claims that "franchise and eligibility for office are the only political rights, and they constitute in modern democracy the very quintessence of citizenship" (RLR 51). The political realm is a realm of equality in Arendt's theoretical model, and she sees the U.S. republic as being based on the equality of all citizens (47). Consequently, it is not only equality before the law, but also equality in political life that is vitally important (ibid.). She elaborates, "The point at stake, therefore, is not the well-being of the Negro population alone, but, at least in the long run, the survival of the Republic" (ibid.).

Concerning the second issue—segregation—it both blurs and crosses the lines of the political, the social, the private, and the public. Since de facto segregation, perhaps more than de jure, is not a political issue, but rather a social issue, the social question (a question Arendt often also associates with class and economics) is raised here in relation to discrimination. Arendt asserts, "Society is that curious, somewhat hybrid realm between the political and the private"; it is the realm through which we pass before we enter "the political realm of equality," and it is a realm that demands discrimination (RLR 51; see also HC 33). Discrimination is to society what equality is to the body politic. Whether this discrimination is based on race, nationality, class, or any other "social" factor, it remains "as indispensable a social right as equality is a political right" (ibid.). Therefore, the question is not how to abolish discrimination, but how to keep it in the social sphere.

Within Arendt's framework, what occurs in the social and private spheres does not and should not concern the political sphere. Consequently, it is a violation of the social right to discrimination when legislation gets involved in social affairs. This is why, according to Arendt, we should allow vacation resorts to be segregated. The decision about what company I choose to keep while on holiday is a social decision that should not be regulated by legislation. Thus she claims, "There cannot be a 'right to go into any hotel or recreation area or place of amusement' because many of these are in the realm of the purely social where the right to free association, and therefore discrimination, has greater validity than the principle of equality" (RLR 52).

Unlike the political or social spheres, the realm of privacy is ruled by exclusiveness rather than equality or discrimination (RLR 52). According to Arendt, "The rules of uniqueness and exclusiveness are, and always will be in conflict with the standards of society precisely because social discrimination violates the principle, and lacks validity for the conduct, of private life" (53). The private realm is where we choose our friends and lovers. We choose what we want to do and with whom we want to do it. The right to privacy should not be violated by social customs or legislation. It is on these grounds that Arendt rejects laws against interracial marriage, asserting, "Social standards are not legal standards, and if legislature [sic] follows social prejudice, society has become tyrannical" (ibid.).

Arendt is not endorsing legalized segregation, even if she thinks discrimination is a social right. She asserts that segregation is not just a southern issue, but is rather "a matter of fact in the whole country and a matter of discriminatory legislation only in Southern states" (RLR 48). Arendt places discrimination in the social realm, but she does take issue with legalized segregation, stating, "The only reason that the Supreme Court was able to address itself to the matter of desegregation in the first place was that segregation has been a legal, and not just a social, issue in the South for many generations" (49). Arendt is clear that discrimination is a social right, but she does not go so far as to claim that it is also a legal or political right. She continues, "For the crucial point to remember is that it is not the social custom of segregation that is unconstitutional, but its *legal enforcement*. To abolish this legislation is of great and obvious importance" (ibid., emphasis in original).[3]

The private realm is ruled by exclusiveness. The social realm is a space where discrimination should be expected and permitted. The political realm is the only realm of equality. But there is some ambiguity around the political, the social, and the private for Arendt in this essay, particularly when she brings in public services like transportation. On the one hand, she claims that there cannot be a right to go into any hotel because these are in the realm of the social, but on the other, she explains that where one sits on the bus, in the railroad car, or in the station along with the right to enter hotels and restaurants in business districts should *not* be subject to segregation because these are in public spaces. She states, "In short, when we are dealing with services which, whether privately or publically [sic] owned, are in fact public services that everyone needs in order to pursue his business and lead his life. . . . Though not strictly in the political realm, such services are clearly in the public domain where all men are equal; and discrimination in Southern railroads and buses is as scandalous as discrimination in hotels and restaurants throughout the country" (RLR 52). But there is no explanation from Arendt for why employment, housing, and education are not also in the public realm.

Arendt's Distinctions and Her Critics

While Arendt's critics may not have agreed with her distinctions and how she applied them, these distinctions were not at all foreign to them. David Spitz begins his commentary by identifying Arendt's central principle to be "that a meaningful distinction must be drawn and maintained between the political, the social, and the private life" (PRB 57). Spitz compares Arendt's distinctions to John Stuart Mill's defense of individual liberty and the difference between self-regarding (private) and other-regarding (social) acts, and denies that there are acts that are so private that they affect only the individual (ibid.). He also calls into question "Miss Arendt's specious idea of freedom," preferring liberty in the Hobbesian ("proper") sense—that is, the absence of chains and constraints (61). Spitz does not engage Arendt on her own terms because he fits her framework into the more familiar theories of Mill and Hobbes. In her reply, Arendt asserts, "Mr. Spitz has misunderstood and misconstrued my argument. . . . my article was not understood on the terms I wrote it, and I shall try to repeat its essential points on a different, less theoretical level" (Reply 179).

The second critic, Melvin Tumin, dismissed by Arendt as having "put himself outside the scope of discussion" because of his abrasive tone, also notes that these distinctions are operating throughout her analysis. Tumin states, "Surely we are not expected to take her distinctions between the public and private domains of life seriously, at least not when they lead her where she has gone with them" (Pie 70). And he reiterates, "We cannot take Miss A's conception of the separate terrains and dominions of society seriously. They lead to conclusions which simply defy elementary logic and human decency" (ibid.).

Of all these critics, Sidney Hook offers the strongest response to Arendt's distinctions and overall argument as presented in "Reflections on Little Rock." We know that Hook's essay "Democracy and Desegregation" is the published revision of his unpublished critique of Arendt's "Reflections." Although Hook does not mention Arendt by name in his revised essay, we can read between the lines to trace her argument and his replies. To begin, Hook identifies opponents to desegregation who make education a private issue that is outside of the law: "The more liberal among these critics make a distinction between the public and private domain according to which it would be wrong to permit segregation on buses and railroads because these lie in the public domain, but wrong to prevent segregation, on the ground of personal freedom in private life. Education, they say, is one of those areas of personal life that are by their very nature outside of the purview of law in a democratic society."[4] He calls into question the application of these distinctions and points out, "The classification which puts transportation in the field of the political, and education in the field of the personal, is completely arbitrary as well as irrelevant."[5]

Hook notes that while he is concerned about personal freedom and the right to privacy, a dividing line between justifiable and unjustifiable discrimination must be drawn. A justifying principle for legitimate and illegitimate discrimination would enable us "to condemn all types of community segregation and at the same time permit a man to choose his friends and control the pattern of his personal and family life."[6] Hook rejects the distinction between segregation as social custom and segregation as discrimination enforced by law, a distinction that is often made by "anti-integregationists" (including Arendt), who simultaneously want to oppose the latter while challenging the legal prohibition of the former.[7] Positioning himself against any social custom that "violates human rights, and imposes unfair and cruel penalties upon individuals," Hook asserts that "the human freedoms that we safeguard by legal action against segregation and unfair discrimination are more important than those we restrict."[8]

Whereas Arendt expresses what Young-Bruehl describes as "moral anger" about school integration, Hook makes a moral argument against segregation, asserting, "If there is any relation between morality and law, the existence of certain evil social practices *may* (not must) justify us in taking legal action to prevent them."[9] For Hook, "the moral question is primary" and cuts across Arendt's arbitrary and irrelevant distinctions. He takes the position that it is on moral grounds that we are justified in adopting a Fair Education Practices Act, a Fair Employment Practices Act, and a Fair Housing Law.[10]

Finally, Hook describes the distinctions between the political, the public, the social, and the personal or private as "vague"—leading to "inconsistencies and confusions."[11] Using references that were probably extracted directly from Arendt's essay, Hook summarizes and then questions these distinctions: "Only the political sphere is the sphere of equality. Focal to it is the right to vote. The social sphere is the sphere in which discrimination is legitimate even if unwise. The public sphere includes both. The private sphere is one of exclusion. But to what sphere, then, belong the inalienable human rights 'to life, liberty, and the pursuit of happiness'?"[12] When framed in this way, it becomes clear that Arendt's attempts to parse segregation within her theoretical grid does not work. The political, private, and social realms are not as clear-cut as her paradigm suggests. Social and political inequalities are interconnected and reinforce one another.

It is curious that while segregation in education is not a political issue for Arendt in "Reflections on Little Rock," what she calls the American crisis in education is delineated as a political problem in "Crisis in Education." And although this crisis is presented as a political problem, she asserts that the connection made between education and politics is a misconception. Education is not "joining with one's equals in assuming the effort of persuasion and running the risk of failure" as is the case with politics (CE 176). Rather, education is "a dictatorial intervention, based upon the absolute superiority of the adult, and the attempt to produce the new as a *fait accompli*, that is, as though the new already existed" (176–177). For Arendt, "Education can play no part in politics, because in politics we have always to deal with those who are already educated." Furthermore, the very word education, "has an evil sound in politics; there is a pretense of education, when the real purpose is coercion without the use of force" (177). In contrast to politics, a private life for adults and children represents home, family, a secure place, and a shield from the public aspect of the world. The life of a child and human life in general needs protection from the public world where persons count but life does not matter (186). The lack of such a private life in the modern world makes things hard for children (188).

While I am sympathetic to Arendt's claims that children's lives and life in general need protection, I am doubtful that this protection is fully realized in segregated schools or altogether denied in desegregated schools. The harsh realities of a white supremacist world exist not only in the education system, but also in housing, transportation, and employment (all social issues for Arendt) as well as in voting, holding political office, and anti-miscegenation laws (the political issues for Arendt). In the Little Rock essay and "Crisis in Education," as in other writings and interviews about similar subjects, Arendt attempts to impose her theoretical framework, which rigidly divides the public, the private, and the social, onto situations that are at once all three or at least are more complex than this rigid framework will allow. If Arendt had been more attentive to the critics of "Reflections on Little Rock," perhaps the framework for her later political philosophy—with its emphasis on the political, the private, the social, and judgment, particularly as these concepts relate to racial oppression and violence—could have been modified. But it has also been suggested that Arendt had warning of the pitfalls of her position elsewhere. Robert Bernasconi argues that "Arendt had evidence at her disposal to enable her to recognize how the distinction between the social and the political had served to secure segregation with all its dire consequences"—based on her own notes on the opening essay of a text titled *The Negro Question* by George Washington Cable.[13]

George Washington Cable: A Curious Connection to Arendt's Distinctions

The son of slaveholders and a former Confederate soldier, Cable wrote novels and short stories about the South as well as two collections of nonfiction essays on the injustice of racial discrimination: *The Silent South* (1885) and *The Negro Question* (1890).[14] This provides some indication that Arendt familiarized herself with the parameters of the Negro question in the United States by use of an unusual source. Cable takes a predictably condescending tone toward African Americans in *The Negro Question*, remarking for example, "Let it be plainly understood that though at least scores of thousands are intelligent and genteel, yet the vast majority of colored people in the United States are neither refined in mind nor very decent in person. . . . For all that is known the black is an 'inferior race,' though how, or how permanently inferior, remains unproved."[15] And yet, when it comes to political rights, Cable (a Louisiana-born former Confederate soldier) is more vehemently critical of the discriminatory rhetoric and actions of southern whites and more defensive of full citizenship for Blacks than is Arendt in "Reflections on Little Rock" and elsewhere.

Cable argues that the South made both a political and a moral error in choosing to subjugate rather than elevate the masses (including not only freed Blacks but also lower-class whites). He attributes this choice to an unsubstantiated white fear that "the freedman would himself usurp the arbitrary domination now held over him and plunder and destroy society."[16] This fear is unsubstantiated because "the struggle in the Southern States has never been by the blacks for and by the whites against a black supremacy, but only for and against an arbitrary pure white supremacy."[17] Cable describes the Negro question in the following way: "Superficially, it is whether a certain seven millions of the people, one-ninth of the whole, dwelling in and natives to the Southern States of the Union, and by law an undifferentiated part of the Nation, have or have not the same full measure of the American citizen's rights that they would have were they entirely of European instead of wholly or partly [of] African descent."[18] For Cable the superficiality of framing the question this way lies in the fact that the answer is quite obviously "no." People of African descent in whole or part who were born in the United States do not have the same full measure of U.S. citizens' rights. He illustrates this point with examples of the separate-but-equal doctrine in public transportation, unequal treatment in the court system, the disproportionate representation of Black boys and men in prisons serving longer sentences for the same crimes as whites, and limited opportunities for education.

Cable asserts that the question to be pursued is not so much the epistemological question of whether this *is* so, but rather the ethical question of *ought*: "Putting aside mere differences of degree, the question is not, Are these things so? but, Ought they be so?"[19] He is clear that the answer to this ethical question is also "no." It ought not be the case that African Americans (a term he uses) are denied U.S. citizens' rights. And although the majority of Americans believe that African Americans should enjoy full citizenship and rights, the problem persists because a large majority of whites in southern states (though a small minority of the nation as a whole) disagree.

Like Arendt, Cable explores this issue from the standpoint of the balance between federal and state power. He explains that a minority made up of white southerners is able to remain entrenched against equal rights for Blacks because in "our scheme of government there is a constant appeal to the majority of the whole people, [but] the same scheme provides, also, for the defence [sic] of local interests against rash actions of national majorities."[20] Northern states, like the southern white-rule party, maintain "that *whether these things ought so to be or not is a question that every state must be allowed to answer for, and to, itself alone.*"[21] Cable goes on, "Thus, by a fundamental provision in the National Government, intended for the very purpose of protecting the weak from the strong, a small national minority has for twenty-five years been enabled to withstand the pressure of an immense majority. Whether this is by a right or wrong use of this provision is part of the open question."[22] Here he differs from Arendt, for whom this is not an open question. In her estimation, this provision is rightly used by southern states in their efforts to maintain segregated public schools. She warns, "The power potential of the Union as a whole will suffer if the regional foundations on which this power rests is undermined" (RLR 54).

Cable's analysis is nuanced not only by the distinction between the "is" and the "ought" but also by his attention to the public, private, and social layers of the Negro question. For example, he asserts that emancipation was limited in part because it destroyed the private ownership of slaves but not public discrimination: "The ex-slave was not a free man; he was only a free negro."[23] Cable associates the "public" with government and the "private" with society. Additional white fears that arise along these lines are the fear of public anarchy and the fear of a confusion of the races in private society. Concerning anarchy, Cable replies, "The freedman, whatever may be said of his mistakes, has never shown an intentional preference for anarchy. . . . He has shown at least as prompt a choice for peace and order as any 'lower million' ever showed."[24] Cable blames the fear about "a confusion of the races in private society" to "the double meaning of the term social and society."[25]

Civil equality in the public realm, which is necessary, should not be confused with social equality or, rather, inequality in the private realm, which is permissible. Cable explains, "The clear and definite term, civil equality, they [the southern states] have made synonymous with the very vague and indefinite term, social equality, and then turned and misapplied it to the sacred domains of private society. If the idea of civil equality had rightly any such application, their horror would certainly be just."[26] However, unlike those in the southern states, Americans in general understand that public or civil society (a realm of impersonal relations in which "all men, of whatever personal inequality, should stand equal") is distinct from private society (a realm that "is personal, selective, assertive, ignores civil equality without violating it, and forms itself entirely upon mutual private preferences and affinities").[27] The collapsing of the terms by southern states has to do with the institution of slavery, which "was both public and private, domestic as well as civil."[28] But rather than fear public equality, that is, "equal public rights, common public liberty, equal mutual responsibility," this form of equality should be embraced as "the greatest safeguard of private society that human law or custom can provide."[29]

There are evident overlaps between Cable and Arendt on the distinction between the public realm of political equality and the private/social realm where inequality and discrimination are expected (even required). Again, Arendt claims in "Reflections," "What equality is to the body politic—its innermost principle— discrimination is to society" (RLR 51). She explains, "In American society, people group together, and therefore discriminate against each other. . . . Without discrimination of some sort, society would simply cease to exist and the very important possibilities of free association and group formation would disappear" (ibid.). And Arendt reiterates, "In any event, discrimination is as indispensable a social right as equality is a political right. The question is not how to abolish discrimination, but how to keep it confined within the social sphere, where it is legitimate, and prevent its trespassing on the political and personal sphere, where it is destructive" (ibid.).

The Public and the Private in *The Human Condition*

A more commonly contemplated source for Arendt's distinctions between the political, the private, and the social is the model of the Greek polis she presents in *The Human Condition*. Hannah Arendt emphasizes six major themes in *The Human Condition*: the functions of labor, work, and action as well as the purposes of the public, the private, and the social. She explores the interconnection and the distinctness of these themes and the myriad of problems that she asserts have arisen due to ignorance of their meaning and relevance. Labor, work, and action are significant concepts in Arendt's political theory because they each play a role in a specific sphere. Labor is limited to the private sphere and work may appear in the public realm, but it is not political. Only action (along with freedom) belongs to the political realm.[30]

In the second part of *The Human Condition*, Arendt outlines the historical role of the public and the private spheres in the Greek polis, while asserting that the diminishing distinction between the two spheres is a consequence of the contemporary rise of the social. According to Arendt, the public sphere corresponds to the realm of the polis, which is the realm of freedom. Throughout *The Human Condition*, Arendt uses the terms public, polis, and political interchangeably (HC 30–33). For example, on one occasion Arendt states, "The public realm itself, the *polis*, was permeated by a fiercely agonal spirit where everybody had to constantly distinguish himself from all others" (41). Arendt also asserts that the public realm was and should be a space of freedom and action. "Freedom" to the Greeks meant that a man did not have to be bothered with the necessities of life because they were mastered in the household, he was not subjugated to the command of another, and he was in command himself (31–32). "Action" corresponds to human plurality, individuality, and political life. The plurality exists because we are all human and yet nobody is the same as anyone else who ever lived, lives, or will live (8).

The Greek public realm allowed for individualization and differentiation among its members. It was an arena of competition in which a man relied on particular deeds and achievements to be distinguished from others. In public a man attempted to exhibit himself as the best. It was the only place that men could show who they were (HC 41). Arendt further asserts that the excellence achieved in the public sphere surpassed any achievement possible in private. This is the case because excellence had to be demonstrated before a formal audience, or in the public presence of others. The activities of the public realm were seen and heard by all, receiving the widest possible publicity. Appearance became reality when it was seen in public. Validation, visibility, and reality were only accessible in public space, and the maintenance of this space preserved it for future generations.

At times Arendt's account of the political seems to place more emphasis on what is to be excluded from the political realm rather than providing a positive account of what belongs to the political realm. But there are instances in which she makes mention of what is properly "political." For example, in "The Social Question" Arendt asserts that the American Revolution was not social but political because the problem posed by the revolutionaries "concerned not the order of society but the form of government" (*OR* 68). She applauds the American Revolution's commitment to the foundation of freedom and the establishment of lasting institutions rather than submitting to necessity or focusing on social issues (92).

Contrary to the public realm of freedom and political equality, the private as described by Arendt was synonymous with deprivation or lack. A Greek man that lived an exclusively private life, "who like a slave was not permitted to enter the public realm or like the barbarian had chosen not to establish such a realm, was not fully human" (*HC* 38). It is not surprising that an exclusively private life constituted a slave-like or barbaric state because those confined to the private were often slaves to labor and necessity. These conditions were forced upon them, in many cases through violence, in order to create a public space independent of necessity. Laborers provided opportunities for free men to leave behind the necessities of life and to engage in public activities (48). To be free from the burden of life's necessities and participate in the polis required the subjugation of others, who were then forced to bear the burdens of the private realm.

According to Arendt, the necessities of life were provided and guaranteed in the private realm. Men were freed from dealing with them because those burdens were forced upon the subjugated. These necessities included bodily functions, labor, and household responsibilities. In the Greek polis, labor was banished and restricted to the private realm in an effort to keep it monitored (*HC* 47). Thus women and slaves were confined to private spaces, separated from the community, and constantly supervised. They were reduced to property and their functions were bodily and laborious (72). Their lives were controlled by necessity.

Confinement to a privatized life meant that one was simultaneously monitored and yet not really seen or heard by anyone in the sense that one's behavior was not displayed in the public realm. Consequently one confined to the private realm was denied those things that are fundamental to a "truly human" life, such as individuation (*HC* 58). The events that occurred in private were unacknowledged and hidden in the shadows. It is not difficult to imagine that those who were confined to privacy longed for validation of their existence. Perhaps they desired to display their excellence, enjoy freedom, or simply to put aside the necessities of life, like those who were privileged to participate in the public realm. Or, more important, they may have desired to experience freedom and agency in the political sense advanced by Arendt. At best, the necessity, futility, and shame associated with the private realm pales in comparison to the freedom, permanence, and honor attributed to the public realm.

The Rise of the Social

According to Arendt, the ancient Greek distinction between the public and the private spheres has been distorted in the modern era, and this is partially a result of what she describes as the "rise of the social."[31] The social realm is a product of the modern age and is neither private nor public. Arendt claims that society seems to have "conquered the public realm" (HC 41). When we substitute the social for the political, we betray the Greek understanding of politics. Before the modern age housekeeping, family matters, and economics were confined to the private sphere. But the rise of society has turned formerly private issues into public concerns. The life process itself, necessity, and economics—which properly belong to the private—have been channeled into the public realm by the rise of the social. Arendt asserts that the emergence of society "has not only blurred the old borderline between private and political, it has also changed almost beyond recognition the meaning of the two terms and their significance for the life of the individual and the citizen" (38).

Another problem that Arendt has with the social as she presents it in *The Human Condition* is that it takes away human plurality and replaces it with a unanimous and simultaneously anonymous general will of all. One used to be able to express a distinct opinion among other differing opinions in the public realm, but the rise of the social has distorted this plurality. Society always demands that its members act as though they were members of one enormous family that has only one opinion and one interest (HC 34). Arendt criticizes society because it expects from each member a certain kind of behavior, imposing rules and normalizing members to make them behave (40). The prevalent concept of the common good is indicative of the absence of a true political realm, and as a result, the public realm is composed of the social rather than the political (35).

Arendt has a problem with the pursuit of one common good because it excludes the possibility and spontaneity of action, as well as any outstanding achievement (HC 40). The true purpose of the public realm (to be a platform to display one's excellence, individuation, and action) becomes eclipsed by the social—a mass of undifferentiated people. Society normalizes everyone's behavior and imposes rules and regulations. According to Arendt this regulation of behavior makes political action virtually impossible. The spontaneous action and outstanding achievement previously possible in the political realm have been replaced with mere behavior.[32] The social realm is like an invisible force that is uncontrolled by man and that paralyzes action. There is no longer a public space for political action; politics has been reduced to no-man rule, rule by an invisible hand, rule by nobody (*HC* 44–45). Arendt warns, "The rule by nobody is not necessarily no-rule; it may indeed under certain circumstances even turn out to be one of the cruelest and most tyrannical versions" (40).[33]

More Contexts for and Critiques of Arendt's Distinctions

Arendt insists that the distinction between the public and private spheres was eroded in the modern age with the rise of the social, yet she simultaneously and incessantly refers to and applies the very distinctions that she has already declared to be eroded. One might ask if these very specific Greek understandings of politics and of the political are applicable to times and to circumstances where such distinctions are no longer adhered to. Some commentators have criticized the role of the Greek polis in *The Human Condition,* while others have rejected these critiques as a misreading of Arendt. In the latter group, Margaret Canovan argues that Arendt makes use of history (and in this case the model of the Greek polis) as "a repository of human experience in which we can find permanent human possibilities that are wider than those known and expected within our own culture."[34] In a later text, Canovan adds that Arendt's theory of action "is not an exercise in her nostalgia for the Greek polis."[35] Likewise, Maurizio Passerin D'Entrèves describes Arendt's return to a Greek version of the political as "an attempt to break the fetters of a worn-out tradition and to rediscover a past over which tradition no longer has a claim."[36] He adds, "Her act of recovery of the central political categories of the Greek and Roman experience must therefore be seen as an attempt to save the modern world from its growing futility."[37]

Richard Bernstein is perhaps the most outspoken in rejecting critical readings of Arendt's analysis of the Greek polis. He asserts that it is "wrongheaded and perverse . . . to think that Arendt's reflections on action and politics have their 'origin' in an idealized nostalgic picture of a Greek polis (that never existed). This misguided, but all too fashionable, view of Arendt is based on a superficial reading of *The Human Condition.*"[38] To be clear, my analysis is aimed at the *principle* of the division and what is required to maintain it rather than the model used to explain the principle. Thus, even if Arendt is not relying on or prioritizing the model of the Greek polis, the division between public and private space as conceived by Arendt still proves to be problematic. Her exclusionary account of the public realm is restrictive because the public-private divide limits political action for those persons who (or those issues that) are confined to the private realm. This dichotomy has long been challenged by feminist theorists like Catharine MacKinnon, Susan Moller Okin, Jean Bethke Elshtain, and Carole Pateman.[39] Seyla Benhabib, Robert Bernasconi, Norma Moruzzi, and Mary Dietz (among others) have criticized Arendt's particular version of the distinction.

Arendt's rigid division between the public and the private spheres will not necessarily prevent the effects of the social that she cautions against, nor will it ensure political activity. This is most obviously the case for those who carry life's burdens in the private realm and are consequently denied political agency. Strict distinctions between the private and the public realms inhibit the very political action that is so important to Arendt. Thus, a rigid division between public and private space, both in Arendt and historically speaking, raises some key concerns. A quandary in Arendt's model of the polis is that women and slaves, along with the necessities of life, are confined to the private realm and consequently are excluded from the political realm. Thus, we are faced with a paradox of public space. The possibility of attaining freedom in the public realm seems to be achievable only through the oppression of others in the private realm. A consequence of their exclusion from the political realm is not only a perpetual denial of their freedom and political action but also a denial of any methods by which they might obtain freedom and act in Arendt's political sense.

In *Situating the Self,* Benhabib identifies two models of public space introduced by Arendt in *The Human Condition:* the "agonistic" model of the Greek polis and the "associational" model of modern politics. In the Greek polis, the public space was political space where appearance became reality, men demonstrated greatness, and men competed with one another for recognition. Women, slaves, laborers, and many others were forced to fulfill life's necessities and therefore were excluded from engaging in political activities. The modern associational view of political space is not significantly different. According to this model, public space "emerges whenever and wherever, in Arendt's words, 'men act together in concert' . . . the space 'where freedom can appear.'"[40] Public space is wherever power and action are coordinated and demonstrated through speech and persuasion among a group of equal human beings.[41] Yet this model is still exclusive because all humans are not seen as equal, and various groups must contend with discrimination in both the private and the public/political realms.

Returning to the Greek model, Benhabib explains that the "political space of the polis was only possible because large groups of human beings like women, slaves, laborers, non-citizen residents, and all non-Greeks were excluded from it and made possible through their 'labor' for the daily necessities of life that 'leisure for politics' which the few enjoyed."[42] By forcing labor and necessity upon those in private space, freedom and action could only be exercised by those in public space. Consequently this distinction "has served to confine women and typically female spheres of activity like housework, reproduction, nurturance, and care . . . to the 'private' domain and to keep them off of the public agenda in the liberal state."[43] Bernasconi has problematized Arendt's agonistic model of public space along similar lines: "The evident problem with this conception of political freedom is, not only that it has historically been confined to the few, but also that, of its nature, it is bought at the expense of others. . . . If to be human is to disclose oneself in the public sphere, and if that possibility is itself dependent on one's being liberated from the necessities imposed by the life-cycle, then it would seem that one of the pre-conditions of being human is the inhumanity of exploiting the labor of others."[44] Bernasconi reinforces the criticism that in order for some to enter the public realm, many must be confined in the private realm. The many are sacrificed to create public space, freedom, and opportunities for political action for the few.

For theorists like Moruzzi and Dietz, it seems obvious that Arendt is aware of the oppressive conditions necessary for the public-private distinction. Yet this awareness does not result in a shift in Arendt's position. Moruzzi in *Speaking through the Mask* explains, "That the toiling private individuals were women and slaves, defined by their status as necessary to but unfit for the political experience, Arendt blandly acknowledged. Her resolute distinction between a public and private realm, her advocacy of the traditional hierarchy between them, and her casual relegation of women to an undervalued private sphere, have led many contemporary readers, especially feminists, to regard Arendt as something of a traitor to her sex."[45] In *Turning Operations* Dietz attempts to uncover "promising directions for feminist speculation" in *The Human Condition* without bracketing the more troubling aspects of Arendt's analysis. According to Dietz, "Arendt seems to have little interest in thinking about male domination and female subordination," and this lack of interest "prevents her from considering how there might be a 'pre-political' despotism, or how the 'political' must be expanded to include those who were not permitted 'into the interlocutory scene of the public sphere,' or how the boundaries of the public were secured through the 'production of a constitutive outside.'"[46] For Dietz, the issue is not whether Arendt acknowledges these realities, but rather that after acknowledging them Arendt "still withholds any direct comment about the justice or injustice of such arrangements in which some living beings are kept in darkness, deprived of or denied the only conditions (politics, plurality, power) that, by Arendt's own lights, render them fully human and free."[47]

Arendt's exclusionary account of the public realm is inadequate because the public-private divide limits political action for those persons who are confined to the private realm. When the private realm is composed of the majority, any strict division between the public and private realms entails the exclusion of the majority from political space and consequently from action as well. But this division remains a problem even if it is the few or the minority who are confined to the private realm. Arendt's clear-cut separation of the private and public realms only crystallizes this paradox of public space. She acknowledges that in order to participate in public/political space, one must be liberated from the burdens of life in the private realm and also that this liberation is most often achieved by forcing life's burdens onto other people. But where does this leave the people upon whom life's burdens have been forced? How do they ever achieve the human condition of freedom through speech and action in the public realm? Where is the political agency of the oppressed (i.e., those carrying life's burdens)? As long as freedom, action, speech, and political influence remain in the hands of those liberated from the necessities of life by exercising domination over others, the persons dominated and subjugated by others will not be free in the political sense that Arendt intends.

These distinctions between the public and the private (and even the political and the social) are not unique to Arendt; they have been made elsewhere—in George Washington Cable's work, as discussed earlier, but also in modern political philosophy more generally (for example, in liberal democratic theory). Although Arendt traces the public-private distinction to ancient Greece and Rome, claiming that it has been lost in the modern era, we find the distinction made later by political theorists like Hegel, Hobbes, Locke, Rousseau, and Mill. So while the Greeks separated (and exalted) the public/political sphere above the disparaged private sphere, liberal theorists have often emphasized the individual and separated the public and private domains in an effort to differentiate spheres of decision making by political institutions versus private individuals.

The uses of the public-private distinction have been fluid, meaning different things in different contexts. Raymond Geuss asserts in *Public Goods, Private Goods*, "There is no such thing as the public/private distinction, or, at any rate, it is a deep mistake to think that there is a single substantive distinction here that can be made to do any real philosophical or political work. When one begins to look at it carefully, the purported distinction between public and private begins to dissolve into a number of issues that have relatively little to do with one another."[48] Geuss also suggests, "To make a practically significant distinction between public and private, a distinction, that is, that deserves to have moral, existential, social, or political standing, we first need a clear idea of the use to which we wish to put the distinction when we have made it."[49] What interests me is Arendt's particular application of these distinctions and the disturbing direction in which they take her analysis of the Negro question.

The divisions between the public, the private, and the social have significant implications not only in *The Human Condition*, but also in "Reflections on Little Rock." The uses to which Arendt puts these distinctions for understanding the Negro question are not only offensive but also counterproductive. Benhabib says about the application of this framework to the Little Rock crisis: "perhaps the episode which best illustrates this blind spot in Hannah Arendt's thought is that of school desegregation."[50] Arendt fails to make the distinction between "public justice—equality of educational access"—and the "issue of social preference—who my friends are or whom I invite to dinner."[51] Benhabib and Bernasconi agree that the consequences of Arendt's insistence on keeping the public and social realms separate are very clear.[52] Arendt emphasizes a rigid division between these realms in the original Little Rock essay, reiterates the division in her "Preliminary Remarks" (added later), and stays firm in her position in "A Reply to Critics" and even in her reply letter to Sidney Hook. This, in spite of all of the warnings about the fallacy of her argument, first from Hook, then from critics David Spitz and Melvin Tumin, and even from several letters to the editors at *Dissent*.

Arendt wears profound blinders when it comes to racial oppression in the United States, a result, in part, of the lines she draws between the public, the private, and the social. Arendt's commitment to this grid distorts her perceptions and inhibits her understanding of anti-Black racism in the United States.[53] Arendt does not problematize the foundation of segregation and racism and the impact of these systems of oppression in the social *and* political lives of African Americans. This restrictive delineation of the Negro question as a social issue is especially alarming given her alternate analysis of the Jewish question, which she insists is political: "Belonging to Judaism had become my own problem, and my own problem was political. Purely political!" (*EU* 12).

4 "The End of Revolution Is the Foundation of Freedom"

Hannah Arendt's *On Revolution* offers an in-depth study of the concept of revolution, including two of the most influential revolutions of the eighteenth century, the American Revolution and the French Revolution. But Arendt's evaluation of the American and French Revolutions in this work is full of inconsistencies.[1] On the one hand, she identifies similarities, for example noting that the early stages of the American and French Revolutions suggest that they initially sought reforms in the direction of constitutional monarchies and that both were eventually driven to the establishment of republican governments (*OR* 134). She explores how the American and French Revolutions were formed and influenced by almost identical traditions, but with different experiences and preparation (119). Both revolutions were concerned with freedom, in America with the notion of "public happiness" and in France with the notion of "public freedom" (ibid.). On the other hand, Arendt describes the French Revolution as a failed one that "ended in disaster" and seems disgruntled that it has had a greater place in our memory and in world history than the "triumphantly successful" American Revolution—perhaps another incorrect assumption on her part (56).

In examining the meaning of revolution Arendt draws distinctions between revolution and rebellion, and between liberation and freedom. The key political themes of freedom and action continue to be emphasized by Arendt as they relate to new beginnings and the foundation of constitutional government. I argue that as in *The Human Condition* and "Reflections on Little Rock" we see Arendt's theoretical framework of the political, the private, and the social operating problematically in *On Revolution*. The framework does not hold as she attempts to apply it to the institution of slavery in the American context. Although slavery is understood to be a crime by Arendt, it is almost simultaneously dismissed as a social question. Accordingly, the founding fathers are celebrated for focusing on political rather than social issues, even while she notes that they understood that the institution of slavery from the beginning had undermined the political principle of freedom. I also challenge her claims about the relationship between race and slavery.

The Meaning of Revolution: Freedom and New Beginnings

Arendt traces the historical meaning of "revolution" back to the time of Copernicus, when it was used in the study of astronomy and referred to the revolving motion of the stars and planets (*OR* 42). After offering the historical meaning of the term "revolution," Arendt differentiates between rebellion (the end of which is liberation) and revolution (the end of which is freedom). Arendt is making two distinctions here: between rebellion and revolution, and between liberation and freedom. The second set of terms is different because liberation is a condition of freedom, but not a promise of freedom (29). Furthermore, although the term "liberation" may imply liberty, it is only a negative notion of liberty, consequently, "the intention of liberating is not identical with the desire of freedom" (ibid.). For Arendt, revolution is not a struggle for liberation, but rather the foundation of freedom (142). Put another way, the "plot" to the story of revolution is freedom (29).

Arendt argues that revolutions in the modern age have as their aim freedom, foundation, and new beginnings—all key concepts within her theoretical framework of the political. Referring to the term's earlier scientific application going back to Copernicus, Arendt explains, "Nothing could be further removed from the original meaning of the word 'revolution' than the idea of which all revolutionary actors have been possessed and dispossessed, namely, that they are agents in a process which spells the definite end of an old order and brings about the birth of a new world" (*OR* 42).[2] The word "revolution" was used as a political term in the seventeenth century to describe a "revolving back" or "a restoration of monarchical power in its former righteousness and glory" (42–43).[3]

Revolution aims at the foundation of freedom, unlike rebellion, which aims at liberation from oppression. Revolution and rebellion are not so much mutually exclusive as they are two stages of the foundation of something altogether new. For Arendt, "There is nothing more futile than rebellion and liberation unless they are followed by the constitution of the newly won freedom" (*OR* 142). While the historian emphasizes "the first and violent stage of rebellion and liberation," the political scientist avoids this pitfall and takes note of "the quieter second stage of revolution and constitution" (ibid.). Thus, she highlights the formation of a constitutional government as a significant achievement of the American revolutionary process.

While Arendt differentiates between rebellion and revolution and between liberation and freedom, she emphasizes the interconnectedness of freedom and the new beginnings resulting from a revolution. For Arendt "the idea that freedom and the experience of a new beginning should coincide" is "crucial" to understanding the modern concept of revolution (*OR* 29). She underscores this point even more by claiming, "Only where this pathos of novelty is present and where this novelty is connected with the idea of freedom are we entitled to speak of revolution" (34). These ideas emerged with the revolutions occurring at the end of the eighteenth century. Arendt is clear that this specifically modern concept of revolution is "inextricably bound up with" a new beginning, history suddenly beginning anew, the unfolding of a story never before told (28). She asserts, "Revolutions are the only political events which confront us directly and inevitably with the problem of beginning" (21). This echoes earlier claims about beginnings in the form of natality in *The Human Condition,* where she explains that the political concept of action "has the closest connection with the human condition of natality; the new beginning inherent in birth can make itself felt in the world only because the newcomer possesses the capacity of beginning something new, that is, of acting" (*HC* 9).[4] In *On Revolution,* Arendt reminds us that beginnings have their challenges, including carrying within them "a measure of complete arbitrariness" and a potential instability with "nothing whatsoever to hold onto" (*OR* 206).[5]

Arendt also takes up freedom and the political in her essay "What Is Freedom?," where she claims that the Greek city-state first discovered the real meaning of the political realm. According to Arendt, the purpose of "the political in the sense of the polis was to establish and preserve a space for freedom. . . . [It was] a realm where freedom is a worldly reality, tangible in words which can be heard, deeds which can be seen, and events which are talked about and remembered" (WIF 154). She then defines the political as that which occurs in public space: "Whatever occurs in this space is political by definition, even when it is not a direct product of action. What remains outside this space of appearances . . . may be impressive and noteworthy, but it is not political strictly speaking" (155).[6] Arendt asserts that in the tradition of philosophy the correct meaning of freedom has been lost. Along with the philosophical tradition, the Christian tradition has also relocated freedom from the external realm of the political to the internal realm of free will or even conscience. But Arendt contends that freedom belongs in the realm of politics, not in the realms of thought or philosophy. Rather than being the aim of political action, freedom is the reason that political organization and action are achievable in the first place. The possibility of participating in politics is contingent on freedom from life's necessities. Again looking at the model of the Greek polis, Arendt claims that freedom in that time meant to be free from the private realm and free to participate in the political realm. According to Arendt, "Without it [freedom] political life as such would be meaningless. The raison d'etre [*sic*] of politics is freedom, and its field of experience is action" (WIF 146).

For Arendt, freedom is not a philosophical notion. It is rather a political notion to be expressed in the political realm through speech (word) and action (deed). We must think of freedom in terms of the public/political realm and in terms of speech and action. If one is free from the necessities of life and still chooses not to participate in the political realm, or chooses not to act, one is not really free because freedom is available only through action in the political realm. The very existence of political institutions depends on men who act.

The American Revolution and the Social Question

Arendt proclaims that the American Revolution "succeeded where all others were to fail, namely, in founding a new body politic stable enough to survive the onslaught of centuries to come" (*OR* 198).[7] More specifically, she contrasts the American and French Revolutions on the basis that the founding fathers posed a political rather than a social problem: "The problem they [America's founders] posed was not social but political, it concerned not the order of society but the form of government" (68). Arendt attributes this focus on the political rather than the social in the American context to the fact that "the predicament of poverty was absent from the American scene but present everywhere else in the world" (ibid.). Framed in this way, the "political" points to the formation of government while the "social" points to poverty. The predicament of poverty is not just deprivation and misery, but inhumanity. Poverty is a dehumanizing agent; to be poor is to be confined to the invisible sphere of the private under the absolute dictation of the body and under the burden of necessity (60). Arendt references John Adams's claim that the predicament of the poor is to be unseen and unacknowledged by mankind (69). This description of the poor is similar to Arendt's description of the private in *The Human Condition,* where she asserts that private men do not appear; it is as though they do not exist (*HC* 58). She adds that the condition of poverty forces a free man to act like a slave (64).

Here, I think it is important to differentiate between the figurative invisibility of the poor or their confinement to the private, and the literal absence of poverty in America. Even if Adams is correct in describing the poor as "unseen and unacknowledged," this does not mean that poverty did not exist in America at the time of the American Revolution. Arendt acknowledges that America had laborers who were poor, but insists they were not miserable or driven by want. For this reason "the revolution was not overwhelmed by them" as was the case in the French Revolution (*OR* 68). While compassion did play a role in the French Revolution and has driven the best men of all revolutions, Arendt claims that "the only revolution in which compassion played no role in the motivation of the actors was the American Revolution" (71).[8] Of course, the portrait that Arendt has painted of America up to this point is missing one very important component, the institution of slavery. To her credit, Arendt quickly notes that "the absence of *the social question* from the American scene was, after all, quite deceptive" and that "abject and degrading misery was present everywhere in the form of slavery and Negro labor" (ibid., my emphasis).

The description of racialized slavery as a "social question" in *On Revolution* is consistent with Arendt's analysis in "Reflections on Little Rock," where she describes racism in education, employment, and housing as discrimination and reduces it to a social or a private issue, but not a political one. It seems that, for Arendt, the Negro question is not only a Negro problem; it is also frequently presented as a social rather than a political problem. But how is it that the founding fathers were able to focus on political issues of government rather than on the social issue of misery, as manifested in slavery and Negro labor? Arendt first suggests that the founding fathers ignored the conditions of the poor and the conditions of slaves because they were rendered virtually invisible and went unnoticed. Following John Adams, she asserts that even worse than the invisibility of the poor was the invisibility of the slaves and explains, "we can only conclude that the institution of slavery carries an obscurity even *blacker* than the obscurity of poverty; the slave, not the poor man, was 'wholly overlooked'" (*OR* 71, my emphasis). (The use of "blacker" here is particularly significant given its racial overtones.) But Arendt also attributes this focus on the political to indifference, stating almost apologetically: "this indifference, difficult for us to understand, was not peculiar to Americans and hence must be blamed on slavery rather than on any perversion of the heart or upon the dominance of self-interest" (ibid.).

"The Primordial Crime upon Which the Fabric of American Society Rested": The Incompatibility of Slavery and Freedom

Although Arendt makes repeated attempts to present slavery and racism as social, rather than political, issues, this framework does not hold. Just as Arendt eventually (even if reluctantly) acknowledges that segregation is at once a social, private, and even a political issue, she also comes to recognize that slavery is not simply a social issue, but a crime with political implications. Recall that in "Reflections" slavery is identified as "the one great crime in America's history" (RLR 46).[9] In the same essay Arendt evokes the founding fathers when responding to her critics about miscegenation laws. She compares white liberals' unwillingness to address the miscegenation laws to the founding fathers' unwillingness to abolish slavery. Arendt states, "All of this calls to mind the earlier reluctance of the founders of the Republic to follow Jefferson's advice and abolish the crime of slavery" (Reply 181). While Jefferson yielded to the slaveholding states, "he, at least, still had enough political sense to say after the fight was lost: 'I tremble to think that God is just'" (ibid.). She elaborates, "He trembled not for the Negroes, not even for the whites, but for the destiny of the Republic because he knew that one of its vital principles had been violated right at the beginning. Not discrimination and social segregation, in whatever forms, but racial legislation constitutes the perpetuation of the original crime in this country's history," namely, slavery (ibid.). In *On Revolution*, Arendt expresses this point again, stating that Jefferson and others "were aware of the primordial crime upon which the fabric of American society rested," and "they were convinced of the incompatibility of the institution of slavery with the founding of freedom" (*OR* 71). Arendt is attempting to simultaneously assert both that slavery was a *social* issue that did not move the founding fathers to pity and that they recognized the *political* truth that slavery was incompatible with freedom.[10]

Aside from pointing out this incompatibility, Arendt does not give adequate attention to the significance of the relationship between slavery and freedom during the American Revolution and beyond. This is ironic given the way in which she underscores this relationship in *The Human Condition*. In her discussion of the Greek polis, the men (and women and laborers) enslaved in the private realm are contrasted with the men who are free to enter the public realm.[11] Arendt also stresses the idea that freedom meant being free from the necessities of the private realm in order to be able to enter the public realm of the political. But she neglects to take up the strong dialectical relationship between freedom and slavery in the United States. I contend that the foundation of political freedom by the founding fathers was possible precisely because it could be juxtaposed with the institution of slavery. The antithesis of slavery and freedom mirrored the antithesis between the political statuses of Black (and other nonwhite groups) and white people. The white image of freedom was defined in contrast to Black slavery, and the Black image of bondage was defined in contrast to white freedom. As Toni Morrison explains in *Playing in the Dark*, "The concept of freedom did not emerge in a vacuum. Nothing highlighted freedom—if it did not in fact create it—like slavery. . . . For in that construction of blackness *and* enslavement could be found not only the not-free but also, with the dramatic polarity created by skin color, the projection of the not-me."[12] Morrison is underscoring the idea that freedom had all the more significance in the United States because it stood in such drastic contrast to slavery. This is a central aspect of the relationship between slavery and freedom in America that Arendt misses.

Slavery's Fundamental Offense against Human Rights

A stronger critique of slavery in the American context can be found in Arendt's earlier work *The Burden of Our Time* (later reissued under the title *The Origins of Totalitarianism*). In *Burden*, Arendt understands:

> Slavery's fundamental offense against human rights was not that it took liberty away (which can happen in many other situations), but that it excluded a certain category of people even from the possibility of fighting for freedom—a fight possible under tyranny, and even under the desperate conditions of modern terror (but not under any conditions of concentration camp life). Slavery's crime against humanity did not begin when one people defeated and enslaved its enemies (though of course this was bad enough), but when slavery became an institution in which some men were "born" free and others slave, when it was forgotten that it was man who had deprived his fellow-men of freedom, and when the sanction for the crime was attributed to nature. (*BOT* 294)[13]

Here Arendt identifies several harms caused by the institution of slavery: it took away liberty, it prevented those who were enslaved from the possibility of fighting for freedom, and it allowed some men to be born slaves and others to be born free—a determination attributed to nature. And finally, slavery was a crime committed by man against his fellow man, not against subhumans or animals.[14]

When we look at the specific case of slavery in the United States we find a system in which *Black* people were born slaves and *white* people were born free. This omission in her analysis is significant because in an earlier section of *Origins*, Arendt asserts that although slavery was "established on a strict racial basis, [it] did not make the slave-holding peoples race-conscious before the nineteenth century. Throughout the eighteenth century, American slave-holders themselves considered it a temporary institution and wanted to abolish it gradually" (*OT* 177). But the opposite is true. America's commitment to slavery and to slaveholders was demonstrated in the drafting of the Declaration of Independence in the late eighteenth century. Given Arendt's focus on Thomas Jefferson, we might look to his writings on this matter. In his autobiography Jefferson attempts to redeem himself, explaining that he included an anti-slavery clause (directed at the king of England) in the Declaration of Independence. But Jefferson's rebukes against the king of Great Britain, who was "Determined to keep open a market where MEN could be bought and sold," were removed because they also represented an indictment against American slavery.[15] He states, "The clause too, reprobating the enslaving of the inhabitants of Africa, was struck out in complaisance to South Carolina and Georgia, who had never attempted to restrain the importation of slaves, and who on the contrary still wished to continue it."[16] Jefferson presents himself as taking a stand against slavery (although he owned slaves), and he reveals how determined slaveholders were to preserve racialized institutional slavery.[17]

It also seems contradictory for Arendt to claim both that slavery was an institution established on a "racial" basis and that slaveholders were not conscious of race. While some may argue that it would be anachronistic to apply the phrase "race consciousness" to slaveholders before the nineteenth century, it is still the case that slaveholders had to be aware of some concept of race, or at least the values of "Black" (or mulatto or Indian) versus "white" skin, which determined which race would consist of the slaveholders and the free, and which would consist of the slaves and the unfree. Racism alongside economic motivations was certainly at the heart of slavery as it developed into a racialized institution assigning a hereditary status that would continue for generations.[18]

The racialized institution of slavery, which determined that white people would be born free and Black people would be born slaves, is something that developed over time with the passing of specific laws that set broad precedents. In *Slavery in the Making of America*, historians James Horton and Lois Horton explain that in "the early colonial period, American concepts about race, slavery and standards for race relations were still being formulated and were not as fixed as they would become in the eighteenth century. Still, by the mid-seventeenth century it was becoming clear that Africans and white servants received different treatment."[19] For example, in 1640 three servants (two white and one Black) ran away from a plantation in Virginia. Once captured, the two white servants were punished with two more years added to their time of servitude. But the Black servant, John Punch, was sentenced to a lifetime of slavery.[20] Edmund Morgan asserts in *American Slavery, American Freedom,* "Whether or not race was a necessary ingredient of slavery, it *was* an ingredient. If slavery might have come to Virginia without racism, it did not. The only slaves in Virginia belonged to races alien from the English. And the new social order that Virginians created after they changed to slave labor was determined as much by race as by slavery."[21]

Over time it became evident that the system of indentured service was disadvantageous to those who exploited others' labor because once the servants were freed, they posed a threat to their former masters. Gradually landowners turned to the establishment of a racialized slave system. According to Horton and Horton, "By the 1660s the Chesapeake colonies began establishing the legal foundation for racial distinctions that created the formal structure for eighteenth century racial slavery."[22] In 1662 it became law in Virginia that children would take on the status of their mother, ensuring multigenerational resources of slave labor.[23] In 1691 South Carolina passed the "first comprehensive slave code . . . [which] defined 'all Negros, Mulattoes, and Indians' sold into or intended for sale . . . as slaves."[24] As previously mentioned, Virginia had anti-miscegenation laws going back to the seventeenth century. By 1705 Massachusetts law prohibited interracial relationships, and the severity of the punishments issued were according to race and gender.[25] The history of slavery, including the laws that transformed it into a racialized institution, reveals a pattern of laws that were used as early as the seventeenth century to oppress and exploit people along what we now describe as racial lines.

From its foundation, the United States has been a country claiming principles of equality in word yet failing to adhere to those principles in deed. Arendt's praise of the American Revolution is especially alarming given the flagrant contradiction between freedom and slavery; the principle of the equality of all men has been belied by the simultaneous and intentional enslavement of a significant portion of the population. For this reason, Frederick Douglass in "What to the Slave Is the Fourth of July?" declares: "I am not included within the pale of this glorious anniversary! Your high independence only reveals the immeasurable distance between us. The blessings in which you, this day, rejoice, are not enjoyed in common. The rich inheritance of justice, liberty, prosperity and independence, bequeathed by your fathers, is shared by you, not by me. The sunlight that brought life and healing to you, has brought stripes and death to me. This fourth [of] July is *yours*, not *mine*. *You* may rejoice, *I* must mourn."[26]

Douglass condemns the hypocrisy of the United States from its very foundation. It is and has always been a nation that believes in equality for a select group at the expense of oppressing several other less-favored groups.

The French Revolution and the Social Question

Standing in contrast to Arendt's praise of the American Revolution for posing a political question is her critique of the French Revolution for emphasizing necessity (including biological processes, changes of the body, and the people's needs) and poverty rather than the foundation of freedom (*OR* 59–60).[27] Prioritizing these needs above freedom is undesirable because poverty and necessity are social, not political, matters. According to Arendt, "No revolution has ever solved the 'social question' and liberated men from the predicament of want, but all revolutions, with the exception of the Hungarian Revolution in 1956, have followed the example of the French Revolution and *used* and *misused* the mighty forces of misery and destitution in their struggle against tyranny and oppression" (112).[28] Arendt acknowledges that "all revolutions" are about a "struggle against tyranny and oppression." But she also claims that poverty and want are not fitting revolutionary aims, and even if they were, a revolution is incapable of solving the social question of poverty. She asserts, "The whole record of past revolutions demonstrates beyond doubt that every attempt to solve the social question with political means leads to terror, and that it is terror which sends revolutions to their doom. . . . To avoid this mistake is almost impossible when a revolution breaks out under conditions of mass poverty" (112). Efforts to deal with economic or social issues by political means not only go against the distinction of the public and the private, but also inevitably result in destruction and doom.

Arendt calls for the exclusion of life's necessities and economics from the political realm: "Since the revolution had opened the gates of the political realm to the poor, this realm had indeed become social" (*OR* 90–91). She leaps from the claim that the question of poverty is a social issue to asserting outright that allowing the poor in the public realm makes it social. The poor bring household issues into the public realm, issues "which, even if they were permitted to enter the public realm, *could not* be solved by political means, since they [are] matters of administration, to be put into the hands of experts, rather than issues to be settled by the two-fold process of decision and persuasion" (91, my emphasis). On Arendt's account, the poor distort the political by raising social problems as political issues, but she reiterates her position that social matters cannot be addressed by political methods.

Arendt explains that when the poor appeared in the realm of politics in the French Revolution, necessity appeared with them. And when Arendt asserts that the "uprising of the poor against the rich carries with it an altogether different and much greater momentum of force than the rebellion of the oppressed against their oppressors" (*OR* 112), it seems that "poor" and "oppressed" along with "rich" and "oppressors" are mutually exclusive terms. In other words, it is suggested that the condition of poverty is not a way of experiencing oppression, and that economic conditions are not a means by which the rich may oppress the poor.[29] Arendt remains consistent with her line of reasoning in *The Origins of Totalitarianism* and *The Human Condition* that mass poverty, economics more generally, and the state of misery that result are social rather than political problems—not solvable by revolutions or political methods.

Arendt acknowledges the austerity of poverty, but poverty is also considered to be the unfortunate (but seemingly acceptable) result of scarcity. This is in contrast to the Marxist argument that poverty is a political issue and the result of exploitation of the proletariat by the bourgeoisie. And while Marx may have persuaded the poor "that poverty itself is a political phenomenon, the result of violence and violation rather than of scarcity," Arendt is critical of Marx for taking this position because in her view poverty is not a political phenomenon, but a social one (*OR* 62–63). She is discontented that after the French Revolution, and even more strikingly through the influence of Marx, the role of revolution was no longer to free men from the oppression of their fellow men, not to found freedom, but to overcome scarcity and turn it into abundance (64). According to Arendt, it was Marx who taught the idea that poverty should help men break the shackles of oppression because the poor have nothing to lose. The men of the French Revolution were inspired by hatred of tyranny and by rebellion against oppression (73).[30]

One additional pertinent criticism of the poor is that poverty makes political plurality, that is, multiple political voices, impossible. Arendt suggests this when she claims that unlike the "social" French Revolution, the "political" American Revolution maintained the plural aspect of "the people." Arendt claims that for the American founders, "the word 'people' retained the meaning of manyness, of the endless variety of a multitude whose majesty resided in its very plurality" (*OR* 93). In contrast to the multitude of voices in the American Revolution, plurality ceased to exist (if it ever existed) in Europe "as soon as one approached the lower strata of the population. The *malheureux* whom the French Revolution had brought out of the darkness of their misery were a multitude only in the numerical sense" (94). Arendt assumes that those whom she labels as the "lower strata," that is, the poor, cannot have a multiplicity of voices. Although a plurality of voices and the presentation of differing opinions are important, even crucial for any politics that takes difference seriously, a major problem that arises here is Arendt's exclusion of those voices that perhaps should count the most, or at the very least should count equally among other voices. The exclusion of poverty and the poor from the political realm is an exclusion of voices that need to be heard in the public arena. Excluding the poor poses limitations on the "plurality" that Arendt claims she wants to achieve.

The social question in *On Revolution* has been analyzed from a variety of perspectives in the literature. Canovan has called Arendt elitist for representing the poor as a mass incapable of plurality and degrading to politics: "A great deal of *On Revolution*, therefore, like a great deal of Hannah Arendt's previous books, seems to be concerned with arguing that political freedom, which is the all-important glory of human existence, is possible only among an aristocratic leisured class . . . and that it has been lost in the modern age because [an] increasing equality of condition has given politics into the hands of the poor and lowly."[31] And yet, Canovan points out, this elitism is contradicted by Arendt's enthusiasm for participatory democracy "amongst those very people whom she has condemned to political oblivion."[32] On a similar note, Bernstein has highlighted Arendt's "paradoxes and unstable tensions" concerning the social question and modern revolutions.[33] He wants to recognize the importance of Arendt's distinctions while also showing that her social-political distinction is "untenable and will not hold up to critical scrutiny."[34] In *On Revolution*, she acknowledges but also wants to suppress or repress the fact that revolutions are born out of struggle for social liberation. Bernstein states, "Although Arendt knows this, she does not do justice to the fact that every revolutionary movement in the modern age has begun with a growing sense of some grave social injustice, with the demand for what she calls liberation."[35] Ferenc Feher has also critiqued Arendt's application of the political-social distinction to the French Revolution because the French could not viably separate the social from the political given the circumstances of that revolution. While conceding the primacy of the political, Feher still contends that the preservation of this exalted position cannot be achieved "by relegating the 'social problem' to the household (which, if realizable at all, is certainly a programme which requires an equally liberticide course of action [as the French Revolution] for its realization)."[36]

My point here is not to present Arendt as heartless or insensitive to the problems of poverty and social oppression. I understand that Arendt saw the French Revolution and other revolutions that followed (including, for example, the Russian Revolution) as making disastrous attempts to solve the social questions of poverty, want, and necessity through violence and terror. But I *am* interested in the implications of this analysis for the Negro question in the overlapping contexts of revolution and slavery. Arendt's emphasis on the social question in the French Revolution distracts from her stronger and more significant critique of the emptiness of the Declaration of the Rights of Man. Furthermore, it is peculiar that Arendt's account of poverty and misery in America leads her to the problem of institutionalized slavery as America's primordial crime, but in her criticisms of the French Revolution (of the poor and the revolutionary leaders' compassion for the poor) she does not address, much less critique, slavery in the French context. The French involvement in the slave trade and French support for slavery are clear cases for Arendt's position that human rights claims without citizenship rights lack substance.

The Declaration of the Rights of Man and Citizen

As with the French Revolution more generally, Arendt is very critical of the Declaration of the Rights of Man and Citizen. Having already differentiated the aims of the American and French Revolutions, she also contrasts the American Declaration of Independence with the French Declaration of the Rights of Man and Citizen. Again she speaks favorably of Americans for proclaiming that rights previously enjoyed only by Englishmen should in the future be enjoyed by all men, that is, "all men should live under constitutional, 'limited' government" (*OR* 149). (Arendt does not revisit the issue of American slavery and who counted as a man here.) Rather than indicating the limits of government, France's Declaration of the Rights of Man and Citizen was assumed to be the foundation of government (148). Arendt says the French version of human rights "meant quite literally that every man by virtue of being born had become the owner of certain rights" (149). For her, the Declaration of the Rights of Man and Citizen is empty because it "proclaims the existence of rights independent of and outside the body politic, and then goes on to equate these so-called rights, namely the rights of man *qua* man, with the rights of citizens" (ibid.). Arendt clarifies her point of emphasis (as with the social question): it is a "fateful misunderstanding" to think that "the proclamation of human rights or the guarantee of civil rights could possibly become the aim or content of revolution" (ibid.).

Arendt has more to say about the Declaration of the Rights of Man and Citizen in *The Origins of Totalitarianism,* where she connects the perplexities of the rights of man to stateless (and therefore rights-less) persons.[37] In the context of the French Revolution, Arendt identifies a contradiction between the declaration of inalienable rights as the heritage of all human beings and the demand for national sovereignty (*OT* 230, 272).[38] The emptiness of these so-called inalienable rights lie in the fact that they seem unenforceable, particularly for stateless persons. When people are in nation-states in which they are not citizens, they are not in a position to appeal to certain rights or to have those rights enforced. She has in mind here the many stateless and rights-less persons who lost their national rights in the aftermath of World War I. But her analysis of the pitfalls of the Declaration of the Rights of Man is readily applicable not only to the condition of slaves and freemen at the time of the French Revolution but also to the French colonial/imperial context before, during, and after two world wars.

This issue is not altogether lost on Arendt: she does acknowledge that rights are not protected in Africa. She states, "The full implication of this identification of the rights of man with the rights of peoples in the European nation-state system came to light only when a growing number of people and peoples suddenly appeared whose elementary rights were as little safeguarded by the ordinary functioning of nation-states in the middle of Europe as they would have been in the heart of Africa" (*OT* 291). But her point of emphasis is not the concession that elementary rights are not guaranteed in Africa, but rather how outrageous it is that the rights of peoples in European nation-states could be dismissed as if they were in the heart of Africa. And while this comment might invite reflections on the ways in which colonialism and slavery also violate the Declaration of the Rights of Man and Citizen, Arendt does not elaborate on this connection. Instead, she explicitly distances slavery (conceived in the U.S. context rather than the French) from statelessness.

According to Arendt, as bad as slavery was for the Negro, the state of the slave was not as bad as the condition of the Jews who are stateless persons without a community. She says, "Even slaves still belonged to some sort of community; their labor was needed, used, and exploited, and this kept them within the pale of humanity. To be a slave was after all to have a distinctive character, a place in society—more than the abstract nakedness of being human and nothing but human" (*BOT* 295/*OT* 297). Arendt is asserting that to belong to the community of slaves within civil society is preferable to the "abstract nakedness" of being "nothing but human." I acknowledge that Arendt is presenting the issue of mere humanity in the European context, specifically the French notion of the rights of man. But the problem that she misses here is that the slave was denied *both* human rights *and* political rights.

Does Arendt really think that one should prefer the subhuman or even nonhuman status of slavery to being nothing but human? It seems she may be leaning in this direction when she later uses the example of a Negro in a white community to explain her point: "If a Negro in a white community is considered a Negro and nothing else, he loses along with his right to equality that freedom of action which is specifically human; all his deeds are now explained as 'necessary' consequences of some 'Negro' qualities" (*BOT* 297/*OT* 302). She adds, "Much the same thing happens to those who have lost all distinctive political qualities and have become human beings and nothing else" (ibid.). At first glance it seems that Arendt sees the reduction of the Negro's deeds to some Negro characteristic as similar to the reduction of certain persons to human beings and nothing else. But when examined more closely, this is not a comparison, but a subtle contrast of the Negro situation with the Jewish situation. In her remark on slavery, Arendt has already described stateless Jewish people as having been stripped down to the "abstract nakedness of being human and nothing but human." Here, in her discussion of the Negro in the white community, she makes explicit reference to the Negro, but only an implicit reference to the Jew. The contrast she is drawing between the two is that the Negro is denied his humanity and reduced to his Negro qualities, but the Jew is denied *not* Jewish qualities, but *political* qualities, and reduced to a human being and nothing else. Again Arendt is overlooking the fact that while the Jew may be denied political qualities, the Negro is denied both human *and* political qualities or rights.

I am not taking a position against Arendt's argument that a declaration of human rights outside of a political system in which those rights can be enforced or defended is empty. On the contrary, I am in strong agreement with Arendt on this claim. I would add that there are some who have been granted citizenship and yet still do not enjoy the full benefit of citizens' rights within the political system. One can readily see the disconnect between the declarations and principles of rights, liberty, equality, and fraternity for all, juxtaposed with the numerous groups of persons denied those rights or excluded from those principles—like slaves (in France and in the French colonies); free Blacks and free *gens de couleur* (the latter being those of mixed race who inherited property and sometimes even owned slaves of their own, and therefore had economic stability but limited or no social and political rights); and perhaps even the white slaveholders and planters in the French colonies. And the gap between the principles and the reality persisted not only in the age of the French Revolution, but also up to and after the First and Second World Wars. Unfortunately, Arendt does not make this connection in *On Revolution* or in *Origins*. Again we see Arendt's simultaneous insight (about the emptiness of the Declaration of the Rights of Man, particularly as it pertains to the Jewish question and statelessness) and gross oversight (about the ways in which the French institutions of slavery and colonialism expose this emptiness far better than the social question of poverty that she so vehemently criticizes).

Slavery and the French and Haitian Revolutions

In emphasizing the social question and critiquing the Declaration of the Rights of Man and Citizen as they relate to the French Revolution, Arendt makes no mention of France's institution of slavery in *On Revolution*. France developed colonies in the Caribbean as early as 1625, and Spain ceded the western portion of Hispaniola (which became the colony Saint-Domingue) to France by 1697.[39] The slave economy generated capital and stimulated growth for France leading up to the French Revolution. Thus, at the forefront of the French Revolution were concerns not only with the social question and the poor, as Arendt posits, but also with the Negro question and the institution of slavery. It is clear that at the time of the French Revolution, slavery, the slave trade, and colonialism (or what Arendt would call imperialism) were all integral parts of France's commerce and political system, presenting France with its own Negro question (and white problem).[40]

The Negro question in France and its colonies at the time of the French Revolution was not only about slavery (in general, those enslaved lived in a state of misery and degradation absent any meaningful political rights), but also about the status and rights of *gens de couleur*—freedmen and their descendants (including free "negroes" and "mulattos"), who were numerically equal to whites in some colonies.[41] The document that provided the parameters for the treatment of both slaves and *gens de couleur* is the colonial ordinance of 1685 known as *Le Code noir*, although Laurent Dubois notes that while *Le Code noir* was theoretically applicable beginning in 1685, "its stipulations on the rights of slaves were consistently ignored by planters."[42] Furthermore, although *Le Code noir* of Louis XIV provided for citizenship rights for classes of freedmen, other rules of custom allowed for various forms of racism and discrimination that undermined these rights and left them unprotected.[43] The provisions of this code remained in effect until the definitive abolition of slavery in 1848. Thus, in addition to Arendt's critiques of the Declaration of the Rights of Man and Citizen as a defining document of the French Revolution, it is necessary to read this declaration alongside (or perhaps against) *Le Code noir*—the earlier, equally emblematic document in France's history, which firmly establishes France's involvement in the trade, institutionalization, and legalization of slavery.

From the very beginning, the Declaration of the Rights of Man and Citizen (which stated, "All men are born and remain free and equal in rights") and the claims about liberty, equality, and fraternity were quite limited when we consider French slavery and colonialism. In *Dark Side of the Light: Slavery and the French Enlightenment*, Louis Sala-Molins repeatedly reminds us that the category "men" in the Declaration of the Rights of Man and Citizen did not constitute the totality of all men: "The Negro slaves and the saleable Negros are (all) not part of that number, unless, of course, those Negroes are not men but movable assets as the *Code noir* specifies."[44] The French representatives did not want to think about the slave because the slave "does not belong to the body that constitutes the citizenship of the citizen, because he was never a member of the group that constituted 'the subjectness' of the subject."[45] Sala-Molins puts the matter of slavery and the French Revolution bluntly, asserting, "The rhetoric of the Enlightenment and of the Revolution is worth absolutely nothing when judged against the only reality that matters: the master is guilty, the slave trade is a crime, slavery is the crime of all crimes."[46]

There were voices that called for the abolition of slavery, including antislavery writings from Montesquieu, Rousseau, and Voltaire. In 1781, the marquis de Condorcet published *Rèflections sur l'eslavage des negroes* (under the pseudonym M. Schwartz). Abbé Raynal published *Historie philosophique et politique des ètablissements et du commerce des Europèens dans les duex Indes* (1782), with contributions from Diderot. In 1788, Jacques-Pierre Brissot de Warville founded the Société des Amis des Noirs. The Friends of the Blacks lobbied against slavery, published pamphlets for their cause, and sought an immediate end to the slave trade followed by a gradual end to slavery. But their voices were practically drowned out by other groups that were in conflict with one another on some matters, but allied on the issue of maintaining slavery in an effort to protect their mutual interests.[47] France did abolish slavery in Saint-Domingue and held a national convention to celebrate in February 1794. Interventions from Jean-Baptiste Belley and others at this convention influenced the decision to decree the abolition of slavery in all of the colonies. But the necessary measures for abolition were not implemented, and Napoleon Bonaparte reinstated slavery by decree on July 16, 1802. French slavery was not abolished definitively until April 27, 1848, long after the French and Haitian Revolutions.

Even more curious than Arendt's silence on France's slavery and colonialism as relevant issues for the French Revolution is her erasure of the Haitian Revolution altogether in a book on revolution.[48] The significance of the Haitian Revolution cannot be overstated, even on Arendt's own terms. Recall that for Arendt we must be attentive not only to the stage of rebellion aiming at liberation, but also to revolution aimed at freedom, new beginnings, history beginning anew, and the unfolding of a story never before told (OR 28–34). The Haitian Revolution sought not only liberation from slavery and from the French colonial order, but also the foundation of freedom for political participation and most certainly new beginnings and the unfolding of a story never before told—the establishment of an independent Black state by former slaves and their free allies. To be sure, Arendt is not alone in ignoring the significance of the Haitian Revolution, but as with other matters related to race and systems of oppression—on which she frequently has keen insight (even if with problematic oversights)—we might expect more from her. On the more general marginalization of the Haitian Revolution, Sibylle Fischer asserts, "One might have expected that the Haitian Revolution would figure prominently in accounts of the revolutionary period, on a par with the revolution in France and the events that led to the foundation of the United States of America. That is not so. To this day, most accounts of the period that shaped Western modernity and placed notions of liberty and equality at the center of political thought fail to mention the only revolution that centered around the issue of racial equality."[49]

Arendt presents an especially intriguing case of this erasure in political theory. As Fischer states, "A particularly interesting example is Hannah Arendt's On Revolution of 1963. Like many others before and after her, she takes the French and American Revolutions as the paradigm and fails to mention the case of Haiti (along with any other nonmetropolitan revolution)."[50] In exploring how such omissions (not only of France's slavery and colonialism but also of the Haitian Revolution) is possible, we are brought back to Arendt's social-political distinction and why it does not hold. According to Fischer:

Revolutionary antislavery combines what in Arendt's language would be the social and the political in ways that make it intractable for her. Considering slavery as a political issue makes her recoil—a symptom of her own inability to make modern racial slavery (and its revolutionary counterpart) fit into her conceptual frame. Slavery, being neither purely political nor purely social, cannot be spoken of. Slaves vanish, first literally, through the institution that cloaks them with invisibility, and then conceptually, in the abyss between the social and the political. Revolutionary antislavery is a contradiction in terms. Haiti becomes unthinkable.[51]

These omissions by Arendt are attributed not only to the social-political distinction, but also to her "deeply engrained Eurocentrism," "racial hierarchies," and "colonialist ways of assessing" what counts or what is important.[52]

Arendt's omissions have also been taken up in *Conscripts of Modernity: The Tragedy of Colonial Enlightenment,* where David Scott compares and contrasts Arendt's analysis in *On Revolution* with C. L. R. James's analysis of revolution in *The Black Jacobins.*[53] Scott notes that while both scholars are interested in the legacy of the eighteenth-century revolutionary tradition, James would disagree with Arendt's claim that the Jacobins brought the French Revolution to its doom and he would find Arendt's silence on the Haitian Revolution, "her complete elision of it and its place in the revolutionary tradition and its legacy," quite objectionable.[54] Using Arendt against herself, Scott explains, "Arendt's oversight is all the more puzzling, and all the more disappointing, because what she is lamenting in *On Revolution* is precisely the failure of memory; she is in fact urging the importance of 'remembrance' to sustaining the spirit of the revolutionary tradition."[55] Looking at James's account of Toussaint Louverture as representative of this lost tradition, Scott argues that the tragedy of Louverture's story is precisely the tragedy of revolutionary tradition that Arendt wants us to remember, only her Eurocentrism prevents her from seeing or recognizing it.[56]

In examining Arendt's analysis of the American and French Revolutions, we are confronted again with her simultaneous insights and oversights. Arendt is ultimately somewhat ambivalent in her characterization of slavery, whether it is a social or a political question in the American context. Although she insightfully recognizes slavery as a crime in America, Arendt is somewhat dismissive of this crime in the grand scheme of the American Revolution, perhaps because slavery is also labeled a social issue. But Arendt is again inconsistent because slavery is not only a social issue and a crime, it is also an institution that is at the core of the foundation of U.S. society and government. How do we reconcile the fact that American rebels were able to engage in a revolution that emphasized freedom and new beginnings while simultaneously maintaining a racialized system of slavery? More important, how does Arendt herself reconcile the incompatibility of slavery and freedom in the context of the American Revolution? Arendt is clear that Jefferson and the other founding fathers *knew* that the institution of slavery was incompatible with the founding of freedom, and she frames their acceptance of these conditions as indifference to those enslaved. Arendt understands that this poses a dilemma, and she names it explicitly in "Reflections on Little Rock" and in *On Revolution,* but offers no solution. All of this exposes the problems that arise from Arendt's limited conception of the public/political sphere and of freedom versus the social realm of necessity and poverty.

While we can problematize Arendt's presentation of slavery as a social and/or political problem in America, we must also be mindful of her egregious omission of the Negro question and slavery in the French context. As Fischer points out, slaves vanish altogether in Arendt's analysis of the French Revolution, and this omission is surpassed only by her erasure of the Haitian Revolution as a relevant subject of inquiry in *On Revolution.* Given Arendt's preference for the *vita activa* of political engagement, Fischer wonders why Arendt does not "raise the question of whether considering slaves politically might have produced some important insight? What prevents her from thinking about slaves as potential political agents? From thinking of the politics of antislavery as part of the revolutionary spirit she studies?"[57] I agree with both Fischer and Scott that Arendt's rigid theoretical framework, which attempts to divide what is properly political from the social question, enables these oversights, which are further undergirded by her Eurocentrism. We will see this Eurocentrism emerge in similar ways in Arendt's analysis of race thinking, racism, and imperialism along with her negative representations of Africa and people of African descent in *The Origins of Totalitarianism.*

5 "A Preparatory Stage for the Coming Catastrophes"

In 1945–1946 HANNAH Arendt began to formulate a proposal for a manuscript with the working title *The Elements of Shame: Anti-Semitism—Imperialism—Racism.*[1] The text would be published with the title *The Burden of Our Time* (1951) in England, but most are familiar with the text as *The Origins of Totalitarianism* (1951). Arendt formulated the proposal for *Origins* a few years after she fled southern France for the United States. Having been transferred from Paris to an internment camp in Gurs, Arendt and Heinrich Blücher made a narrow escape, which forced them to leave in 1941 for Lisbon and then New York without Martha Arendt.[2] I do not take lightly Arendt's situational knowledge about the rise of Nazism and her integration of this knowledge into her understanding of the interrelationships between antisemitism, imperialism, and totalitarianism. It is also important to note the timing of the writing of *Origins:* not only in the aftermath of totalitarianism but also in the face of anti-imperialism, or what is often described as decolonization.

In her preface to the first edition of *Origins* (dated "Summer 1950"), Arendt writes, "Antisemitism (not merely the hatred of the Jews), imperialism (not merely conquest), totalitarianism (not merely dictatorship)—one after the other, one more brutally than the other, have demonstrated that human dignity needs a new guarantee which can be found only in a new political principle, in a new law on earth, whose validity this time must comprehend the whole of humanity while its power must remain strictly limited, rooted and controlled by newly defined territorial entities" (*OT* ix). Young-Bruehl explains that, for Arendt, the analysis in *Origins* is not historical writing insofar as such writing seeks to offer a justification; there is no justification for antisemitism, imperialism, and racism. But at the other end of the spectrum, the book was also not intended as a simple condemnation, which Arendt thought could be taken as cynical and therefore unconvincing.[3]

I am interested in Arendt's *Origins* as one of her major political writings on the Negro question—a question that arises throughout the text in her examination of imperialism, race thinking, and racism. In part 2 of *Origins,* Arendt utilizes her usual method of distinction making by differentiating colonialism and imperialism along with race thinking and racism. But the systematic oppression that occurred during the "colonial" era in the Americas had "imperialist" undertones, and the groundwork for race thinking and racism was laid long before what Arendt considers to be the age of imperialism—between 1884 and 1914. In addition to the colonialism and imperialism distinction, there is also a relationship between imperialism and totalitarianism. While there are places where it seems Arendt is offering a continuation argument concerning imperialism in Africa and totalitarianism in Europe, it is also the case that she emphasizes the uniqueness of Nazism and the totalitarian Holocaust as altogether different from and more brutal than imperialism. I want to challenge a hierarchy-of-oppressions approach between imperialism and totalitarianism by taking seriously Michael Rothberg's use of multidirectionality as a conceptual model to imagine "how it is possible to remember the specificities of one history without silencing those of another."[4] Despite the fact that Arendt seeks to take a position against racism, there are still traces of racism in her analysis. This is marked in part by her frequent use of the term "savage" and by the way that she naturalizes Africans, asserting that they are pure nature and suggesting that they are somehow not capable of culture and the formation of (or participation in) the political.[5]

Colonialism and Imperialism

In *Origins* Arendt asserts that the difference between colonialism and imperialism has been neglected along with the distinctions between commonwealths and empires, plantations and possessions, and colonies and dependencies (*OT* 131). The differences between colonialism, or colonial trade, and imperialism that Arendt emphasizes include the following: when she speaks of colonialism, she has in mind the European colonization of America and Australia, and when she speaks of imperialism, she has in mind the expansion of European countries into Africa and Asia and the racism, exploitation, and violence that occurred there. For Arendt, "colonialism" involved more of an extension of the laws and ideals of the mother country into the colonial territory, while "imperialism" often denied the extension of these laws, denied efforts to assimilate the foreign country, and focused on economic expansion for the mother country at the expense of the conquered country through racist ideologies and through violence.[6] She dates the period of imperialism from 1884 to 1914 (between the "scramble for Africa" and the pan-Africa movements), and argues that the political ideals of imperialism have "expansion as a permanent and supreme aim of politics" (*OT* 125).

According to Arendt, imperialism grew out of colonialism and, with the help of Cecil Rhodes, took expansion for the sake of expansion as its focal point no earlier than 1884. She emphasizes that although imperialism may have grown out of colonialism, imperialism represents something that is radically different and new in the history of political thought and action (*OT* 125). But even if we acknowledge that imperialism is quite possibly a new concept, the relationship between colonialism and imperialism still needs to be underscored. When we consider the genocide of Native people in the Americas and of Aboriginals in Australia, along with the enslavement and mass murder of Africans (in Africa, through the

Middle Passage, and in the Americas), it is evident that colonialism before 1884 shares many violent and expansionist characteristics with imperialism. While imperialism may differ from colonialism in its timing, some of its motivations, and its role as a precursor to totalitarianism, it is also the case that, like imperialism, colonialism in the Americas and Australia employed violent, religious, and racist tactics for the purpose of economic expansion.

Arendt seems to overlook this aspect of colonialism when she denies that these continents had any precolonial history or culture: "Colonization took place in America and Australia, the two continents that, without a culture and a history of their own, had fallen into the hands of Europeans" (*OT* 186). However, later (in the expanded edition of *Origins*, but not in *The Burden of Our Time*) Arendt acknowledges the violent and oppressive circumstances surrounding colonization, saying, "through centuries the extermination of native peoples went hand and hand with colonization in the Americas, Australia and Africa" (440). Arendt does recognize (even if she does not emphasize) the similarities between the motivations and oppressive methodologies of colonialism in the Americas and Australia, and the later phenomenon of imperialism in Africa and Asia. But her analysis leads her to connect racism to imperialism rather than identifying the seeds of racism that were already planted during colonialism.

Arendt does not draw the connection between race thinking and racism already at work both in precolonial slavery and during colonialism. Colin Palmer in "Rethinking American Slavery" explores this relationship: "By the fifteenth century, the Spaniards, Portuguese, and probably other Europeans had already assumed a posture of superiority over black Africans, based on cultural or phenotypical (racial) differences. . . . some scholars are now suggesting that by the end of the European Middle Ages the terms *slavery* and *race* were becoming interchangeable and negative 'racial' characteristics began to be applied to Africans in intellectual and public discourse."[7] This relationship between race thinking and slavery took place long before race thinking and racism were used as tools for imperialism and totalitarianism. While Arendt suggests (and some contemporary race theorists and historians would agree) that there was not a cohesive theory of race before and during the colonial era, I am arguing that the genocide, oppression, and aggression characteristic of this era operated along the lines of categories that we now classify as racial.[8]

Addressing Arendt's position on the timing of race thinking, racism, and imperialism, Richard King asserts: "The idea that there were biological differences among peoples that justified slavery and made extermination easier had clearly emerged in the Western hemisphere by the seventeenth century, much earlier than Arendt's focus on the 'second' imperialism of the late nineteenth century would suggest. . . . Arendt was essentially correct to make a strong connection between racism and European expansion, but hierarchical racism, as opposed to horizontal race-thinking, emerged much earlier and much more decisively than she allowed."[9] Arendt bypasses the development of race thinking and racism in the colonial context, and instead attributes racism to imperialism, which she sees as a precursor to totalitarianism. For her, the period of imperialism was a "preparatory stage for the coming catastrophes" of totalitarianism (OT 123).

Imperialism and Totalitarianism

Operating in the background of this analysis of imperialism and totalitarianism is Arendt's attempt to elucidate Nazism and the Holocaust. Arendt is able to identify the relationship between the bourgeoisie, racism, and imperialism, on the one hand, and antisemitism and the attempted obliteration of the Jewish people, on the other—a connection that has less often been made by white scholars (or, better stated, a connection that is frequently altogether ignored by white scholars). As Charles Mills has pointed out, from the Third World perspective an insistence on the uniqueness of the Jewish Holocaust "represents an astonishing white amnesia about the actual historical record. . . . The dark historical record of European imperialism has been forgotten."[10] Mills notes that "the Racial Contract makes the Jewish Holocaust—misleadingly designated *the* Holocaust—comprehensible, distancing itself theoretically both from positions that would render it cognitively opaque, inexplicably sui generis, and from positions that would downplay the racial dimension and assimilate it to the undifferentiated terrorism of German fascism."[11]

The connection between imperialism and Nazism has been readily visible to and highlighted by Black scholars. To give just two examples, we can look at the intellectual and educator W. E. B. Du Bois (*The World and Africa,* 1946) and the political theorist and Negritude poet Aimé Césaire (*Discourse on Colonialism,* 1955). Along similar lines as Mills, Du Bois and Césaire challenge the claim that there was something unique about Nazi totalitarianism. In Du Bois's words: "There was no Nazi atrocity—concentration camps, wholesale maiming and murder, defilement of women or ghastly blasphemy of childhood—which the Christian civilization of Europe had not long been practicing against colored folks in all parts of the world in the name of and for the defense of a Superior Race born to rule the world."[12] Du Bois is not denying the horror of Nazism; rather, he is denying its uniqueness in the history of "the Christian civilization of Europe."[13]

Likewise, Césaire (who uses the term "colonialism" rather than "imperialism") describes colonization as comparable to Nazism against people of color. Hitler's words and sentiments were preceded by similar sentiments from colonizers about the colonized. According to Césaire, European/Western civilization has caused two problems that it cannot solve: the problem of the proletariat and the colonial problem.[14] Césaire explains that the bourgeoisie has awakened to a boomerang effect of its actions, namely, Nazism. His analysis is worth quoting at length:

The gestapos are busy, the prisons filled up, the torturers at work.... People are surprised, they become indignant. They say: "how strange! But never mind—it's Nazism, it will pass!" And they wait and they hope; and they hide the truth from themselves . . . that it is Nazism, yes, but that before they were its victims, they were its accomplices; that they tolerated that Nazism before it was inflicted on them, that they absolved it, shut their eyes to it, legitimized it, because, until then, it had been applied only to non-European peoples; that they have cultivated that Nazism, that they are responsible for it, and that before engulfing the whole edifice of Western, Christian civilization in its reddened waters, it oozes, seeps, and trickles from every crack.[15]

Césaire asserts that the colonial system created by Europeans and targeting "non-European peoples" eventually ushered in Nazism, which targeted European peoples. For Césaire, the twentieth-century bourgeois railing against Hitler is being inconsistent. Europeans, particularly the bourgeoisie, are the accomplices of both colonialism and Nazism.

There is some debate in the literature about Arendt's analysis of imperialism and totalitarianism—whether she is emphasizing a causal connection between these two phenomena, presenting imperialism as a foreshadowing of totalitarianism, or whether she is insisting on the absolute uniqueness of totalitarianism (more specifically, the Holocaust) in contrast with imperialism. According to Dana Villa, for Arendt, "Nazi and Soviet totalitarianism were not aberrations born of peculiarly dysfunctional national characters or political histories; rather, they were phenomena made possible by a particular constellation of events and tendencies within modern European history and culture."[16] These events and tendencies included the expansionist model of imperialism as well as the evolution and spread of racism, particularly by those in the West. It seems clear that Arendt's analysis reveals the ways in which the origins of imperialism are closely related to the origins of totalitarianism. But King suggests that Arendt's position is not as straightforward as it might appear: "it is not clear whether, for instance, Arendt is claiming a causal connection between the enslavement and mass murder of Africans by Europeans (English, French, Germans, and Belgians) in the late nineteenth and early twentieth century and the emergence of the concentration/extermination camp system in Europe; or whether she intends the African experience to serve as a foreshadowing of the Holocaust, a hint of what was to come, but without strong causal links."[17]

Other scholars have explicitly rejected Arendt's version of the uniqueness-of-the-Holocaust argument. Shiraz Dossa explains that, for Arendt, "the absolute uniqueness of the Holocaust is contained in the parallel assaults on the public structure of 'normal reality,' and the personal structure of individuality and freedom."[18] But Dossa argues that even on Arendt's own terms, "the absolute uniqueness of the Holocaust becomes very doubtful because human plurality has been violated more effectively in the past."[19] In a more recent essay, A. Dirk Moses (like Dossa) challenges Arendt on the absolute uniqueness of the Holocaust: "Far from proposing a 'boomerang' thesis about the corrosive effect of colonialism in Africa on the German and European metropole, Arendt was advancing an alternative continuity argument in service of a broader agenda about the *discontinuity* between what she called 'the Western tradition' and totalitarian crimes."[20] For Dossa and Moses, as for Du Bois, Césaire, and Mills, it is difficult to make the case for the uniqueness of the Holocaust against the historical context of colonialism, imperialism, and genocide—even as outlined by Arendt herself.

Michael Rothberg uses the notion of multidirectionality to offer a framework for appreciating the significance of both genocidal imperialism and the totalitarian Holocaust, which helps explain and even push beyond the uniqueness-versus-continuity debate. Looking at the work of Arendt, Césaire, and Du Bois (among others), Rothberg reminds us to "consider the epistemological as well as political problems of writing comparative cultural and historical analysis."[21] In distinguishing Césaire's *Discourse* from Arendt's *Origins*, Rothberg asserts that the former "refuses to naturalize colonialism or genocide in the figure of culture-less human beings; it recognizes the catalyzing role of Europe's disavowal of colonial violence; and it maps out the movement from colonialism to Nazism to decolonization as a multidirectional constellation in which each term modifies the others."[22] But for Rothberg, both Césaire and Arendt have great insights as well as problematic oversights.

Rothberg sees Du Bois as an exemplar of multidirectionality based on the analysis Du Bois presents in "The Negro in the Warsaw Ghetto." Rothberg argues, "Du Bois provides both an example and a method for conceptualizing memory beyond the logic of competition."[23] In the Warsaw essay Du Bois presents an analysis of the Jewish problem and the Negro problem that goes beyond his 1946 comments in *The World and Africa*. He notes that his visit to the Warsaw ghetto resulted in "a real and more complete understanding": "the problem of slavery, emancipation, and caste in the United States was no longer in my mind a separate and unique thing."[24] Du Bois adds that his conceptualization of the race problem was now enlarged and "cut across lines of color and physique and belief and status and was a matter of cultural patterns, perverted teaching, and human hate and prejudice, which reached all sorts of people and caused endless evil to all men."[25] These reflections bring us back to Arendt's analysis of the race problem in imperialism and totalitarianism—for her, presented in terms of race thinking and racism.

Race Thinking and Racism

In "Race-Thinking before Racism," Arendt claims that it was not race thinking but the new era of imperialism that gave rise to racism. She distinguishes between "race thinking," such as pseudoscientific and anthropological studies about racial hierarchies and origins, and "racism," which she describes as the ideology eventually used as a justification for the national political agendas of imperialism (*OT* 160). Furthermore, race thinking is largely a matter of free opinion, while racism is more ideological because it permeates public opinion and leads people to abandon concrete facts for racist principles. For Arendt, ideologies are "systems based upon a single opinion that proved strong enough to attract and persuade a majority of people and broad enough to lead them through the various situations of an average modern life" (159). Ideologies differ from opinions in that an ideology claims to have the key insight into or knowledge of history, all the world's problems, or universal laws. According to Arendt, the ideology of race "interprets history as a natural fight of races" (ibid.).

While Arendt sees race thinking as a political tool, she tends to emphasize its political aspects in France and Germany more than in Britain and the United States. In the case of France, Arendt traces the "germs" of "the nation destroying and humanity-annihilating power of racism" to the comte de Boulainvilliers, whom she describes as a nobleman of France. According to Arendt, during the eighteenth century Boulainvilliers's theory of two distinct peoples of France was used to "counteract the new national idea" (*OT* 162). She adds that at the beginning of the French Revolution these thoughts about race were used for political purposes (ibid.). For Arendt, these ideas about race are forms of race thinking, not racism.

Arendt juxtaposes the race thinking in France, which was used as "a weapon for civil war and splitting a nation," with that in Germany, which she asserts was useful to unite Germans against the domination of foreign elements (*OT* 165). Race thinking in Germany became a rallying point for the joining together of various German states. Consequently, Arendt explains, in Germany it is hard to distinguish "mere nationalism and clear-cut racism" because "harmless national sentiments expressed themselves in *what we know today* to be racial terms" (ibid., my emphasis). Race thinking in Germany "developed outside of the nobility, as a weapon of certain nationalists who wanted the union of all German-speaking peoples and therefore insisted on a common origin" (166). In the early nineteenth century there was a shift in the meaning of "common origin" from common language to terms like "blood relationship," "family ties," "tribal unity," and "unmixed origin" (ibid.). German intellectuals sought social status through "innate personality"—given by birth rather than merit (169).[26] Arendt claims that German racism and imperialism did not fully develop until after 1870 and contends that Nazism is not the same as German nationalism (165).

As a transition from French and German race thinking to English race thinking, Arendt uses Arthur de Gobineau who, she claims, "invented racism almost by accident" (*OT* 172).[27] Gobineau is well known for his influential and racist work *The Inequality of Human Races* (1853–1855). Arendt's summation of Gobineau's thesis is that "the fall of civilization is due to a degeneration of race and the decay of race is due to a mixture of blood. This implies that in every mixture the lower race is always dominant" (*OT* 172–173). She also says in passing that Gobineau tried to get a larger audience in the United States by siding with slavery.[28]

In England, Arendt argues, the seeds of race thinking were developed during the French Revolution. But she also claims that the English and German versions of race thinking had more similarities to one another than to the French version insofar as both England and Germany tended to reject the invented ideals of *liberté, égalité,* and *fraternité* and the "Rights of Man" (*OT* 175). One idea that did appeal to the English is Edmund Burke's concept of entailed inheritance, contained in his argument against the abstract principles of the French Revolution. The English connected this notion of inheritance to liberty and nationalism, bringing with it a "curious touch of race-feeling" (*OT* 176). Arendt draws a correlation between the more historical concept of inheritance and the more modern concept of eugenics (ibid.).

Let us return to the distinction that she makes between race thinking and racism and consider how these concepts operate in her analysis of imperialism. Recall that Arendt describes race thinking as a matter of opinion that often uses pseudoscience and anthropology to support claims to racial hierarchies. Racism, on the other hand, is ideological, abandons facts for racist principles, and interprets history as a fight of the races.[29] She claims that racism is not so much a byproduct of race thinking as it is a byproduct of imperialism. And since imperialism needed justification, racism would have been invented even in the absence of race thinking. She correctly identifies racism as a tool used by Europeans to justify exploitation and oppression in the form of imperialism. However, her analysis is limited because it discounts the possibility that race thinking utilizing science, anthropology, or any other such tool to support claims about racial hierarchies, which are in turn used to justify or excuse racial oppression based on those hierarchies, is already racist, even if it has not yet been developed into a fully accepted ideology. And furthermore, Arendt's analysis of race thinking and racism in relation to imperialism does not take into account the fact that this very possibility was the reality of racialized institutions of slavery and early colonialism long before race became the excuse for imperialism.

Another difference Arendt highlights between race thinking and racism is how each relates to nationalism and to principles of equality. For Arendt, not only is racism not equivalent to nationalism, racism actually undermines nationalism. While I would not argue that racism is the same as nationalism, because it is not the case that all nationalisms are racist, it must also be acknowledged that racism and nationalism are not as mutually exclusive as Arendt posits. She states:

> From the very beginning, racism deliberately cut across all national boundaries, whether defined by geographical, linguistic, traditional, or any other standards, and denied national-political standards as such. Historically speaking,

> racists have a worse record of patriotism than the representatives of all other international ideologies together, and they were the only ones who consistently denied the great principle upon which national organizations are built, the principle of equality and solidarity of all peoples guaranteed by the idea of mankind. (*OT* 161)

It is suggested here that since racism cuts across national boundaries, is somehow unpatriotic, and rejects principles of equality, it follows that a person or a nation may *not* be racist if that person or nation accepts the principle of equality, which Arendt describes as the central pillar of genuine nationhood. For example, Arendt identifies Nazism as a form of racism but denies that Nazism is a form of German nationalism.

Arendt seems to overlook the many cases where a person or nation accepts the principle of equality in theory, but intentionally and systematically rejects this principle in practice. And she overlooks the many cases where a person or nation accepts the principle of equality among certain groups (or races) of people, but rejects notions of equality and solidarity of all peoples. These points are not intended to prompt an abstract thought experiment; rather, they direct us to situations in which this line of thinking is deeply engrained in a country's history from its inception. Two obvious examples are the United States of America, where the foundation of freedom and the principles of equality coexisted with the development of racialized slavery, and France, where similar principles coexisted with slavery and colonialism. One additional example is the racist Afrikaner nationalism of the Boers.

The Boers and South Africa

The Boers are an example of nationalism founded in racism.[30] In "Prelude to Disaster: An Analysis of the Racial Policies of Boer and British Settlers in Africa before 1910," Okon Edet Uya describes several characteristics of the Boers' Afrikaner nationalism. First, the Boers were violently oppressive toward the native population of South Africa. Second, the Boers were antagonistic toward the British. And third, the Boers came to see South Africa as their own fatherland. Citing Floris van Jaarsveld, Uya argues that the Boers became unified in South Africa before the nineteenth century by both anti-African and anti-British sentiments. The former sentiment was fed by a sense of racial superiority buttressed by claims that they were God's chosen people and that racial discrimination was the will of God. The latter sentiment was an expression of their disdain for the principle of equality that the British came to represent (in theory, if not in practice) and a response to the interference of the British government in South Africa.

Uya explains that the conflict between the Boers and the British can be interpreted as a competition for control over South Africa. Ironically, the coherence of the Boers in the form of Afrikaner nationalism was stimulated more by the conflicts with the British than by their racist attitudes of superiority over the

South Africans. And although these conflicts may suggest otherwise, the mindset of the Boers and the British toward Africans were not that distinct from one another. Uya states, "The actions of the British settlers in Natal tend to show that, where fundamental issues were concerned, the attitude of the British settlers toward Africans was not very different from that of the Boers."[31]

The section in *Origins* titled "Race and Bureaucracy" examines the Boers in South Africa as a representative model of the evils of imperialism. It is remarkable that Arendt points out the fallacy of race thinking and the lack of foundation for racial stereotypes and yet she incorporates this thinking into her own description and characterization of Africans. She constantly refers to Africans as savages, backward, and lacking in history and culture. Arendt incorporates these stereotypes into her investigation of the actions of the Boers, who are described as "the only European group that ever, though in complete isolation, had to live in a world of black savages" (*OT* 191). In her description of the Boers' practice of slavery, Arendt states: "First of all, slavery, though it domesticated a certain part of the savage population, never got hold of all of them, so the Boers were never able to forget their first horrible fright before a species of men whom human pride and the sense of human dignity could not allow them to accept as fellow-men. This fright of something like oneself that still under no circumstances ought to be like oneself remained at the basis of slavery and became the basis for a race society" (192).

Rather than making a commentary about slavery and race society in general, Arendt is focusing specifically on slavery (though she claims that slavery "is a very inadequate word to describe what actually happened"; *OT* 192) and the race society established by the Boers in South Africa. The case could be made that in the latter part of the quote in the previous paragraph, Arendt is not giving her own description, but rather thinking from the perspective of the Boers. However, the first part of the quote seems to represent Arendt's position and not the Boers' and it remains problematic that Arendt describes slavery as a means to "domesticate" what *she* calls the "savage population."[32]

Gale Presby has criticized these analyses in an essay titled "Critic of Boers or Africans?" Although Arendt is explicitly critical of imperialism for bringing economics into the political realm and for making expansion a national agenda, Presby problematizes what Arendt *neglects* to criticize about imperialism (and even forms of slavery that resulted from imperialism), particularly in the actions of the Boers and the British. Presby charges: "[Arendt] does not say that what the Boers and the British did was wrong because: (1) they practiced slavery; (2) they engaged in unfair discriminatory labor practices; (3) they appropriated for themselves all of the land, which they acquired through the use of force; (4) they committed massacres and conducted cruel and unusual punishments."[33] Presby questions the basis of Arendt's analysis and suggests that if the Boers had relied on slave labor in order to engage in political activity (in the ancient Greek sense), then "Arendt might have praise for them."[34] Presby may be exaggerating here by suggesting that Arendt would have praised the Boers for their political activity, but she raises an important point. Rather than criticizing the methods (or means) of exploitation, Arendt criticizes the ends of the exploitation.

This is true in Arendt's critique not only of the Boers and the British, but also of the French brand of imperialism. Arendt asserts that if France's methods and motives for imperialism had been along the same lines as Rome's, the "events that followed" would have been "more humanly tolerable" (*OT* 132). Here Arendt is prioritizing the political over economics, which for her is social rather than political.[35] If imperialism had aimed at empire building, allowing the conquering nation to spread its form of government and politics abroad, the oppression required to do so perhaps would have been more acceptable. But since imperialism was largely an economic and expansionist venture, the oppressive means used to achieve these economic ends were not as tolerable to Arendt. Of course, it should not be surprising that Arendt presents a paradigm that prioritizes the political over economics (or the social), given the way she later builds on this model in *The Human Condition* (1958) and *On Revolution* (1963). In both of these works Arendt argues that the concept of the political (which is marked by a distinction between public and private space) has been distorted by what she describes as the rise of the social (which includes attempts to bring issues of economics, poverty, and racial oppression into the public realm). We see the earlier stages of this framework throughout *Origins*.

But beyond the economic critique, Presby also challenges Arendt's historical claims about imperialism and the population demographics in South Africa along with her account of the British and the Boers' agenda there. Presby notes that although some of Arendt's most severe criticisms of capitalism are contained in her analysis of imperialism in *Origins*, these criticisms are less effective when Arendt seemingly excuses the actions of European expansionists, accusing them of absent-mindedness rather than intentional harm. For Presby, "This suggestion that the British were not 'conscious' of what they were doing, although not intended to absolve them from responsibility for the consequences of their actions, can sound very much like apologetics."[36]

The idea that Arendt's analysis sometimes seems to blame the victims rather than the offenders for detestable events in history is not new. Arendt's general representation of Jews in *Origins* as well as in her report on the Eichmann trial has also been criticized along these lines. For example, Seyla Benhabib explains in "Arendt's *Eichmann in Jerusalem*" that this report by Arendt, in comparison to all her other writings, has resulted in "by far the most acrimonious and tangled controversy, which has since cast a long shadow on her eventful but otherwise respectable and illustrious career."[37] But Presby explains that unlike what has been written critiquing Arendt's position on Eichmann, "where many intellectuals were outraged over her suggestion that Eichmann did not intend evil but was merely *thoughtless*, there has been little or no outrage in the intellectual community over Arendt's repeated suggestions that the British did not intend evil when they expanded their empire but were merely being thoughtless."[38]

While Presby may be right about the lack of "outrage" over Arendt's suggestion that the British did not intend evil toward the people of Africa, I would like to offer more nuance to the notion of thoughtlessness as used by Arendt. The case can be made that, for Arendt, thoughtlessness may be worse—or at least more disturbing—than intentional harm. Arendt is thinking within the framework of moral or ethical philosophy, where thought or the act of thinking is related to judgment or the act of judging. When Arendt accuses Eichmann of thoughtlessness, she is criticizing his claim that he was merely doing his job well *and* his failure to judge his actions as wrong. Following this line of thinking, one might argue that, for Arendt, the British and the Boers were responsible for a similar failure of judgment: they did not see their actions in South African as wrong. However, although Arendt may judge the violent actions of the Boers and the British as wrong, she is disturbingly sympathetic to their reactions to what she perceives to be savagery in the "dark continent" of Africa.

Dark Hearts, Dark Continents

Arendt is clear that one of the major problems faced by Europeans, the British or others, who claimed to include all people in the concept of humanity, was that they had to contend with the differences between Europeans and non-European "others," who they treated as subhuman, as animals, or as property. She asserts that the crucial question became "whether the Christian tenet of the unity and equality of all men, based upon common descent from one original set of parents, would be kept in the hearts of men who were faced with tribes which, as far as we know, never had found by themselves any adequate expression of human reason or human passion in either cultural deeds or popular customs, and which had developed human institutions only to a low level" (*OT* 176–177). Arendt appears to be speaking in her own voice here and she uses the pronoun "we" rather than "they," suggesting that she agrees with claims that some groups of people (specifically, African tribes) did not adequately express human reason, passion, culture, or customs.[39]

Arendt goes on to say, "The great horror which had seized European men at their first confrontation with native life was stimulated by precisely this touch of inhumanity among other human beings who apparently were as much a part of nature as wild animals" (*OT* 194). She makes it clear that the separation between the "savages" and the rest of humanity is not an issue of skin color, but one of behavior. She explains, "What made them [Africans] different from other human beings was not at all the color of their skin but the fact that they behaved like a part of nature, that they treated it as their undisputed master, that they had not created a human world, a human reality" (192). This is Arendt's personal description of Africans, not just an adaptation of a European perspective. And yet, even if Arendt *is* describing the perspective of Europeans or imperialists toward Africans, and not her own, it is problematic that she presents this view uncritically (or, in Presby's words, almost as an apologetic).

Some have suggested that Arendt's account is troublesome because she is providing a narrative that is not representative of her perspective. Villa argues that Arendt is simply taking us into the minds of the racist Europeans and their initial encounter with the people of Africa.[40] But Anne Norton has rejected such defenses of Arendt outright: "It is in her own voice that Arendt denies history and politics to the Africans. . . . Arendt put herself in the minds and circumstances of the Boer. She left the African silent."[41] Norton continues, "Yet if Arendt had written these words in another voice, marking them as foreign to her own sentiments, one would still have reason to question her views of racial difference and their significance for her political theory."[42]

Both Moruzzi and Presby assert that part of the problem is Arendt's use of Joseph Conrad's novel *Heart of Darkness* (which Arendt describes as "the most illuminating work on actual race experience in Africa"; *OT* 185) as a representation of the Boers' attitudes in particular and of African behavior in general. Arendt uncritically accepts Conrad's depiction of Africa as a savage world with creatures who "were as incomprehensible as the inmates of a madhouse" (*OT* 190, quoting *Heart of Darkness*). But *Heart of Darkness* is a thoroughly racist text, even if it also functions to expose and possibly condemn imperialism. Conrad's novel, like Arendt's *Origins*, (re)presents the ravaging effects of imperialism, yet without satisfactory reprimand or reproach.[43] The fact that Arendt accepts and embraces this racist image of Africa undermines her efforts to position herself against racism.

Eurocentrism, Ethnocentrism, and Antiprimitivism

As critical of racism as Arendt is throughout *Origins,* she seems nonetheless convinced that racism is a fathomable response by Europeans toward Africans, who (in her estimation) lacked civilization, reason, culture, history, and political institutions. Race became "the emergency explanation of human beings whom no European or civilized man could understand and whose humanity so frightened and humiliated the immigrants that they no longer cared to belong to the same human species" (*OT* 185). In this passage Arendt acknowledges Africans as human beings while suggesting that they were frightening and uncivilized. Arendt describes European xenophobia at the sight of Africans, their unwarranted fear and contempt for those who became defined as different and "other," as the impetus for raced societies and perhaps also for racial oppression.

Arendt explains, "Race was the Boers' answer to the overwhelming monstrosity of Africa—a whole continent populated and overpopulated by savages" (*OT* 185). But the use of race, or rather racism, to answer the question concerning the "savages" of Africa quickly resulted in massacres of Africans (ibid.). Imperialist racism offered massacre as an acceptable policy for handling foreign affairs. But Arendt excuses Europeans' use of violent racism against Africans when she asserts that Africans were "'natural' human beings who lacked the specifically human character, the specifically human reality, so that when European men massacred them they somehow were not aware that they had committed murder" (192). She further plays down the heinous nature of these violent massacres of Africans by Europeans when she states that Africans had already been killing each other.[44] Arendt claims, relying on accounts given by C. W. de Kiewiet and Selwyn James, "The senseless massacre of native tribes on the Dark Continent was quite in keeping with the traditions of these tribes themselves" (ibid.).

Arendt also suggests that such violent forms of racism (genocidal massacres) are acceptable instruments to use against Africans, but not against Asians and other groups, particularly Jews. She states that these instruments of violence and racism were first used against Africans and then spread to Asians and others. But for Arendt, the crime was not what was done to Africans, because that was natural and comprehensible. What was incomprehensible to her was that the same methods could be extended toward non-Africans—because in the latter case Europeans should have known better. So racism and genocidal massacres are understandable when exercised against "the African savages who had frightened Europeans literally out of their wits," but "there could be no excuse and no humanly comprehensible reason for treating Indians and Chinese as though they were not human beings" (*OT* 206). She then makes the oft-cited claim, "In a sense, it is only here that the real crime began, because here [in Asia, unlike Africa] everyone ought to have known what he was doing" (ibid.).[45]

It is worth returning to Du Bois and Césaire here, since they anticipated and rejected this position. Du Bois considers myths like the "European gentleman" and the "Golden Rule" and the ways that these concepts were utterly undermined in Asia and Africa "by indulging in lying, murder, theft, rape, deception, and degradation, of the same sort and kind which has left the world aghast at the accounts of what the Nazis did in Poland and Russia."[46] He underscores the continuity of the crimes in Asia and Africa with those in Europe, rather than seeing a discontinuity between the violent racism in Africa compared to Asia and Europe. Likewise, Césaire understands, "At bottom, what he [the European bourgeois] cannot forgive Hitler for is not the *crime* in itself, *the crime against man*, it is not *the humiliation of man as such*, it is the crime against the white man, the humiliation of the white man, and the fact that he applied to Europe colonialist procedures which until then had been reserved exclusively for the Arabs of Algeria, the 'coolies' of India, and the 'niggers' of Africa."[47] This seems to capture precisely Arendt's stance in her claims about when the "real" crimes began.

It has been rightly noted by George Kateb that Arendt's analysis of Africans and the violence used against them is "upsetting to an unusual degree," and "there is an indigestible quality to Arendt's analysis [and] to her act of generosity toward the Boers, Germans, Belgians, and other European exploiters and imperialists."[48] King states that Arendt's position has an "ethnocentric strain" but is not Eurocentric "per se" because although she allows for the brutal treatment of Africans, she draws the line at similar treatment for Chinese and Indians.[49] This suggests that Arendt's position is somehow less Eurocentric because she asserts that there is no excuse for using violent racism against Chinese and Indians (i.e., other non-European peoples) as though they were not human. But others are more critical, describing Arendt's analysis as Eurocentric and classically Orientalist. For example, Dossa has argued that Arendt's ethnocentrism is evident in her understanding of the totalitarian Holocaust as unique, and furthermore it is explicit "in her reading of imperial history and implicit in her normative political theory."[50] Moruzzi asserts, "The description Arendt gives of it [this encounter], while repudiating brutal excess, is structured by her empathic participation in a descriptive discourse that is fundamentally Eurocentric and emotionally charged."[51] Jimmy Casas Klausen acknowledges ethnocentrism and racial prejudice in Arendt's writings, but also calls attention to her antiprimitivism: "I am *not* interested in calling Arendt racist, but I do claim that her texts' antiprimitivist tropes produce racial and dehumanizing effects: primitives are and are not human, and the 'racial' difference between Hottentots and the Boers who became like them turns less on skin color than moral capacity."[52]

As with "Reflections on Little Rock" and *On Revolution,* Arendt's analysis of the Negro question in *Origins* is both insightful and problematic. She is insightful because she seems to be able to get into the minds of the oppressors. But this also proves problematic, because she is somehow unable to take a step back and separate herself from their racist characterizations and constructions of Africans. I am not attempting to dismiss Arendt's thought altogether and label her as a racist.[53] In *Origins* Arendt thinks through difficult questions and attempts to make sense of difficult times and circumstances. In many cases, her line of inquiry is extremely helpful and productive, including her ability to trace totalitarianism back to the violent system of imperialism. But there are also some major shortcomings in her analysis, particularly when it comes to the issue of anti-Black or anti-African racism. Arendt's association of racism with imperialism ignores the problems of racism that were already part of race thinking during the colonial era, including the creation of racial hierarchies, the transatlantic slave trade, and the resulting establishment of racial systems of slavery. It would have been more accurate for Arendt to note that long before imperialism the racialized institution of slavery gave rise to racism in both Europe and the Americas. And Arendt's attempt to criticize the race thinking and the racism used to justify imperialism is weakened by her inability to distance herself from a very racist (even essentialist) characterization of African people.

6 "Only Violence and Rule over Others Could Make Some Men Free"

THE THEME OF violence can be traced throughout Arendt's major political writings, such as *The Human Condition* and *On Revolution*, where she draws connections between war, violence, and necessity (or liberation from necessity); *The Origins of Totalitarianism*, where she examines Europe's use of violence in concentration camps and imperialist massacres in Africa; and of course, *On Violence*, where she condemns the violence of the Black Power movement and of anticolonialism. Patricia Owens notes in *Between War and Politics* that Arendt "was the theorist of political speech and action and claimed on numerous occasions that violence was mute and brought death to politics. Yet, we also find in Arendt's work praise for the experience of war as the quintessential moment for humans to be most fully alive and political."[1] In this chapter I examine this double-sided approach to violence by Arendt. More specifically, I parse how Arendt presents violence uncritically in some contexts and hypercritically in other contexts.

In *The Human Condition* there is a troublesome relationship between violence and the private and public spheres, or the use of violence to leave the private realm and to make entry into the political realm possible. Likewise in *On Revolution* Arendt attempts to situate violence outside of the political realm even while acknowledging the constitutive role of violence in the creation of a political realm. Additionally, in *The Jewish Writings* Arendt's argument for a Jewish army is made in explicitly political terms—linking self-defense to fighting for freedom and equal rights. Yet in *On Violence* Arendt critiques Fanon and Sartre for their stances on anticolonial violence in *The Wretched of the Earth* (1963) and *Critique of Dialectical Reason*, volume 1 (1960). Arendt, Fanon, and Sartre are each clear that European expansion in Africa was violent. But Arendt presents an uncritical view of the violence against Africans deployed by Europeans (in *Origins*), while Fanon and Sartre critique the violent colonial system, taking into account the role of violence in establishing the colonial system and the corresponding role of revolutionary counterviolence against this system.[2] Using Arendt against herself, I juxtapose her presentation of the violence used to master necessity and to enter political space with her vehement critiques of the violence used by the colonized (whom she characterizes as violent). Arendt's apologetics for European violence and her insistence on the formation of a Jewish army as a political issue, on the one hand, contrasted with her criticism of Sartre and Fanon concerning counter-violence, on the other, further confirms her biases.

"While Violence Can Destroy Power, It Can Never Become a Substitute for It"

Hannah Arendt's distinction between violence and power can be added to the list of distinctions in her political thought, and we see it developed across several of her writings. In *On Violence,* Arendt draws distinctions between power, strength, force, authority, and violence, all of which she describes as ways by which man rules over man. According to Arendt, "power is the human ability to act in concert. . . . It belongs to a group and remains in existence only as long as the group keeps together" (*CR* 143; see also *HC* 202–203). Power is inherent in political communities and requires legitimacy, but not justification. Arendt asserts that "legitimacy" is derived from the initial organization of acting in concert, but "justification" is derived from a future end. Not only does Arendt stress that violence does not equal power, she adds that politically speaking the two terms are opposites. Power does not entail any form of violence. This is so much the case that to speak of nonviolent power is, for Arendt, redundant. She explains that power and violence cannot rule simultaneously: "Violence appears when power is in jeopardy and ends in power's disappearance" (*CR* 155). While power needs legitimacy and not justification, violence always stands in need of justification and will never be legitimate. Power belongs only to a group and points to that group's ability to act in concert, but violence is merely a means and is by nature instrumental. Arendt asserts that the ends of violence are always in danger of being overwhelmed by the means that they justify and that are needed to reach them (106). Furthermore, Arendt warns that within violence there is an arbitrariness, or an "all-pervading unpredictability," that will not allow for any certainty (ibid.).

In *The Human Condition* she asserts that power exists in its actualization and in this regard differs from instruments of violence, which may be stored up and reserved for later use (*HC* 200). According to Arendt, "Power is what keeps the public realm, the potential space of appearance between acting and speaking men, in existence" (ibid.). She explains that the only alternative to power is force (particularly in cases where force is monopolized through violence), but Arendt is clear that "while violence can destroy power, it can never become a substitute for it" (202). In *On Revolution,* she distinguishes power (which resides with the people) and violence (which is outside of political organization).[3] In the same text Arendt states, "Power comes into being only if and when men join themselves together for the purpose of action, and it will disappear when, for whatever reason, they disperse and desert one another" (*OR* 175).

Although Arendt goes out of her way to distance the concepts of power and violence, usually privileging the former over the latter, she does not deny that they "have the same function" (*CR* 142) and "usually appear together" (151). She claims that power, which is intrinsic in political communities, does not entail any form of violence—yet at the same time notes that the use of violence in the private realm creates the possibility for one's entrance into the public realm. She even suggests that there would not be a political sphere without the use of violence in the private realm.

The Human Condition and Violence

In part 2 of *The Human Condition*, Arendt distinguishes between the public and the private realms in the Greek polis. Violence emerges as a focal point in her presentation of thought, speech, and action in the public/political realm. Arendt couples political action and speech, both of which are contrasted with and remain outside of the sphere of force and violence (*HC* 26). She asserts that, for the Greeks, decisions were made through words and persuasion within the polis, while force, violence, and command "were prepolitical ways to deal with people characteristic of life outside of the *polis*" (27). Put another way, force, violence, and command were reserved for the home, family, laborers, and slaves, on the one hand, and for despots and barbarians, on the other (ibid.).[4] She claims that Greek philosophers took for granted "that necessity is primarily a prepolitical phenomenon, characteristic of the private household organization, and that force and violence are justified in this sphere because they are the only means to master necessity—for instance, by ruling over slaves—and to become free" (31).[5] According to Arendt, "Because all human beings are subject to necessity, they are entitled to violence toward others; violence is the prepolitical act of liberating oneself from the necessity of life for the freedom of the world" (ibid.). In this instance, Arendt suggests that violence is justified, not only in efforts to master necessity, but also in efforts to liberate oneself from necessity.[6]

In part 3 of *The Human Condition*, in addition to turning her attention to a distinction between labor and work, Arendt also analyzes justifications for violence and slavery in antiquity. She asserts that slavery was defended and justified among the Greeks on the grounds that it allowed some men to "win" their freedom to enter the public sphere by dominating others and using force to confine these others to the private sphere of labor and necessity (*HC* 85). Referencing Plato, Arendt describes this ability to keep oneself free from the necessity of labor, or to force that necessity onto others, as an "art" (128). The art of violence in particular was "required of the master of a household who [had to] know how to exert authority and use violence in his rule over slaves" (129). And the aim of the art of violence was to enable the master to remain free. The art of violence, including torture, could not be exerted against free citizens, but could be used readily against slaves and non-citizens, both already subjected to necessity. Arendt explains, "It was the arts of violence, the arts of war, piracy, and ultimately absolute rule, which brought the defeated into the services of the victors and thereby held necessity in abeyance for the longer period of recorded history" (ibid.).

Contributing to the diminished distinction between the public and the private spheres, the modern age has not only glorified labor, but has also devalued the arts of war and violence, and decreased the use of the instruments of violence (*HC* 129). Arendt warns that the "growing elimination of violence throughout the modern age almost automatically opened the doors for the re-entry of necessity" (130). The danger is that the ushering in of labor and necessity will not result in freedom, but rather will force all mankind "for the first time under the yoke of necessity" (ibid.). What she seems to be suggesting is that the use of man-made violence to force necessity on some for the freedom of others is preferable to the elimination of violence in the private sphere, which has the danger of subjecting everyone to necessity and labor.

Arendt goes on to posit that even if slaves, laborers, or animal laborans were liberated from necessity in antiquity, their free time would only be wasted. She contends, "The spare time of the *animal laborans* is never spent in anything but consumption, and the more time left to him, the greedier and more craving his appetites" (*HC* 133). In the modern era, the laborer is characterized not only as an insatiable consumer, but also as a destroyer of the public realm. Arendt insists, "The rather uncomfortable truth of the matter is that the triumph the modern world has achieved over necessity is due to the emancipation of labor, that is, to the fact that the *animal laborans* was permitted to occupy the public realm; and yet as long as the *animal laborans* remains in possession of it there can be no true public realm, but only private activities displayed in the open" (133–134). The presence of the animal laborans forecloses the possibility of a public space. Furthermore, the laborer or slave is described as "worldless and herdlike" and therefore "incapable of building or inhabiting a public, worldly realm" (160).[7]

Arendt contrasts the laborer with the craftsman or builder. Unlike the animal laborans, the homo faber "is fully capable of having a public realm of his own," namely, "the market place where his products are displayed" (*HC* 160).[8] In addition to their different relationship to (or distance from) public and political space, the animal laborans and the homo faber also have differing relationships to violence. Whereas the animal laborans is on the receiving end of violence (i.e., violent labor and the violence from the head of house to keep him in the private realm of necessity), it is the very workmanship of the homo faber that harbors an element of violence. According to Arendt, "Fabrication, the work of *homo faber*, consists in reification" (139). There is an element of "violation and violence" in all fabrication, and "*homo faber*, the creator of the human artifice, has always been a destroyer of nature" (ibid.). Means and ends determine making and fabrication so much that the ends not only justify the means, but also organize them (143, 153, 157). For example, "the end justifies the violence done to nature to win the material, as the wood justifies killing the tree and the table justifies destroying the wood" (153).

Arendt's emphasis on the importance of keeping necessity and labor in the private realm, where she thinks they belong, has been well theorized and documented. But it is also important to call attention to her complicity with the violence required to contain necessity in the private realm in order to preserve a separation of the public and private spheres. A question to be asked here is why Arendt offers such a lucid description of the role of violence without criticism. She identifies violence as a prepolitical phenomenon that forces the family, laborers, and slaves to remain in the private realm in order to enable free men to enter the public and political realms. She also acknowledges the violence against nature inherent in fabrication and workmanship.[9] In both cases, Arendt appears to justify the use of violence. Her observation is not only an "uncomfortable truth," but also a deeply disturbing one. Arendt makes similarly problematic observations about violence and truths in *On Revolution*.

On Revolution and Violence

In the introduction to *On Revolution*, war and revolution are described as the two central political issues of the twentieth century. Wars are old phenomena and make use of violence (for the purpose of liberation), but revolutions are modern phenomena and aim at freedom (*OR* 12). These concepts are not only *distinct*—"revolution, in distinction to war, will stay with us into the foreseeable future" (17–18)—but are also *interrelated* inasmuch as revolutions "either were preceded and accompanied by a war of liberation like the American Revolution, or led into wars of defense and aggression like the French Revolution" (17). Arendt explains that although wars and revolutions are not "completely determined by violence," it is still the case that they are "not even conceivable outside the domain of violence. . . . Violence is a kind of common denominator for both" (18). Thus, "in so far as violence plays a predominant role in wars and revolutions, both are outside of the political realm, strictly speaking" (19). It is interesting to observe how Arendt wants to situate violence outside of the political realm.

As already noted, in *The Human Condition* Arendt is clear that violence is necessary to subjugate some so that others may be free. Although Arendt does not present it in these terms, her analysis effectively exposes the constitutive violence of the polis. First, she insists that violence is prepolitical, then that it is outside of the political, but then she acknowledges that violence *is* operating in the political when she describes it as "a marginal phenomenon in the political realm" (*OR* 19). This admission is made in the context of her coupling violence with silence (in contrast to the power of speech). Arendt contends, "Where violence rules absolutely, as for instance in concentration camps . . . everything and everybody must fall silent" (18). It is the silence of violence that makes it marginal, because the political realm is the realm of thought, speech, and action. According to Arendt, "The point here is that violence is incapable of speech, and not merely that speech is helpless when confronted with violence" (19).

But the issue of constitutive violence reemerges when Arendt analyzes the relationship between revolutions, beginnings, and violence. Arendt rejects the theoretical state of nature that is explored in social and political philosophy because it is not historical fact and it presents the problem of a beginning separated from the violence that follows (*OR* 19–20, 38). She underscores the fact that beginnings "must be intimately connected with violence" and that "no beginning could be made without violence, without violating" (20). At least twice, Arendt refers to fratricidal violence, noting: "whatever brotherhood human beings may be capable of has grown out of fratricide, whatever political organization men may have achieved has its origin in crime" (20, 208).

Remaining consistent with her line in *The Human Condition,* Arendt again argues that in order for some to have access to the political realm, many have to be confined to the private realm—and this is also achieved through force and violence (*OR* 114). She contends, "All rulership has its original and *most legitimate* source in man's wish to liberate himself from life's necessity, and men achieved such liberation by means of *violence,* by forcing others to bear the burden of life for them" (ibid., my emphases). Again making the connection to slavery, Arendt continues, "This was the core of slavery and it is only the rise of technology, and not the rise of modern politics as such, which has refuted this old and *terrible truth that only violence and rule over others could make some men free*" (ibid., my emphasis).[10] Whereas in *On Violence* Arendt claims that violence can never be legitimate, in *On Revolution* she states that the most legitimate source of rulership, here conceived as the desire to emancipate oneself from life's necessity, is achieved through violence.

Arendt suggests that freedom and emancipation from necessity are achievable by one of two methods: either by subjugating others through force and violence or through the rise of technology. But she does not criticize this conclusion. Arendt acknowledges that freedom in public space (as she conceives it) is attained by the few through violence and force against the many, who are confined to the private sphere. Her recognition of the role of violence in maintaining the public-private division, or in the political realm in general, is significant. The question is whether Arendt is merely revealing the role of violence or going a step further and validating the role of violence. If the latter is the case, and Arendt is validating or in some way condoning the role of violence in emancipating oneself from the necessities of life, then it confirms that Arendt does not object to all forms of violence in all circumstances. But even if Arendt is not validating, but rather revealing, how violence is used to maintain the public-private division, she is nonetheless uncritical of its role. These issues are important in relation to Arendt's overall position concerning violence.

Returning to the second option of technology: although violence may be required for one to be freed from necessity and to maintain the public-private distinction, it is not clear how technology refutes the "terrible truth" that only violence allows some to be free at the expense of oppressing others. And in some instances the rise of technology may exacerbate rather than solve this problem insofar as access to the political realm is not simply an issue of being liberated from necessity and labor in the private realm. For example, in the case of slavery in the United States the rise of technology, specifically the cotton gin, contributed to the expansion of slavery rather than to its abolition. This technological advance made the production of cotton more economically lucrative at a time when manual separation of the cotton boll fibers from the seeds was too time consuming and economically unviable. With this new technology came the expansion of the slave states and increased demand for and consumption of cotton.[11]

Technology also could not solve the problem of colonialism, a system in which the freedom of the colonizers was obtained by the subjugation of the colonized with the use of technology and the tools of violence. In this case, far from refuting the "terrible truth" of rulership through force and violence, technology actually reinforced it. Jean-Paul Sartre highlights the role of technology in his essay "Colonialism Is a System" (1956). He explains how Europeans set out to occupy a territory in Africa, take the land, and exploit the people for labor and resources. But improvements in technology, or an increase in mechanization, only worsened the problem because even cheap labor became too expensive and the very right of the colonized to work (even if under exploitative conditions) was taken away.[12] The "rise of technology" does not help the colonized and empower them to enter the public sphere. It just leaves them even more impoverished and trapped in the colonial system. Although Arendt does not explain exactly how technology can address the problem, Sartre is clear about how technology can make it worse.

Expansion of the National Instruments of Violence

Arendt is aware of the violence used to establish and maintain what she calls imperialism, and yet she is not as critical of the oppressors' violence as she is of the revolutionary counterviolence of the colonized. Before taking up her critiques of Fanon and Sartre in *On Violence*, I want to underscore Arendt's insistence on the connection between violence and freedom (through armed uprisings and the formation of an army for defense) in *The Jewish Writings* and then revisit her insightful analysis of the violence of imperialism in *Origins*. We tend to emphasize the violence-power distinction in Arendt's work and understate the violence-freedom connection. For example, writing in the context of the Holocaust and World War II (at the center of which were also colonial considerations), Arendt argues that Jews must defend themselves as Jews and fight for freedom using weapons through the formation of a Jewish army under a Jewish flag (*JW* 137–138). She asserts that it is utopian to think that Jews can profit from the defeat of Hitler if they are not also contributing to his defeat "with weapons in [their] own hands" (138, 143).[13] Arendt explicitly links the formation of a Jewish army to political engagement: "The storm that will be unleashed in our own ranks by the formation of a Jewish army with volunteers from around the world will make clear to those in honest despair that we're no different from anyone else, that we too engage in politics, even if you usually have to extract it painfully from the murky code of the petitions of Jewish notables and charitable organizations, and despite the fact that our politics has been especially adept at alienating itself from the Jewish people" (138).[14]

In addition to articulating the need for a Jewish army, Arendt also quite justifiably celebrates the Jewish uprisings in the Warsaw ghetto and elsewhere. She explains that these armed uprisings led to "a series of armed revolts in concentration camps and ghettos, followed shortly thereafter by the organization of Jewish guerilla [sic] bands with their own Jewish flag. Something for which Jews around the world, and especially Jews in the Palestinian *yishuv* had petitioned for years— the formation of a Jewish army—was suddenly created by those from whom we would have least expected such deeds, people broken in body and spirit, the future inhabitants of asylums and sanitoriums, objects of worldwide Jewish charity" (*JW* 199, April 21, 1944). She adds: "Honor and glory are new words in the political vocabulary of our people" (ibid).[15] I draw attention to these claims in an effort to contrast her position in this context with her more critical position concerning anticolonial violence in the colonial context.

Going back to *The Origins of Totalitarianism*, recall that, for Arendt, violent racism was not just a result of the Europeans' fear of Africans; it was the direct result of their aims to control, subjugate, and exploit Africans. The use of race to answer the question concerning the "savages" of Africa quickly resulted in racism in the form of violent massacres of Africans (*OT* 185). Not only does Arendt acknowledge imperialist racism as a form of violence, she also recognizes that imperialism was only achievable through violence in the form of military presence in imperial territories. She correctly notes, "Only through the expansion of the national instruments of violence could the foreign-investment be rationalized, and the wild speculations with superfluous capital, which had provoked gambling of all savings, be reintegrated into the economic system of the nation" (*OT* 136). Arendt is even cognizant of the consequences of the use of violence for imperialist aims. She states that one major outcome of the exportation of the tools of violence, that is, the police and the army, was that they no longer had any political or national limitations on how they were used in foreign lands. Arendt explains that the framework of the nation and the national institutions that controlled the police and the army within the nation were now separated from them, allowing violence much more latitude in "backwards regions without industries and political organization" (ibid.). She also explains: "The state employed administrators of violence soon formed a new class within the nations and, although their field of activity was far from the mother country, wielded an important influence on the body politic at home. Since they were actually nothing but functionaries of violence they could only think in terms of power politics" (137). They were the first to claim that power was the essence of every political structure. But Arendt asserts that this predominance of violence and the discovery of power as a basic political reality was nothing new because "violence has always been the *ultima ratio* in political action and power has always been the visible expression of rule and government" (ibid.).

And while Arendt describes all of these modes of violence without criticism, she is highly critical of revolutionary counterviolence in the context of decolonization. Just as I previously contrasted Arendt's critical stance toward Black parents (in "Reflections on Little Rock") with her reflections on how her own mother protected her dignity against antisemitism (in the interview with Günter Gaus), we can also contrast Arendt's position on the Jewish army and Jewish armed uprisings in the Warsaw ghetto and elsewhere with her critiques of anticolonial violence in the colonial context. In *On Violence* Arendt launches an attack against Frantz Fanon and Jean-Paul Sartre on the matter of anticolonial violence. She misinterprets Fanon's and Sartre's analyses of violence, and her critique of violence in the works of both authors is biased. Arendt rejects their arguments for the use of violence to overcome the violent system of colonialism and accuses them of glorifying violence for violence's sake.

Critiquing Fanon

In *Black Skin, White Masks* (1952), Fanon is clear (like Aimé Césaire before him) that the negative contacts between the Negro and the white man are a direct consequence of the racial oppression and economic exploitation created and maintained by the colonial system.[16] Continuing his analysis in *The Wretched of the Earth* (1963), Fanon describes the colonial system as a "Manichean" world defined by dichotomy and segregated into two compartments.[17] Although the two zones are opposed to one another, they still "follow the principle of reciprocal exclusivity."[18] The settler's town is strongly built, brightly lit, and clean with a good infrastructure. Rather than having strong and sturdy houses, the colonized live in crowded huts. The inhabitants are barely clothed and suffer from hunger. Viewed as two distinct species, the colonizers and the colonized inhabit two distinct zones in the colonial world.

The colonized are expected to stay in their place and within the boundaries set by the colonizers. They are always on alert and always presumed guilty. But

Fanon assures us that they do not accept this guilt and they agree to no accusation. The colonized are able to see that these stereotypes are false. While treated as inferiors, they are not convinced of their inferiority.[19] The colonized recognize that they can only escape the immobilizing effects of colonization by ending it, and that they must be the agents to bring the history of the nation and the history of decolonization into existence.[20] This is achieved through violent resistance to the colonial system. Fanon explains that violence is a remedy to the accusation of inferiority: "It frees the native from his inferiority complex and from his despair and inaction; it makes him fearless and restores his self-respect."[21]

In her critique of Fanon, Arendt asserts that he is one of a few authors (along with Sorel and Pareto) who "glorify violence for violence's sake," and she attributes this glorification to a "deeper hatred of bourgeois society" and a "radical break with its moral standards" (CR 162).[22] Arendt also describes Fanon as praising the practice of violence, but this is far from the case. Rather than glorifying or praising violence, Fanon is describing the struggle for liberation in Algeria from a historical, philosophical, and psychological standpoint, analyzing the events that are opening up before him. Or, as Sartre states in the preface, "Fanon is merely an interpreter of the situation, that's all," so we need not think that he has "an uncommon taste for violence."[23] Arendt does not see the struggle for freedom in Algeria as an instance of one attempting to liberate oneself from necessity, as self-defense, or as a method to properly balance the scales of justice.

According to Arendt, Fanon is misled because he believes that a new community together with a "new man" will arise out of "the strong fraternal sentiments [that] collective violence engenders" (CR 166). This line of thinking is misleading, according to Arendt, because the brotherhood that arises out of collective violence is merely transitory. Arendt misses the nuance and insight of Fanon's analysis of violence, brotherhood, and the formation of a new humanity. His starting point for the phenomenon of intragroup violence and the collective violence of decolonization is the violence of the colonial system. Fanon explains that the violence of the colonizers against the colonized is internalized with the psychosomatic effects of muscular tension and cramping. The colonized do not initially exercise even self-defense against the violence of the colonizer. Consequently, the aggression and violence that the colonized man has learned from the colonizer is first manifested against his own people.[24] This intragroup violence results from the colonial system. Because the colonized are not permitted to exhibit any violence (or self-defense) toward the colonizers, their anger festers without an outlet.[25]

Fanon posits that the colonized must figure out how to turn the atmosphere of violence into something productive for decolonization, how to utilize and organize these forces to convert them into action.[26] Violence becomes a unifying agent for the colonized when they all take hold of that violence as a tool against their oppressors instead of one another. Decolonization alters beings, transforms spectators into actors, and creates new men, a new generation, a new language, and a new humanity.[27]

In addition to challenging Fanon's conceptions of community and brotherhood, Arendt also attempts to distance Fanon (and, later, Sartre) from Marxism. She asks, "Who could possibly call an ideology Marxist that has put its faith in 'classless idlers,' believes that 'in the *lumpenproletariat* the rebellion will find its urban spearhead,' and trusts that 'gangsters will light the way for the people'?" (*CR* 122). However, her selective quotation of Fanon takes his words out of context. Fanon actually states:

> The *lumpenproletariat,* once it is constituted, brings all its forces to endanger the "security" of the town, and is the sign of the irrevocable decay, the gangrene ever present at the heart of colonial domination. So the pimps, the hooligans, the unemployed, the petty criminals, urged on from behind, throw themselves into the struggle for liberation like stout working men. These classless idlers will by militant and decisive action discover the path that leads to nationhood.[28]

> In fact the rebellion, which began in the country districts, will filter into the towns through that fraction which has not yet succeeded in finding a bone to gnaw in the colonial system. The men whom the growing population of the country districts and colonial expropriation have brought to desert their family holdings circle tirelessly around the different towns, hoping that one day or another they will be allowed inside. It is within this mass of humanity, this people of shanty towns, at the core of the *lumpenproletariat,* that the rebellion will find its urban spearhead.[29]

> For example, the gangster who holds up the police set on to track him down for days on end, or who dies in single combat after having killed four or five policemen, or who commits suicide in order not to give away his accomplices—these types light the way for the people, from the blue prints of action and become heroes.[30]

Arendt, possibly as a consequence of her desire to exclude those who are oppressed on the basis of economics and race from the revolution, fails to see the lumpenproletariat, the class idlers, and the gangsters as revolutionaries. But they represent those in the colonial system who have nothing to lose and therefore are willing to risk what they have—their lives—in the struggle for freedom.

Critiquing Sartre

Arendt compares Sartre's account of violence in his preface to *The Wretched of the Earth* to Georges Sorel's *Reflections on Violence,* asserting that, like Sorel, Sartre thought about class struggle in military terms. Arendt points out that although Sartre goes beyond Sorel (and even Fanon) "in his glorification of violence," he still mentions "Sorel's fascist utterances" in this preface.[31] She also claims that Sartre is unaware of his basic disagreement with Marx on the question of violence, especially when he states that "'irrepressible violence . . . is man recreating himself,'[32] [and] that it is through 'mad fury'[33] that 'the wretched of the earth' can 'become men'" (CR 114). Contrary to Arendt's claim, Sartre was well aware of his disagreement with Marx, but this disagreement had more to do with the issue of scarcity than the issue of violence.[34]

While Sartre claims that man is able to recreate himself through violence, Hegel claims that man can recreate himself through thought and Marx claims that this is possible through labor. But, Arendt asserts, a gulf separates the essentially peaceful activities of thinking (Hegel) and laboring (Marx) from all deeds of violence (Sartre) (CR 115). In making this assertion, Arendt takes for granted that labor is peaceful. However, it can be violent—particularly for the proletariat and especially for colonized workers. Furthermore, Arendt's presentation of Marx here as nonviolent differs from her analysis in "The Social Question," where she said Marx "unmasked necessity as man-made violence [and] . . . reduced violence to necessity" (OR 64). She does not see how Sartre's analysis is an extension of this idea. Sartre presents the notion of necessity in terms of scarcity and the violence it induces. Another difference between Sartre and Marx, according to Arendt, is Sartre's claim that "to shoot down a European is to kill two birds with one stone . . . there remain a dead man and a free man."[35] Arendt says this is a sentence Marx could never have written. To further support her theory that Sartre has abandoned Marx, Arendt cites Leonard Schapiro and Raymond Aaron, who consider Sartre's emphasis on violence to be a kind of backsliding or an unconscious drifting away from Marxism (CR 186).

Arendt critiques Sartre's account of violence in the preface to *The Wretched of the Earth* in the body of *On Violence*, reserving her criticisms of his *Critique of Dialectical Reason* for the second appendix at the end of *On Violence*. But while she claims to be addressing Sartre's account of violence in the *Critique*, she gives no indication that she has actually read it. All of the quotes that she attributes to Sartre are extracted from Laing and Cooper's *Reason and Violence: A Decade of Sartre's Philosophy 1950–1960*, which was published in 1964. This text is a highly condensed version of three major works by Sartre: *Saint Genet: Comédien et martyr* (1952), *Questions de méthode* (1957), and *Critique de la raison dialectique* (1960).[36] In fact, *Reason and Violence* is so condensed that it summarizes all three works in about 175 pages!

In their introduction, Laing and Cooper point out, "Condensation to about one-tenth of the scale of the original clearly creates its own difficulties" (9). They attempt to follow Sartre's lines of argument without reference to Sartre's examples, which they describe as very lengthy. Nevertheless, Arendt quotes Laing and Cooper at length in her criticisms of Sartre, substituting their volume for Sartre's *Critique*. To complicate things further, she provides few references to page numbers, which may lead the reader to believe that she is actually quoting Sartre. When possible,

I have provided in the endnotes the page numbers that reference the passages in both *Reason and Violence* and the *Critique*. I will also point to the differences in Laing and Cooper's summary of the *Critique* and Sartre's actual arguments. While reading a condensed version of Sartre may be acceptable for someone wishing to grasp a few basic concepts before committing the time and effort required to examine his actual works, clearly Laing and Cooper's volume should not serve as the basis on which one launches a critique against Sartre for his stance on violence.

Arendt describes Sartre as giving a Hegelian espousal of violence in the *Critique*. But this statement undermines her previous claim that "a gulf separates" Sartre's account of violence from Hegel's thought (*OV* 115). She asserts that Sartre's Hegelian point of departure is that "need and scarcity determined the Manicheistic basis of action and morals" in present history, "whose truth is based on scarcity [and] must manifest itself in an antagonistic reciprocity between classes."[37] Arendt is quoting from *Reason and Violence,* but what Sartre actually states in the *Critique* is, "I believe that, at the level of need and through it, scarcity is experienced in practice through Manichean action, and that the ethical takes the form of destructive imperative: evil must be destroyed."[38] The difference is that Sartre is examining the ethical implications of violence in scarcity rather than celebrating violence for its own sake as Arendt previously asserted. He is exploring how scarcity gives rise to violence.

Arendt adds that under such circumstances violence is no longer a marginal phenomenon: "Violence and counter-violence are perhaps contingencies, but they are contingent necessities, and the imperative consequence of any attempt to destroy this inhumanity is that in destroying in the adversary the inhumanity of the contraman, I can only destroy in him the humanity of man, and realize in me this inhumanity."[39] What Sartre actually states is:

> Violence always presents itself as *counter-violence,* that is to say, as a retaliation against the violence of the Other. But this *violence of the Other* is not an objective reality except in the sense that it exists in all men as the universal motivation of counter-violence; it is nothing but the unbearable fact of broken reciprocity and of the systematic exploitation of man's humanity for the destruction of the human. Counter-violence is exactly the same thing, but as a process of restoration, as a response to a provocation: if I destroy the non-humanity of the anti-human in my adversary, I cannot help destroying the humanity of man in him, and realizing his non-humanity in myself.[40]

But Sartre does not stop here. He adds, "In other words, it is undeniable that what I attack is man as man, that is, as the free *praxis* of an organic being. It is man, and nothing else, that I hate in the enemy, that is, in myself as Other; and it is myself that I destroy in him, so as to prevent him destroying me in my own body."[41] Arendt is missing an important point being made by Sartre concerning exploitation and violence against men. Sartre is emphasizing that exploitation and violence are attacks on the humanity of all men, as well as a kind of self-destruction. Exploitation and violence cannot be reduced to treating man as non-human or even as an animal. Sartre is building on his earlier assertion (not mentioned by Arendt) that "in order to treat a man like a dog, one must first recognize him as a man."[42]

This is what Sartre describes as the contradiction of racism, colonialism, and all forms of tyranny. He explains, "The concealed discomfort of the master is that he always has to consider the *human reality* of his slaves (whether through his reliance on their skill and their synthetic understanding of situations, or through his precautions against the permanent possibility of revolt or escape), while at the same time refusing them the economic and political status which, *in this period,* defines human beings."[43] This point is also illustrated by the debate about baptizing slaves. If slaves have a soul and are in fact persons, then they should be baptized, but of course that also means that they should *not* be enslaved.

Having ignored all these points, Arendt then says that Sartre claims, "Whether I kill, torture, enslave . . . my aim is to suppress his freedom—it is an alien force *de trop*."[44] But Sartre actually states, "I may try to kill, to torture, to enslave, or simply to mystify, but in any case my aim will be to eliminate alien freedom as a hostile force, a force which can expel me from the practical field and make me into 'a surplus man' condemned to death."[45] This statement must be understood in the context of Sartre's analysis of scarcity. But Arendt ignores that analysis and leaps to Sartre's analysis of collectives, which is presented over a hundred pages later. Arendt is either neglecting the analysis of scarcity altogether or she is conflating his analysis of scarcity with his analysis of collective, series, and group. Arendt claims that Sartre's model for a condition in which "each one is one too many . . . each is *redundant* for the other"[46] is a bus queue, the members of which obviously "take no notice of each other except as a number in a quantitative series."[47] Here Laing and Cooper may be paraphrasing the passage where Sartre states that "there are not enough places for everyone,"[48] so each passenger on the bus becomes too many. The idea of redundancy may be a paraphrase of Sartre's claim that "everyone is the same as the Other in so far as he is Other than himself."[49] Or the claim that "identity becomes synthetic: everyone is identical with the Other in so far as the others make him an Other acting on the Others; the formal universal structure of alterity produces the formula of the series."[50]

After this misquotation and misinterpretation of Sartre's analysis, Arendt casually adds that the flaw in Sartre's argument should be obvious: "There is all the difference in the world between 'not taking notice' and 'denying,' between 'denying any link' with somebody and 'negating' his otherness; and for a sane person there is still a considerable distance to travel from this theoretical 'negation' to killing, torturing, and enslaving" (*OV* 186). Arendt is trying to navigate between different examples used by Sartre to explain different analyses, but she has the wrong map. The description of the unity of the people waiting at the bus stop is but one example that leads to other examples of serial unities. There are points at which Laing and Cooper remain very close to Sartre's text, and Arendt still chooses to oversimplify Sartre's analysis; this may point to a willful distortion of Sartre. She selected bits and pieces from *Reason and Violence* that fit her critique, but she is not fair or true to the analysis presented in *Reason and Violence* or the *Critique*.

The Violent System of Colonialism: Critiquing Arendt

Arendt's critiques of Fanon and Sartre are a byproduct of problems in her analysis of the political in general (e.g., the public-private distinction) and her analysis of the interconnection between violence, race, racism, and colonialism in particular (e.g., her understanding of racial oppression in the colonial system). Although Fanon, Sartre, and Arendt each identify the central role of violence in the colonial system, they are not led to the same conclusions. Rather than learn from Fanon and Sartre, she remains critical of their descriptions of violent resistance to oppression. By using Fanon's and Sartre's arguments concerning violence and the colonial system, we can formulate a clear critique of Arendt's one-sided condemnation of violence.

What is striking about Arendt's account is that she does not endorse rebellion or revolution in any form (violent or otherwise) against colonization. Unlike her discussion of Jewish resistance, there is no call for an army or an armed uprising, no assertion that "death with weapons in hand can bring new values" (*JW* 217). On the contrary, in *On Violence* Arendt denounces anticolonial violence and uses Fanon and Sartre as examples of those who endorse and glorify it. While it may appear at first glance that Arendt is offering a universal condemnation of violence, in reality she is only rejecting *some* forms of violence, namely, revolutionary violence against colonial oppression. I have already shown that Arendt acknowledges the role of violence in various systems of oppression, including imperialism/colonialism, but she is not as critical of the oppressors' violence as she is of revolutionary violence. I have also shown her endorsement of the formation of a Jewish army and the uprisings in the Warsaw ghetto. In order to fully appreciate the significance of Arendt's uncritical relationship to violence in colonialism, I want to underscore Fanon's and Sartre's accounts. It is on the foundation of the argument that colonialism is a system of violent oppression that they are able to assert that the revolutionary violence of the colonized is really *counter*violence. The ferocity of the violence within colonial oppression broadens the justification for counterviolence.

Fanon is clear that the colonized learned violence from the colonizers. He states, "The settlers said that the native only understands the language of force and the native decides to give utterance by force. The settler, through his violence, has shown the native that violence is the only way that he can be free."[51] Since the colonized are oppressed through violence, they come to understand that violence will be required to overcome colonialism and attain freedom. Fanon explains, "The argument the native chooses has been furnished by the settler, and by an ironic turning of the tables it is the native who now affirms that the colonist understands nothing but force."[52] The violence that was once used to oppress is appropriated as a tool for liberation.

Fanon is adamant: "The uprising of the new nation and the breaking down of colonial structures are the result of one of two causes: either of a violent struggle of the people in their own right, or of action on the part of surrounding colonized peoples which acts as a brake on the colonial regime in question."[53] The destruction of the colonial world is not to open lines of communication or for cohabitation because "the destruction of the colonial world is no more and no less [than] the abolition of one zone, its burial in the depths of the earth or its expulsion from the country."[54] For these reasons, "National liberation, national resistance, the restoration of nationhood to the people, commonwealth: whatever may be the headings used or the formulas introduced, decolonization is always a violent phenomenon."[55] Decolonization is the meeting of two opposed forces, the colonizer and the colonized: "Their first encounter was marked by violence and their existence together—that is to say the exploitation of the native by the settler—was carried on by dint of a great array of bayonets and cannons."[56]

In an effort to discourage resistance among the colonized, the colonizers respond with greater violence, increasing the police and military presence. The colonizers have at their disposal machine guns, airplanes, and bombardment from the fleet, and the impacts of these weapons "go far beyond in horror and in magnitude any answer the natives can make."[57] The colonized are confronted with the setbacks of using violent resistance against colonizers who are able to exert a higher magnitude of violence sanctioned by the state. The colonized remain caught in an atmosphere permeated by violence, but they are not without hope. The magnitude of the oppressors' resources against those of the oppressed does not thwart the revolution. Fanon asserts, "The violence of the native is only hopeless if we compare it in the abstract to the military machine of the oppressor. On the other hand, if we situate that violence in the dynamics of the international situation, we see at once that it constitutes a terrible menace for the oppressor."[58]

We see Sartre's analysis of violence as a counterresponse to violence in "Colonialism Is a System," where he asserts that colonialism is the shame of France.[59] Rather than passively supporting colonialism, Sartre asserts that the French must *help it die.* He adds that the only thing that they can and ought to do is to fight alongside the Algerian people to deliver Algeria and France from colonial tyranny.[60] In the same essay, Sartre also claims that the first violence is the colonizers': "the colonists themselves have taught their adversaries [e.g., the colonized

Algerians] . . . that no solution was possible other than force."[61] Even the oppressive colonizer recognizes that it is *his* oppressive violence that is manifested in the revolutionary violence of the colonized natives, and he becomes appalled at it.[62]

In *Critique of Dialectical Reason*, Sartre describes the system of colonialism as an infernal machine in which "violence and destruction were an integral part of the desired objective."[63] He adds that it is the objective violence of colonialism that defines the system itself as a "practico-inert hell."[64] Sartre asserts that the colonizer's violence is the only violence, and it emerges as an infinite necessity even in the absence of violence on the part of the colonized. In 1961 Sartre built on the analysis of an original violence in his preface to Fanon's *The Wretched of the Earth*.[65] Again he asserted that the first violence is always the colonizers' violence because it is the colonizer who sets the tone in colonialism. Thus, when the colonized respond with violence, it is always counterviolence, a means of resistance, and a means to regain humanity.

Sartre's position is a disturbing one not only for Arendt but for many others as well, because he exposes the persistence of violence. In spite of the fact that the colonial system (like much of the world) is always already constituted by violence, many condemn the use of violence to confront violence and appeal to nonviolent resistance on the part of the oppressed. But to appeal to nonviolence (an appeal which is often one-sided, i.e., aiming at the violent resistance of the oppressed rather than at the violent system of oppression which they are confronting) or to pose the problem in terms of violence versus nonviolence is to present a false dilemma. Violence (and the threat of violence, which is itself violence) is already at the heart of most of our institutions (consider the police, military, prison system, education, media and entertainment, or capitalism in general). Thus, it is not a question of *whether* there will be violence, but rather *whose* violence will be endorsed and whose will be condemned. To condemn the violent self-defense of the oppressed is to, perhaps inadvertently, endorse the violence used to oppress.

"There Are Situations in Which the Very Swiftness of a Violent Act May Be the Only Appropriate Remedy"

Although Arendt warns against the unpredictability of violence, in *On Violence* she does allow for the use of violence in self-defense, explaining that no one questions this use of violence because the danger is not only clear but present, and the end justifying the means is immediate. On at least three occasions in this text she even notes that nonviolence does not work in all circumstances. The first is when she states, "If Gandhi's enormously powerful and successful strategy of nonviolent resistance had met with a different enemy—Stalin's Russia, Hitler's Germany, or even pre-war Japan, instead of England—the outcome would not have been decolonization but massacre and submission" (*CR* 152). This suggests that the best use of violence or nonviolence may depend on the enemy that is being confronted or resisted rather than on the conditions of oppression. I would push this even more to stress that when a group is confronting a violent oppressor (or a violent oppressive system), then nonviolent methods may have to be replaced with violent methods of resistance.

On another occasion Arendt concedes, "In private *as well as public* life there are situations in which the very swiftness of a violent act may be the only appropriate remedy" (*CR* 160, my emphasis). Here Arendt concedes that violence can be a remedy in certain (undisclosed) situations in both the private realm of necessity and the public realm of political action. Finally, Arendt acknowledges, "Under certain circumstances *violence*—acting without argument or speech and without counting the consequences—is the *only* way to set the scales of justice right again" (161, my emphasis).[66] So not only does Arendt concede that nonviolence does not always work, she also concedes that violence is in some cases a remedy and in other cases the "only way" to address certain situations. I contend that the violent system of colonialism is one such case, where revolutionary violence may be a more "swift" and appropriate remedy and "the only way to set the scales of justice right again."

But even Fanon, who emphasized the violent aspects of decolonization, moves beyond this phase of violence and calls for politicization. This is an important point that Arendt misses in Fanon's analysis. He critiques national leaders and the national bourgeoisie for imitating the European bourgeoisie and failing to develop meaningful connections with the people after fighting for independence.[67] He notes that they do not understand the economy of the country and their knowledge is academically abstract. The national leaders exploit agriculture workers without offering any modernization of agriculture, development plans, or initiatives.[68] They perpetuate the divisions and racisms of the colonial period and are harsh toward the masses. Fanon challenges political leaders to learn from and educate the people without claiming, as the colonizers did, that the people are too slow.[69] He demands that the people be educated politically, making the totality of the nation a reality to each citizen.[70] Although Fanon explains that violence was an important part of achieving consciousness in Algeria, he also acknowledges that similar results have been achieved elsewhere with methods like political struggles and information campaigns.[71]

By now Arendt's bias concerning violence should be evident. Arendt revealed the role of violence in the private sphere to master necessity in *The Human Condition* (*HC* 31). As Dossa states, "To suffer and inflict suffering is for her quite normal: she is reconciled and somewhat inured to the practice of violence among men."[72] In *On Revolution* she claimed that it is a "terrible truth" that "only violence and rule over others could make some men free" (*OR* 114). In *The Origins of Totalitarianism* she acknowledged the major role of violence in the colonial system. And while Arendt describes all of these modes of violence without criticism, she denounces the colonized as violent. So in *On Violence,* it is not only Arendt's critique of Sartre and Fanon in relation to violence, but also her analysis and judgment of the colonized and their use of violence that I am questioning here. Arendt is uncritical of the role of violence in the private realm and the use of violence to enter the public realm, but when it comes to the use of violence by the colonized, she takes a much more critical stand. If Arendt had followed her account of violence in *The Human Condition* to its conclusion, then she should have argued in *On Violence* that the colonized were also entitled to violence to liberate themselves from necessity and poverty. Rather than making this claim, Arendt takes the opposite position and criticizes the colonized revolutionaries for doing what she previously claimed all humans were entitled to: use force and violence to liberate themselves from necessity.

As with her analysis in "Reflections on Little Rock," in *On Violence* Arendt is unwilling to connect her insights on the importance of forming a Jewish army, the need for Jews to fight Hitler with weapons in their hands, and the significance of the armed uprisings in the Warsaw ghetto to Fanon's and Sartre's insights about the violent system of colonialism and the counterviolence of the colonized to combat it. But the issue is not only Arendt's biased critique of violence. Even if Arendt were to take a critical stance against the violence about which she has been uncritical up to this point, her distinctions and categories—including the public-private distinction, the account of the rise of the social, and even her distinction between violence and power—all perpetuate an uncritical relationship to the violence that is central to colonialism, as emphasized by Sartre and Fanon. Her exclusionary categories perpetuate and even legitimize violence, racism, and colonialism in a way that allows the violence of the oppressors to go unchecked.

7 "A Much Greater Threat to Our Institutions of Higher Learning than the Student Riots"

Hᴀɴɴᴀʜ ᴀʀᴇɴᴅᴛ ᴡʀᴏᴛᴇ "Reflections on Violence" in 1969, a decade after the publication of "Reflections on Little Rock." But Arendt's later reflections have not changed much from her earlier reflections. If anything, her views seem to have gotten worse. And yet Arendt's claims about Black students and higher education in *On Violence* (the expanded version of the 1969 "Reflections") have not received as much critique as those in "Reflections on Little Rock."[1] Although Arendt describes without criticism several uses of violence (including torture) in the private realm—oppressing others to facilitate one's entrance into the political realm—and although she acknowledges the violence of racism, she denounces the violence in student protests and the Black Power movement. As with her analysis of anticolonial resistance, Arendt is again presenting a biased critique of violence. She asserts that "violence pays," but it pays indiscriminately for "soul" courses, instruction in Swahili, and even "real" reforms (*CR* 176–177).

Here, I examine Arendt's unwavering position on integration (in education and in residential neighborhoods), her claims about Black students' intellectual abilities (along with the establishment of Black studies programs), and her negative representation of Black students and the Black community as violent. I challenge Arendt's wholesale characterization of Black students as academically unqualified and violent, and I bring attention to the symbolic violence of her representation of them.

"Our Specialty—The Negro Question"

In personal correspondence with Mary McCarthy (December 21, 1968), Arendt ruminates on what she calls "our specialty—the Negro question." Arendt writes to McCarthy: "I am pretty convinced that the new trend of Black Power and anti-integration, which comes as such a shock to liberals, is a direct consequence of the integration that preceded it."[2] As long as integration was token, standards of admission were not threatened, but "the general civil rights enthusiasm led to integrating larger numbers of Negroes who were not qualified."[3] According to Arendt's reasoning Black people started to become anti-integration because they realized that they were not qualified to attend white schools, but at the same time they were seeking to lower the standards in order to gain admission to white institutions. From her perspective Black students want to take over white institutions *and* adjust the standards to their (lower) level, and on this basis they present "a much greater threat to our institutions of higher learning than the student riots."[4]

We find similar sentiments in a 1970 interview with Adelbert Reif, which was translated and published in *Crises of the Republic* under the title "Thoughts on Politics and Revolution." Again taking up the issue of integration and education, Arendt explains: "The middle-class liberals have put through laws whose consequences they do not feel. They demand integration of the public schools, elimination of neighborhood schools (black children, who in large measure are simply left to neglect, are transported in buses out of the slums into schools in predominately white neighborhoods), forced integration of neighborhoods—and send their own children to private schools and move to the suburbs, something that only those at a certain income level can afford" (*CR* 226). This is consistent with Arendt's position in "Reflections on Little Rock," where she rejects arguments that segregation ought to be limited to private schools (while public schools are integrated) on the basis that it is unfair to poor white families. Arendt asserts that private schools "would make the safeguarding of certain private rights depend upon economic status and consequently underprivilege those who were forced to send their children to public schools" (RLR 55).

When asked in the same interview about American laborers' support of the U.S. engagement in Vietnam, Arendt responds by talking at length again about racial integration and "the color problem":

> In the eastern and northern parts of the country integration of the Negroes into the higher income groups encounters no very serious or insuperable difficulties. . . . The same integration in the middle and lower levels of middle-class, and especially among the workers . . . leads to catastrophe, and this indeed not only because the lower middle class happens to be particularly "reactionary," but because these classes believe, not without reason, that all these reforms relating to the Negro problem are being carried out at their expense. This can best be illustrated by the example of the schools. . . . In the big cities this public school system, under the weight of a very numerous, almost exclusively black *Lumpenproletariat*, has with very few exceptions broken down; these institutions, in which children are kept for twelve years without even learning to read and write, can hardly be described as schools. (*CR* 225)

Arendt adds that Black families destroy entire neighborhoods and turn them into slums: "Now if a section of the city becomes black as a result of the policy of integration, then the streets run to seed, the schools are neglected, the children run wild—in short, the neighborhood very quickly becomes a slum" (ibid.). But Anne Norton has rightly pointed out what Arendt neglects to mention: "Arendt erases the role of white flight in the changing racial balance of neighborhoods.

Her description of decay erases the role of discriminatory distribution of public services and private capital in neighborhood deterioration. These concealed erasures make integration the cause of blackness and blackness the cause of decay."[5] Given Arendt's portrayal of a Black *lumpenproletariat* that weighs on schools to the point of breaking them down and wild children who cannot be taught the basic skills of reading and writing, it is not surprising that Arendt's negative characterization is extended to Black college students.

In her discussion of Black students on college campuses in *On Violence*, Arendt asserts that the majority of Negro students admitted to colleges and universities were admitted without academic qualifications and that within the Black community the Negro's goal was to lower academic standards (*CR* 120). For Arendt, lowering academic standards included attempts to create courses in African and African American studies, which she calls "soul courses" (a phrase she borrows from Bayard Rustin), and instruction in languages such as Swahili (177). Arendt describes Swahili as "a nineteenth century kind of no language spoken by the Arab ivory and slave caravans, a hybrid mixture of a Bantu dialect with an enormous vocabulary of Arab borrowings"—using the 1961 *Encyclopedia Britannica* as her source (192).[6] She predicts that "in about five or ten years this 'education' in Swahili . . . , African Literature, and other nonexistent subjects will be interpreted as another trap of the white man to prevent Negroes from acquiring an adequate education" (ibid.).

Arendt attempts to reinforce her claims about Black students and soul courses with reference to a 1969 *Daily News* commentary by Bayard Rustin, a civil rights leader who studied Gandhian passivism in India and trained civil rights activists in nonviolent resistance tactics. Rustin was the principal organizer of the 1963 March on Washington, but was forced into the background because of left-wing associations from his youth (he was a former communist) and because he was gay.[7] He rejected the identity politics of the Black Power movement and was hesitant to help Martin Luther King Jr. with a rally in Jackson, Mississippi, because Stokely Carmichael (later, Kwame Ture) was also participating. Rustin was "sure that Carmichael intended to use the rally for his own purposes, as a forum for black nationalism."[8] Arendt quotes Rustin at length in the appendixes to *On Violence*, where she explains that he "has said all that needed to be said on the matter" (*CR* 191).[9] But Rustin's comments are not all that needs to be said on the matter. His remarks, mostly critical of the Black students protesting on college campuses, represent the differences (in part generational and in part philosophical) that were manifesting in private and public between the civil rights generation and the Black Power generation. But as Young-Bruehl points out, Arendt "assumed that his was a solitary voice."[10]

Arendt's (and Rustin's) claims here ignore the fact that *qualified* Black students were denied admission to colleges and universities on the basis of their race. The blanket critique of Black students as unqualified to enter institutions of higher education and of Black studies courses as "soul courses" fails to capture the problem of racist discrimination against qualified Black students coupled with the systematic erasure of Black intellectuals from history, literature, arts, sciences, and classroom discourse in general. There was (and still is, in spite of views to the contrary)[11] a legitimate need to offer courses in African and African American studies because academic disciplines have been and continue to be overwhelmingly whitewashed. Mainstream (white) curriculum often reduces Black history to slavery and to brief tributes to increasingly depoliticized Black iconic figures without regard for the histories and civilizations that flourished on the African continent before the transatlantic slave trade and without reference to the broader contributions of "the Negro in the making of America."[12]

Norton offers an incisive critique of Arendt on each of these points. In describing Swahili as a "no language," Arendt places Africans and African Americans outside of language, and in doing so also "places them outside of politics, outside reason, in the 'dark background of mere givenness.'"[13] Norton continues, "Arendt's easy dismissal of African history, African literatures, African languages; her readiness to ascribe academic inferiority to black students, and squalor, crime, and ignorance to the black community, are innocent of evidence. They evince an uncharacteristic, and profound, indifference to the historical record and the evidence available on these subjects in her time."[14]

Judith Butler addresses this problem in "I Merely Belong to Them," where she underscores the continuity of Eurocentricity in Arendt's earlier and later writings. Butler offers this scathing analysis:

> In the 1930s and early 1940s, the non-Jew Arendt has in mind is, of course, the European gentile. . . . Her views throughout this period are emphatically Eurocentric. . . . A presumption about the cultural superiority of Europe pervades much of her later writings too, and is clearest in her intemperate criticisms of Fanon, her debunking of the teaching of Swahili at Berkeley, and her dismissal of the black power movement in the 1960s. She clearly does not have racial minorities in mind when she thinks about those who suffer statelessness and dispossession. She appears to have separated the nation from the nation-state, but to the degree that the conception of "minorities" is restricted to national minorities, "nation" not only eclipses "race" as a category, but renders race unthinkable.[15]

What is clear—both in the extended quotes from Arendt herself and in Norton's and Butler's critiques—is the consistency of Arendt's position concerning the Negro question. For Arendt, from "Reflections on Little Rock" to "Reflections on Violence" and "Thoughts on Politics and Revolution," integration amounts to the degradation and contamination of white space (physical and intellectual) by Black bodies. Again, the Negro question is a Negro problem and not a white problem.

1968: The Year the World Caught Fire

It is worth exploring for a moment the climate in which Arendt's "Reflections on Violence" was written. In 1968 there was a tremendous amount of aggression, protest, and resistance in the United States and globally. For example, in January North Korea captured the USS *Pueblo* (a U.S. Navy intelligence vessel) and its crew of eighty-three, who would not be released until December of the same year. Also in January, North Vietnam launched the Tet offensive at Nha Trang, South Vietnam, which became a major turning point in American public opinion about the war. In March Howard University students staged a sit-in and took over a building. Martin Luther King Jr. was assassinated in Memphis, Tennessee, on April 4. He had delivered the antiwar speech "Beyond Vietnam" at Riverside Church in New York City exactly one year prior to his assassination. The student protests at Columbia University in which five buildings are taken over lasted for about a week in April. In May there was "Bloody Monday," one of the most violent days of student protests in France. Robert Kennedy was assassinated in June in Los Angeles. In August, Chicago police attacked protesters at the Democratic National Convention. In October, students protesting in Tlatelolco Square in Mexico City were injured or killed by police. Days later, the Summer Olympic Games commenced in Mexico City, though they were boycotted by many African nations. American athletes Tommie Smith and John Carlos raised their black-gloved fists during a medal ceremony. Richard Nixon was elected president in November, and *Apollo 8* was launched into space in December.

This is by no means an exhaustive itemization of the events of that watershed year, but it should provide some context for Arendt's contentious claims about the admissions process for Black students into higher education, the shift in language and posture from the civil rights movement to the Black Power movement, and the establishment of Black studies programs at colleges and universities across the country. Noliwe Rooks, *White Money/Black Power* (2006), and Fabio Rojas, *From Black Power to Black Studies* (2007), also put the 1960s student protests on college and university campuses in context. Rooks goes back to the 1940s and reminds us that colleges and universities across the United States experienced growing student populations from diverse social classes as a result of the G.I. Bill after World War II, which covered tuition expenses for veterans. Rooks explains, "The overall number of university and college students more than doubled in the decade between 1955 and 1965. . . . This included unprecedented growth in the number of African American students."[16] The increase of African American students resulted from both aggressive recruitment (especially in northern universities, which "lowered standards for admission and established remedial programs specifically aimed at increasing [the] numbers of African Americans") and increases in financial aid (e.g., through "the Higher Education Act of 1965, which provided funds for education through the Work Study Program, Educational Opportunity Grants, and the Guaranteed Student Loan Program").[17]

The institutions of higher learning expected gratitude from students for these opportunities, but this gratitude was mixed with "resentment toward the overwhelmingly white curriculum and [was] combined with a revolutionary fervor wrought by the political changes and rhetoric of both the civil rights and Black Power movements sweeping the country."[18] Rojas notes: "Before the 1960s, there was a substantial amount of black scholarship and intellectual work, but it was rarely taught in college courses. . . . But during the 1960s, a number of events, such as the civil rights mobilization, encouraged students and intellectuals to demand the institutionalization of knowledge about black culture."[19]

In the aftermath of white terrorism in the South in response to nonviolent resistance to white supremacy, there was a decisive shift from the civil rights philosophy of nonviolence and integration to the Black Power emphasis on power and armed self-defense, as well as to Black nationalism and separatism. Martin Luther King Jr. takes up this shift in "The Social Organization of Nonviolence," where there is an adjustment in the presentation of his nonviolent philosophy as he attempts to make room for the ideals of Black Power.[20] The escalation of white terrorism in response to the civil rights movement is captured in *Where Do We Go from Here: Chaos or Community?* "James Meredith has been shot!" is the opening line of "Black Power," the second chapter of that text. King asserts that this shooting was "the latest evidence that a Negro's life is still worthless in many parts of his own country."[21] King also describes his debates with Stokely Carmichael on the issue of Black Power and the bitterness expressed by students in an atmosphere of false promises, deferred dreams, and violence toward Blacks without repercussion.

It is in this context that students contributed to the development and proliferation of Black studies programs, departments, and institutes. Rooks points out, "Those of an earlier generation, such as Kenneth Clark and Bayard Rustin, argued passionately, persuasively, and vehemently against any type of revolutionary or ideological significance for what was merely a field of study."[22] She continues, "While that generation railed long and hard against any attempt to organize Black Studies as a separatist field, their arguments were drowned out by the sheer persuasive eloquence of those aligned with more militant sentiments."[23] Rojas explains the contrasting views: "Those who strongly identified with civil rights as it had been articulated until the 1960s believed that integration would solve these problems [i.e., various grievances with American institutions]. . . . In contrast, more radical black intellectuals felt this approach worked at the expense of the specific needs of the black community, which included a cultivation of black history and identity."[24] There were numerous student protests at colleges and universities throughout the country, demanding Black studies and calling for a relevant education that could help confront and end racism in America—including the protests at Columbia University about which Arendt writes in *On Violence*.

According to Elisabeth Young-Bruehl, Arendt was initially excited about the protests at Columbia in April 1968, but within days she became disappointed about the course of events.[25] On the one hand, Arendt was impressed with the push to sever ties between the university and war-related research but, on the other, she "was not sure what they meant with their calls for the university to be more responsible in its relations with the surrounding community of Harlem, which was alive with mourning for Martin Luther King, Jr., who had been shot on 4 April."[26] While Arendt did not object to the students' occupation of buildings, "she did object to the threat of armed revolt that came when Columbia's Hamilton Hall was taken over by black students allegedly supplied with arms from the Harlem community."[27] This image of armed Black students would be reinforced by the student protests at Cornell University in April 1969. In 1970, Steve Starr won a Pulitzer Prize for his photograph of armed students, reinforcing the view of Black students as violent and the association of Black studies programs with "upheaval, militancy, unrest, and violence."[28]

Rooks captures the misperceptions of Black studies programs well when she states: "The creation and institutionalization of Black Studies is sometimes viewed as a result of the capitulation of well-meaning white college administrators to militant, angry, and ungrateful African American students who were recruited to Northern colleges and universities during the late 1960s. . . . The role of Black Studies in such universities is often thought of . . . as glorified affirmative action programs useful for insuring an easy ride for unqualified Black students."[29] Arendt certainly fits into this description of those with misperceptions about Black studies and Black students. Utterly unable to see any value in Black students, let alone Black studies, Arendt writes that in the United States the established power yielded to "nonsensical and obviously damaging demands—such as admitting students without the necessary qualifications and instructing them in non-existent subjects" (*CR* 177). But Rooks offers a significant corrective to these perceptions, noting that the first Black studies program, established at San Francisco State University, resulted from protests by Black, white, Native American, Asian, and Latino students working together to support a common goal. With this in mind, Rooks states, "Black Studies is rarely viewed as a successful example of social justice, a means of multiracial democratic reform, or a harbinger of widespread institutional and cultural change in relation to race, integration, and desegregation at the postsecondary level. That is precisely what these programs were."[30]

Black Violence and Riots, White Guilt and Backlash

Arendt does not see the nonwhite student protesters as acting together in concert and attributes the yielding of the established power "to nonsensical and obviously damaging demands" to Black violence. Arendt asserts that violence was the method by which Black students hoped to lower academic standards and create "non-existent" subjects and disciplines. Contrasting the United States with other Western countries, Arendt claims that elsewhere there is no popular support of violence in a movement, but in the United States the Black community endorses it: "there is a large minority of the Negro community behind the verbal or actual violence of the black students" (*CR* 121). Arendt is astonished that the colleges and universities respond to such violence: "It seems that the academic establishment, in its curious tendency to yield more to Negro demands, even if they are clearly silly and outrageous, than to the disinterested and usually highly moral claims of the white rebels, also thinks in these terms and feels more comfortable when confronted with interests plus violence than when it is a matter of nonviolent 'participatory democracy'" (ibid.). Here we find very different characterizations of white students and Black students. For Arendt, the demands of the "violent" Negro students are "silly and outrageous," whereas the demands of the white rebels, through "nonviolent participatory democracy," are highly moral.

Arendt is critical of the police violence on campuses in response to protesters. She concedes that police brutality was a form of violent intervention in nonviolent (white) demonstrations in the student movements, but asserts that "serious violence" did not enter the scene until the Black Power movement appeared on college campuses (*CR* 120). This is problematic because it wrongly suggests that police brutality is not "serious violence" and furthermore that the Black Power movement was exclusively a violent movement in which violence "was not a matter of theory or rhetoric" (ibid.). She describes the Black students as "new militants" inspired by Sartre and Fanon and deceiving themselves about the "Unity of the Third World": "To think, finally, that there is such a thing as a 'Unity of the Third World,' to which one could address the new slogan in the era of decolonization 'Natives of the World Unite?' (Sartre) is to repeat Marx's worst illusions on a greatly enlarged scale and with considerably less justification. The Third World is not a reality but an ideology" (123). She adds in a footnote that in the case of the Black Power movement, "its ideological commitment to the nonexistent 'Unity of the Third World' is not sheer romantic nonsense. They have an obvious interest in a black-white dichotomy; this too is of course mere escapism—an escape into a dream world in which Negroes would constitute an overwhelming majority of the world's population" (123–124n37).[31]

In addition to dismissing Black claims about the unity of the Third World, Arendt also rejects white liberal declarations that "we are all guilty" (*CR* 162). She explains, "Where all are guilty, no one is" (ibid.). The notion that all white men are guilty—which she describes as racism in the reverse—serves "to give the very real grievances and rational emotions of the Negro population an outlet into irrationality, an escape from reality" (ibid.).[32] Arendt asserts that feelings of guilt in the white community have allowed Black demands to be met and then warns against confessions of group guilt because "Black Power has proved all too happy to take advantage of this 'confession' to instigate an irrational 'black rage'" (ibid.). Of course, white guilt—in the absence of protests, the civil rights movement, and the Black Power movement—never produced any positive widespread institutional changes in the conditions of the American Negro. White guilt is neither a necessary nor a sufficient condition for Black liberation.

Not only does Arendt reject the idea of white guilt, she also warns about the possibility of white backlash—presented as part of her analysis of the relationship between racism and violence. In *On Violence,* Arendt is clear that racism "is fraught with violence by definition because it objects to natural organic facts—a white or black skin—which no persuasion or power could change" (*CR* 173). She also asserts that "violence in interracial struggle is always murderous" and that violence is "a logical and rational consequence of racism" (ibid.). This is a significant claim by Arendt because she maintains that, contrary to popular belief, violence is often rational and calculated. Though people may choose to believe that the murderous nature of violence is thoughtless and irrational, the opposite is more often the case. She adds, "But even today's violence, black riots, and the potential violence of white backlash are not yet manifestations of racist ideologies and their murderous logic" (173–174).

Arendt asserts that if there were a backlash from the white community in response to the Black Power movement, it would be "the perfectly rational reaction of certain interest groups which furiously protest being singled out to pay the full price for ill-designed integration policies whose consequences their authors can easily escape" (*CR* 174). What she calls "Black racism" could "provoke a really violent white backlash" that would result in the "transformation of white prejudices into [a] full-fledged racist ideology" (ibid.).[33] It seems to escape Arendt's attention that Black students were already in the throes of a full-fledged anti-Black racist ideology. Far from seeing the (sometimes) violent resistance of student protesters as a form of backlash from segments of the Black community against white racism and violence, Arendt identifies riots and protests as a form of Black anti-white racism that invites white backlash. When she claims that white prejudice *could* turn into racism, she is denying that white prejudice was usually accompanied by white racism and was already a problem.

Reflections on the "Highly Successful Civil Rights Movement" and Civil Disobedience

Arendt's characterization of Black students and the Black Power movement as violent becomes more problematic when juxtaposed with her pithy remarks about the civil rights movement. She mentions and criticizes the civil rights movement and Martin Luther King Jr. (not only in *On Violence* and "Thoughts on Revolution" but also in "Civil Disobedience"), yet Arendt does not really discuss the significance of the movement nor the nonviolent philosophy behind it. For example, Arendt talks about a "split in the civil rights movement into 'black' and 'white'" over the Vietnam War in the interview "Thoughts on Politics and Revolution." She states: "The white students coming from good middle-class homes at once joined the opposition, in contrast to the Negroes, whose leaders were very slow in making up their minds to demonstrate against the war in Vietnam. This was true even for Martin Luther King" (CR 226). These claims allow her to simultaneously celebrate "good" middle-class white students and casually dismiss King as late to demonstrate against the Vietnam War without mentioning his other significant contributions (including his public denunciation of that war). When she examines the problematic role of conscience in "Civil Disobedience," arguing that one conscience simply stands against another conscience, Arendt puts King in the same category as Mississippi governor Ross Barnett.[34]

When Arendt distinguishes between racism and prejudice in *On Violence*, asserting that prejudice may yield under pressure as evidenced by the "highly successful civil rights movement" (CR 173), this fleeting note of success is undermined by her more sustained critique of Black Power and her repeated characterizations of Black students as violent. Arendt argues: "While boycotts, sit-ins, and demonstrations were successful in eliminating discriminatory laws and ordinances in the South, they proved utter failures and became counterproductive when they encountered the social conditions in the large urban centers—the stark needs of the black ghettos on the one side, the overriding interests of white lower income groups in respect to housing and education on the other" (ibid.). And Arendt remains consistent with her position in "Reflections on Little Rock" that these are not solutions to social questions.[35]

There are also overlaps in Arendt's analysis of racial oppression and Black people's objectives in "Reflections on Little Rock" and the later "Civil Disobedience." In the latter she again notes the troubled history of anti-Black racism in the United States going back to slavery. Acknowledging the tacit exclusion of Blacks from the "tacit *consensus universalis* of the nation," Arendt insightfully asserts: "We know the result, and we need not be surprised that the present belated attempts to welcome the Negro population explicitly into the otherwise tacit *consensus universalis* of the nation are not trusted" (CR 91). Yet this insight is again undermined by her myopic and monolithic representation of Black people as violent and having misplaced priorities. Shifting from the context of the racial integration of public schools in "Reflections on Little Rock," where Arendt assumed that Black parents' primary motivation was social climbing, to the anti-integration stance held by many Black Power leaders, in "Civil Disobedience" Arendt argues: "At any rate, attempts of integration often are met by rebuffs from black organizations, while quite a number of their leaders care little about the rules of nonviolence for civil disobedience and, often, just as little about the issues at stake—the Vietnam war, specific defects in our institutions—because they are in open rebellion against all of them" (92). Once more Arendt makes passing mention of nonviolence and civil disobedience, in this case to make dismissive assumptions about where Black leaders' "cares" do and do not lie.

It is clear that Arendt's account of Black student protests, violence, and the Black Power movement misses the mark when it comes to the Negro question, and it is part of a pattern in Arendt of underanalyzing anti-Black racism coupled with a biased critique of violence. Arendt's dismissal of African histories, literatures, and languages as nonexistent subjects is troubling. Her characterization of Black students on college and university campuses as violent and unqualified academically, along with her denial of their capacity for political action, is a problem. She presents Blacks as trapped in a dream world of escapism and suffering from irrational rage, while describing a "potentially" violent backlash from the white community as perfectly rational. And as with her analysis of the violence of imperialism/colonialism and the violence of decolonization, Arendt is far less condemning of the oppressors' offensive violence than she is of the defensive violence of the oppressed.

Conclusion

The Role of Judgment in Arendt's Approach to the Negro Question

THROUGHOUT THIS BOOK I have made several arguments. I argued that Arendt sees the Negro question as a Negro problem rather than a white problem, meaning that Arendt frames the issues of slavery, segregation, and colonialism/imperialism in a way that presents Black persons as the problem rather than situating white people's anti-Black racism as the problem (as did Richard Wright, James Baldwin, Ralph Ellison, and Gunnar Myrdal, for example). I also argued that Arendt does not constructively connect her analysis of the Jewish question to her analysis of the Negro question, even though the former has implications for the latter. For example, Arendt does not connect her childhood experience with antisemitism and the ways her mother equipped her to confront antisemitism with Black children's experiences of anti-Black racism and Black parents' abilities to do for their children what Arendt's mother did for her. Instead she chooses to view Black parents as social parvenus who allowed their children to integrate white schools for upward social mobility. Likewise, while Arendt puts her arguments for the formation of a Jewish army in political terms and claims that the armed uprisings in the Warsaw ghetto transformed people broken in body and spirit into political actors fighting for the freedom of Jews, she does not apply this analysis to uprisings staged by colonized resisters. She is keenly aware of the violent oppression in the colonial system (which she calls "imperialism") but criticizes Fanon and Sartre as theorists glorifying violence for the sake of violence. Additionally, although Arendt insists that antisemitism and Jew hatred are political, she holds that most forms of anti-Black racial oppression are private and at times social issues, but not specifically political problems.

With this in mind, I have also argued that Arendt's description of the Jewish question as political and the Negro question as private or social raises doubts about her criteria for what is political, private, or social. Her theoretical framework dividing up the political, the private, and the social guides her analysis of the Negro question in a way that undermines her understanding of and judgments about it. Consequently, Arendt's approach to the Negro question as a private or social issue prevents her from recognizing that anti-Black racism (like Jew hatred) is a political phenomenon. I want to connect these broader arguments concerning Arendt and the Negro question to her analysis of judgment and representational thinking, which inhibits rather than enhances her understanding of this question. My starting point is Arendt's Kantian (or Kant-influenced) conceptualization of judgment and representational thinking. Judgment involves being in public space, communicating one's opinions, reaching agreement with others, and considering other viewpoints to move beyond private opinions and interests. While Arendt imagines that she has many standpoints present in her mind and that she thinks in the place of absent others, instead she represents the views only of those allowed in the public realm while misrepresenting (or not making present at all) the views of those confined to the private or social realms. The limitations of the concepts of judgment and representative thinking are evident in Arendt's representation of African Americans and Africans across her political writings. Rather than representing and making present the absent standpoints of the oppressed, Arendt occupies and represents the standpoints of those already present in the public realm, the oppressors.

A Political Activity: "To Think in the Place of Everybody Else"

In "The Crisis in Culture," Arendt uses Immanuel Kant's *Critique of Practical Reason* to show that the faculty of judgment implies political rather than merely theoretical activity.[1] She then turns to Kant's *Critique of Judgment* to explore representational thinking or enlarged mentality, that is, the ability to "think in the place of everybody else" (*BPF* 219). For Arendt, "The power of judgment rests on potential agreement with others," or reaching agreement through communication with others in public/political space (220).[2] This judgment "must liberate itself from 'the subjective private conditions'" and be thought about in anticipation of communication and potential agreement with others (ibid.). Already Arendt has situated this concept into her framework of the political (reaching agreement with others in public space) and the private (moving beyond private opinions that are not valid in the public realm). According to Arendt, "Judgment may be one of the fundamental abilities of man as a political being insofar as it enables him to orient himself in a public realm, in the common world" (221).[3] Thus, the capacity to judge is identified by Arendt as a specifically political ability, "the ability to see things not only from one's own point of view but in the perspective of all those who happen to be present" (ibid.).[4]

Arendt's emphasis on the relationship between judgment and the communication or agreement between those *present* (or those one imagines would be present and potentially agreed with) raises questions about judgment and the representation of viewpoints that are *absent* from political space. How does one anticipate communication and agreement with a subject who is (or historically has been) absent from the political space in which opinions are exchanged? This question brings us back to Arendt's political-private distinction. The common world of the public realm (the political) is an exclusionary world open only to the few. Those present in the public realm and common world do not just happen to be present; they are present at the cost of the absence of others (see chapter 3).

Arendt offers a possible reply to this question concerning the absent other with the concept of representational thinking. In "Truth and Politics," again using and interpreting Kant, she describes the capacity for representational thinking as an "enlarged mentality" that enables men to judge. She asserts: "Political thought is representative. I form an opinion by considering a given issue from different viewpoints, by making present to my mind the standpoints of those who are absent; that is, I represent them" (BPF 241).[5] So there is a slight shift from communication and potential agreement with those who happen to be present, to considering and representing the viewpoints of those who are absent. This does not solve the problem of their absence, but does seem to be an attempt to represent their views in the public space from which they are absent and excluded. But we have to remember that in Arendt's model of public space, the absent others (and their absent viewpoints) are not and will not be anticipated because they are deemed unfit for the public realm of appearances and exemplarity.

This potentially promising idea of representational thinking becomes even more problematic when Arendt elaborates on what she means (or rather what she does not mean) by representation: "This process of representation does not blindly adopt the actual views of those who stand somewhere else, and hence look upon the world from a different perspective; this is a question neither of empathy, as though I tried to be or to feel like somebody else, nor of counting noses and joining the majority but of being and thinking in my own identity where I actually am not" (BPF 241).[6] Representational thinking is *not* adopting the views of those absent (excluded), it is *not* looking at the world from another perspective, and it is *not* empathy. What, then, is representational thinking? Arendt continues, "The more people's standpoints I have present in my mind while I am pondering a given issue, and the better I can imagine how I would feel and think if I were in their place, the stronger will be my capacity for representative thinking and the more valid my final conclusions, my opinion" (ibid.).

All of this suggests that representational thinking amounts to validating one's own conclusions and opinions by imagining oneself in the place of others but without ever adopting their viewpoint, seeing things from their perspective, or empathizing with them. Representational thinking displaces their standpoint while inserting one's own, imagining oneself in their place, but never inquiring about their own experience in their place. Arendt concludes, "The very process of opinion formation is determined by those in whose places somebody thinks and uses his own mind, and the only condition for this exertion of the imagination is disinterestedness, the liberation from one's own private interests. . . . I remain in this world of universal interdependence, where I can make myself the representative of everybody else" (*BPF* 241–242). The goal is not to bring those who are (or have historically been) absent and excluded into the political space to express their opinions. It is not to communicate and potentially agree with those who are absent, nor is it to represent their views on their terms in the political space. Rather, the goal of representational thinking is to form a judgment about the absent others using one's own imagination and disinterestedness.

Arendt claims that she forms opinions considering different viewpoints (including those that are absent). But she does not make the case that the absent viewpoint should be made present (that is, should be brought into the space of deliberation). Rather, she asserts that she can represent the absent viewpoints. And while this might be less problematic if those absent were actually consulted about their viewpoints, the problem is that the absent viewpoints are summarily dismissed. Arendt does not "blindly adopt the actual views of others," "look upon the world from a different perspective," or even try "to be or feel like someone else" (*BPF* 241). So what is she actually doing? What is the foundation of this representational thinking if the viewpoints of others are neither presented by the others (because they are absent) nor represented by those present? Imagining how "I" would feel in someone else's place, while intentionally ignoring how this absent other actually feels or sees her situation, is not (to me, even if it is to Arendt and Kant) inclusive representative thinking. If anything, this is a model for exclusive misrepresentative thinking.[7] We see a myriad of problems from such misrepresentative thinking in Arendt's judgments concerning the Negro question: in her analysis of segregation and her characterization of African Americans in "Reflections on Little Rock," in her analysis of slavery in the context of the American Revolution (*On Revolution*), in her racist representations of Africans in her examination of racism and imperialism (*Origins*), in her descriptions of Fanon and Sartre as glorifiers of violence, and in her characterization of African Americans as violent (*On Violence*).

Judging, Representing, and Imagining the Negro

Arendt's "Reflections on Little Rock" together with her "Preliminary Remarks" and "A Reply to Critics" are integral (not incidental) to Arendt's political thought and writings. In the Little Rock essay we find the fundamental strategies that organize Arendt's thought (see chapters 1, 2, and 3). Her reflections are not simply naïve remarks from someone unfamiliar with racial oppression in America. Nor are they an abstract theoretical exercise. On the contrary, these works present her "judgments" (which for her constitute a political, not merely theoretical, activity) and her "representational thinking" about racial segregation in general and the situation in Little Rock in particular. Arendt is quite consciously judging Black parents and the NAACP in the Little Rock essay as she defends whites' right to segregation in public education against Blacks' right to equal educational opportunities.

In the "Preliminary Remarks" to "Reflections on Little Rock," Arendt tries to situate herself as an outsider (outside of the American framework of racism, which she calls prejudice): "I should like to remind the reader that I am writing as an outsider" based on the fact that she "never lived in the South," and because of her European, not Jewish, origin she has "difficulty in understanding, let alone sharing, the common prejudices of Americans in this area" (RLR 46). Arendt attempts to distance herself from American racism with an air of moral superiority, but after claiming to be an outsider in the "Preliminary Remarks," Arendt presents herself as a representative thinker in "Reply to Critics." Recall that her reflections unfolded around three questions: "What would I do if I were a Negro mother?," "What would I do if I were a white mother in the South?," and "What exactly distinguished the so-called Southern way of life from the American way of life with respect to the color question?" (Reply 179–181). These questions indicate Arendt's attempt to view the situation from multiple perspectives in order to achieve an enlarged mentality, or representative thinking.

Let us examine more closely Arendt's attempts to situate herself as an outsider (not American, not familiar with American racism, and therefore not implicated in shared racist attitudes) and as a representative thinker (making present in the public realm standpoints that are absent and representing them). Although Arendt assumes that she is writing from the position of a disinterested or unbiased outsider representing standpoints that are absent, the position she occupies and represents in the Little Rock essay is actually the position of white racists. That is, she is inside the racist American system and mentality. Her arguments about segregation and her ordering of priorities are in line with what Myrdal called the white man's rank order of priorities. The standpoints of Black parents and NAACP members remain absent and their positions are not accurately represented. In fact, Arendt misrepresents their motives altogether.

One could argue that in Arendt's estimation, the absent voices are those of the segregationists. These voices are being drowned out by the "routine repetition of liberal clichés" against which she positions herself. In this way, she is imagining and representing the segregationists' absent positions. But where are the absent Black standpoints? We might consider several possibilities: (1) Arendt assumes that the voices of the Black community are actually present (represented by white liberals); (2) she believes that she has in fact represented the absent Black standpoint through the faculty of imagination—that is, imagining and putting herself in the place of Black people (without empathy); or (3) she assumes that Black voices ought to remain absent—that is, Black voices, positions, and standpoints are not worthy of consideration in public discourse, perhaps because they are merely social. But I would argue that it is the Black parents and children who are actually in the outsider position and therefore in the better position to make judgments about segregation. Thus, the issue is not (as Arendt claims) that "oppressed minorities were

never the best judges on the order of priorities" but rather that the white segregationists are not the best judges on how to dismantle the Jim Crow systems of segregation in which they are actors, insiders, and beneficiaries. Consequently, it is
precisely the oppressed minorities, by virtue of their outsider position, who are
the best judges.

Furthermore, despite asserting an outsider position, Arendt attempts to simultaneously present herself as having an insider position (inside a framework
of oppression because she is Jewish) when she states, "as a Jew, I take my sympathy for the cause of the Negroes as for all oppressed or under-privileged peoples
for granted and should appreciate it if the reader did likewise" (RLR 46). But it is
clear that Arendt's sympathies are with white parents, white children, and state
politicians faced with government-enforced desegregation, not with the African
Americans enduring anti-Black racism in the South and throughout the country.
She is quite unsympathetic to Black parents whom she judges are putting their
children in harm's way. As Anne Norton astutely notes, "The uneasy fit between
her writings on race and her disavowal of complicity in an unjust racial order
shows the danger of taking one's sympathies for granted."[8] This may explain part
of the reason that Arendt's "Reflections on Little Rock" goes so terribly wrong.

The misrepresentations of and judgments about the absent Black other, however, extend beyond the Little Rock essay. In *On Revolution,* Arendt praises the
founding fathers for focusing on the political problem of freedom rather than on
the social problem of misery among Black slaves. She is as capable of representing
the position of the founding fathers (even noting the incompatibility of proclaiming freedom while preserving a racialized system of slavery) as she is incapable
of representing the position of those enslaved. In forming judgments about the
American Revolution, she presents the founding fathers as indifferent to slaves
and the institution of slavery. But Arendt does not attempt to make present the
standpoint of those enslaved. She does not include their views on the institution
of slavery or the American Revolution or the foundation of freedom for some, but
not all. There is no enlarged thought or representative thinking about the absent
viewpoints of those enslaved. This is also the case in her extraction of the Negro
question in the form of slavery for France and the French Revolution as well as
the complete absence of the Haitian Revolution in her study of revolutions.

We find more of the same in Arendt's analysis of race thinking, racism, and
imperialism in *The Origins of Totalitarianism.* In describing the encounters between Europeans and Africans, Arendt demonstrates with ease her ability to see
from the perspective of the Europeans. To Arendt, it is obvious that the Africans
lacked civilization, reason, culture, history, and political institutions. Race and
racial oppression were understandable emergency explanations and rational responses by Europeans to their encounters with frightening and uncivilized African tribes. But again, there is no representative thinking or enlarged mentality that

includes the very absent perspectives of the African tribes. There is no attempt by Arendt to liberate her judgments from subjective private interests in order to see the standpoint of the Africans being confronted with European xenophobia and racism. She imagines how she would think or feel in the place of Europeans but not in the place of Africans. Her characterization of Africans is not impartial.

This one-sided representative thinking continues in Arendt's uncritical account of the constitutive role of violence in the political realm, along with the use of violence to keep necessity in the private realm. She even offers a clear analysis of the expansion of the national instruments of violence through imperialism/ colonialism. But despite all of these insights, in *On Violence* Arendt is hypercritical not only of Fanon's and Sartre's views of violence, but also of the colonized and their use of anticolonial counterviolence to liberate themselves from necessity in their fight for freedom from the violent system of colonialism.

She takes a similar approach in her discussion of college and university campus protests. Arendt thinks in the place of white students and administrators, seeing things from their perspective. White administrators are well-meaning. White students are making highly moral claims and demands through nonviolent participatory democracy. She assumes that white students are (perhaps by definition) highly qualified academically. Additionally, Arendt thinks it perfectly rational that there would be backlash in the white community, that white prejudices would be transformed into racist ideologies against Black students and the Black Power movement. But she makes a very different representation of the Black students, who are described as angry, ungrateful, lacking academic qualifications, and desiring to take over institutions so that they can lower academic standards— an effort that presents a greater threat than even their riotous violence. Arendt represents the demands of Black students as nonsensical and damaging. Given these opinions about white students versus Black students, it is difficult to see her as an impartial observer liberated from private interests and making present the absent standpoints. Arendt has not made herself the representative of everybody. She has made herself a representative of white Americans, affirming a negative image of Blackness that persists in the white imagination, an image that is at the foundation of the white problem.

Arendt's representation of the Negro question as a Negro problem rather than a white problem is an indication of her poor judgment. She does not adequately imagine nor represent the standpoint of African Americans or Africans. This may be because her image of Black people is always already distorted and partial. She represents African Americans as unconcerned with political issues and preoccupied with social issues for the purpose of upward social mobility. She represents Blacks as violent, apolitical, unintelligent, and seekers of admission to public and higher education without qualification. She represents Africans as savages and mass murderers, lacking history and ruled by nature. These images and representations are not a matter of demonstrating a lack of empathy. Nor are these imagined representations a matter of disregarding private interest or self-interest.

Hannah Arendt argues that we expose ourselves through judging: "By his manner of judging, the person discloses to an extent also himself, what kind of person he is, and this disclosure which is involuntary, gains in validity to the degree that it has liberated itself from merely individual idiosyncrasies" (*BPF* 223). In expressing her judgments about the Negro and the Negro question, Arendt has indeed exposed and disclosed herself, though it appears that she has not liberated herself from her individual idiosyncrasies.

Notes

Preface

1. Arendt protests the label "philosopher" in her 1964 interview with Günter Gaus: "I do not belong to the circle of philosophers. My profession . . . is political theory. I neither feel like a philosopher, nor do I believe that I have been accepted in the circle of philosophers" (*EU* 1). In the same conversation she claims that there is a tension between philosophy (man as a thinking being) and politics (man as an acting being), so much so that philosophy has enmity toward politics. Arendt rejects this enmity and states, "I want to look at politics, so to speak, with eyes unclouded by philosophy" (2).

2. Alice Walker, *In Search of Our Mothers' Gardens: Womanist Prose* (New York: Harcourt Brace, 1983), 13 (emphasis in original). Also cited by Patricia Hill-Collins in *Black Feminist Thought: Knowledge, Consciousness, and the Politics of Empowerment* (New York: Routledge, 1990), 13.

Introduction

1. Richard Bernstein, *Hannah Arendt and the Jewish Question* (Cambridge, MA: MIT Press, 1996), 10 (hereafter, *HAJQ*). For a thoughtful review of Bernstein's book, see Robert Bernasconi, "Richard Bernstein: Hannah Arendt's Alleged Evasion of the Question of Jewish Identity," *Continental Philosophy Review* 32(4) (October 1999):472–478.

2. *HAJQ* xi. See also *JW*.

3. See Jacob Toury, "'The Jewish Question'—A Semantic Approach," *Publications of the Leo Baeck Institute, Year Book* 11 (1966):85–106. Toury locates the phrase in the mid-eighteenth century with reference to a pamphlet, *Reply to the Famous Jewish Question,* published in London in 1754. See also Charles Zueblin, "Ethics of the Jewish Question," *International Journal of Ethics* 2(4) (July 1892):462–475. With all of its problematic claims, this article offers an interesting example of the ways in which the Jewish question was thought about alongside race problems, race mixing, and intermarriage in the United States in the late eighteenth century. Zueblin claims, "In studying the growth of this people [Jewish people], we may learn not only our duty toward them but also the solution of the many race problems now confronting the American people" (462). He later declares, "We must recognize our duty to the Jew for the altruistic reason that we should aid the oppressed, and for the egoistic reason that the solution of this problem will enable us to solve the greatest question before our nation—the assimilation of the races. We must see the Jew as an opportunity" (474–475).

4. See Derrick Bell, *Faces at the Bottom of the Well: The Permanence of Racism* (New York: Basic, 1993). I use "colonialism/imperialism" here because Arendt calls imperialism what others (like Jean-Paul Sartre, Aimé Césaire, and Frantz Fanon) refer to as colonialism. I have in mind the invasion of lands, enslavement of persons, and exploitation of resources by Europeans (and "Americans") under the guise of discovery and civilization missions.

5. The importance of the Negro question compared to and contrasted with the Jewish question is readily apparent in *The Origins of Totalitarianism,* but implicit in essays like "Reflections

on Little Rock." The question also looms in Arendt's interviews, personal correspondence, and political writings, such as *On Revolution* and *On Violence*.

6. At the end of *Anti-Semite and Jew: An Exploration of the Etiology of Hate* (New York: Schocken, 1995), Sartre states: "Richard Wright, the Negro writer, said recently: 'There is no Negro problem in the United States, there is only a White Problem.' In the same way we must say that anti-Semitism is not a Jewish problem; it is our problem" (152).

7. Gunnar Myrdal, *An American Dilemma: The Negro Problem and Modern Democracy* (New York: Harper, 1944), 669 (my emphasis).

8. Alfred Schutz, "Equality and the Meaning of the Structure of the World," in his *Collected Papers*, vol. 2 (The Hague: Martinus Nijhoff, 1964).

9. See Hazel Rowley, *Richard Wright: The Life and Times* (New York: Holt, 2001), 326. Dorothy Norman was the founder and editor of *Twice a Year: A Semi-Annual Journal of Literature, the Arts and Civil Liberties*. She was also known for her poetry, photography, and activism.

10. James Baldwin, "Letter from a Region in My Mind," *New Yorker* (November 17, 1962):59–144, reprinted in *The Fire Next Time* (New York: Vintage International, 1963) (hereafter, LRM and *FNT*). There is an article titled "Nation: The Root of the Negro Problem" in *Time* magazine (May 17, 1963) on Baldwin, his role as a reluctant Negro leader, and the so-called Negro problem (available at http://www.time.com/time/magazine/article/0,9171,830326,00.html, accessed June 22, 2012). Baldwin asks, "What do people mean when they say, 'the Negro problem'? I have never quite known what they meant, but whatever they had in mind overtook them and I was thrown up as a kind of public figure by the internal pressures of life in the United States" (82). He continues, "There isn't any such thing as a Negro. . . . but when you go on to say 'the Negro problem,' you create a great big monolith, and beneath this wall are thousands of millions of human beings' lives which are being destroyed because you want to deal with an abstraction" (ibid.).

11. In *Making It* (New York: Harper Colophon, 1967), Norman Podhoretz asserts that Baldwin had agreed to write a piece for *Commentary* but instead sent it to the *New Yorker* and was paid $12,000 for it—twenty times more than *Commentary* could have paid (340). He explains, "When the piece came out a few weeks later—it was, of course, *The Fire Next Time*—and I saw what a precious item had been stolen from me, my fury knew no bounds" (341). He continues with the story, adding to it an encounter with Arendt about Baldwin's piece: "As if my gall needed an additional poisonous ingredient, Hannah Arendt—feeling understandably benign toward the *New Yorker* for having just agreed to send her to Jerusalem to cover the Eichmann trial—told me solemnly over lunch before I had a chance to recount my tale of woe that the *New Yorker* was the *only* magazine in America which would have had the courage to publish so inflammatory an article as Baldwin's; I, 'of course,' could never have risked printing it in *Commentary*" (ibid.).

12. LRM 60/*FNT* 21. Baldwin also mentions the lack of love in the church and the hypocrisy of the instruction to love everybody when those offering these instructions do not really mean *everybody* (LRM 80/*FNT* 40). Baldwin describes love as that which "is so desperately sought and so cunningly avoided" (LRM 138/*FNT* 95). He notes that "relatively conscious" whites and Blacks must "like lovers, insist on, or create the consciousness of others" (LRM 144/*FNT* 105).

13. LRM 141/*FNT* 100.

14. Baldwin writes, "The American Negro has the great advantage of having never believed that collection of myths to which white Americans cling: that their ancestors were all freedom-loving heroes, that they were born in the greatest country the world has ever seen, or that Americans are invincible in battle and wise in peace, that Americans have always dealt honorably with Mexicans and Indians and all other neighbors or inferiors, that American men are the world's most direct and virile, that American women are pure" (LRM 142/*FNT* 101).

15. LRM 60/*FNT* 22.

16. LRM 137/*FNT* 94. Baldwin identifies one of the "striking ways" in which this attitude is revealed: the claim about the possibility of there being a Negro president (which was *not* a real possibility at the time he wrote the remarks). One wonders what he would have said about the election of Barack Obama to the office of the president of the United States in 2008.

17. Ralph Ellison, "The World and the Jug," in his *Shadow and Act* (New York: Vintage, 1964), 108. Ellison is responding to Irving Howe's essay "Black Boys and Native Sons," *Dissent* (Autumn 1963), and asserting that, like Arendt, Howe goes astray. See Kenneth W. Warren, "Ralph Ellison and the Problem of Cultural Authority," *boundary 2* 30(2) (Summer 2003):157–174. According to Warren, "This Olympian distance, which derived from Arendt's (and Howe's) lack of cultural knowledge of the Negro's situation in the South, had been fatal to the accuracy of their analyses. Both writers, Ellison contended, had missed the full human dimension of the situations they were observing" (159). See also Ross Posnock, "Ralph Ellison, Hannah Arendt and the Meaning of Politics," in *Cambridge Companions Online* (Cambridge: Cambridge University Press, 2006). Posnock notes, "Ellison's phrase 'Olympian authority' should not be construed as a compliment; it is his sarcastic euphemism for the arrogance of those such as Howe and Arendt 'who would tell us the meaning of Negro life' without ever bothering 'to learn how varied it really is'" (201).

18. She quotes the first two lines of William Blake's poem "Never Seek to Tell Thy Love": "Never seek to tell thy love / Love that never told can be" (*HC* 51–52). Continuing with her penchant for distinction making, love in the private sphere is distinguished from respect ("a kind of 'friendship' without intimacy and without closeness") in the larger domain of human affairs (243).

19. Arendt seems to conflate two types of love here. On the one hand, she discusses love as an intimacy shared by "lovers," the product of which might be a child (*HC* 242). On the other hand, she discusses love and forgiveness as Christian concepts introduced by Jesus. Arendt quotes a Bible verse from Luke 7:47: "Her sins, which are many, are forgiven; for she loved much: but to whom little is forgiven, the same loveth little" (238–242). Perhaps Arendt ultimately rejects both types of love (love as intimacy and love as forgiveness) in politics, but I think the difference between the two is important for Baldwin's project. Arendt offers the concept of respect as sufficient for forgiveness and as an alternative to love. She states, "Respect, at any rate, because it concerns only the person, is quite sufficient to prompt forgiving of what a person did, for the sake of the person" (243). For an analysis of Arendt on forgiveness and action (compared with Ralph Ellison), see Posnock, "Meaning of Politics," 209–210.

20. I am curious about the claim that "as a people"—I take Arendt to be talking about Black people here—we can only afford hatred and love so long as we are "not free." One possible explanation of this point can be found in *The Human Condition* when Arendt claims, "Compared with the reality which comes from being seen and heard, even the greatest forces of intimate life—the passions of the heart, the thoughts of the mind, the delights of the senses—lead an uncertain, shadowy kind of existence unless and until they are transformed, deprivatized and deindividualized, as it were, into a shape to fit them for public appearance" (*HC* 50). Arendt often connects this notion of a "shadowy existence" in the private realm to a lack of freedom (a kind of slavery), and in a footnote she explains, "This is also the reason why it is impossible 'to write a sketch of any slave who lived. . . . Until they emerge into freedom and notoriety, they remain shadowy types rather than persons'" (50n41). She does not explain here exactly *how* these "forces of intimate life" can be "transformed, deprivatized, and deindividualized."

21. Elisabeth Young-Bruehl, *Hannah Arendt: For the Love of the World* (1982; rpt., New Haven, CT: Yale University Press, 2004), 419 (hereafter, *HALW*).

22. Ellison's comments on Arendt are in the interview transcribed in "Leadership from the

Periphery," in Robert Penn Warren's *Who Speaks for the Negro?* (New York: Random House, 1965).

23. *JW* 136 (emphasis in original).

24. *HAJQ* 11.

25. Ibid., 85.

26. Aimé Césaire, *Discourse on Colonialism*, translated by Joan Pinkham (New York: Monthly Review Press, 2000), 37. Originally published as *Discours sur le colonialisme* (Paris: Présence Africaine, 1955).

27. *HAJQ* 20.

28. Ibid., 17.

29. Arendt explains this point: "For the parvenu, being innocently liked is a triumph, being innocently disliked an offense. . . . The 'great poison of all insight and outlook' which the parvenu could never admit to himself in any circumstance was this: that he was gnawed at by a multitude of things which he did not even really want, but which he could not bear to be refused; that he had to adapt his tastes, his life, his desires to these things; that in nothing and not for a single minute did he dare to be himself any longer. He had to be something, anything else, had to want to attain everything, had heroically 'to tolerate' what he had 'not made' and even 'despised'" (*RV* 241).

30. She offers four prototypes of the pariah: Heinrich Heine, Bernard Lazare, Charlie Chaplin, and Franz Kafka.

31. Arendt praises Heine because he does not abandon his people through assimilation or to become a parvenu and states, "Just because he refused to give up his allegiance to a people of pariahs and schlemiels, just because he remained consistently attached to them, he takes his place among the most uncompromising of Europe's fighters for freedom" (*JP* 282). But let us revisit Arendt's claim that the pariah group seeks refuge in nature. She says that the pariah "gauges things so consistently by [the] criterion of what is really and manifestly natural," and this allows the pariah to "detect the weak spot in his opponent's armor" (*JP* 280). In "The Jew as Pariah," nature is presented as desirable or positive, but Arendt seems to reverse her attitude toward nature and the natural in her description of Africans in *The Origins of Totalitarianism*. In *Origins*, Arendt does not claim that Africans sought refuge in nature in an effort to identify their opponent's weakness or hold up a mirror to the political world. Rather, Arendt says, what made Africans "different from other human beings was not at all the color of their skin but the fact that they behaved like a part of nature, that they treated nature as their undisputed master, that they had not created a human world, a human reality, and that therefore nature had remained, in all its majesty, the only overwhelming reality. . . . They were, as it were, 'natural' human beings who lacked a specifically human reality" (*OT* 192).

32. *HALW* 311.

33. Ibid., 312.

34. *HAJQ* 17. He continues, "This is one of the most fundamental distinctions in her political thinking (even though it was to undergo several transformations in the course of her development)" (ibid.).

35. Hanna Pitkin, *The Attack of the Blob: Hannah Arendt's Concept of the Social* (Chicago: University of Chicago Press, 1998), 19. See also Pitkin, "Conformism, Housekeeping, and the Attack of the Blob," in *Feminist Interpretations of Hannah Arendt*, edited by Bonnie Honig (University Park: Penn State University Press, 1995).

36. This goes against more positive readings of Arendt's notion of judgment, for example by Linda M. G. Zerilli in "Toward a Feminist Theory of Judgment," *Signs: Journal of Women in Culture and Society* 34(2) (2009):295–317.

1. "The Girl, Obviously, Was Asked to Be a Hero"

1. Of course, Europe also has a slave history. Europeans brought the transatlantic slave trade to the Americas, and the slave trade was not abolished in Britain until 1807. See Wim Klooster, ed., *Migration, Trade, and Slavery in an Expanding World* (Leiden: Brill, 2009). Also, the United States of America has been and remains a participant in the crimes of colonialism and imperialism. See Alfred W. McCoy and Francisco A. Scarano, eds., *Colonial Crucible: Empire in the Making of the Modern American State* (Madison: University of Wisconsin Press, 2009). These facts are not mentioned by Arendt.

2. Hannah Arendt, "Reflections on Little Rock," *Dissent* 6(1) (Winter 1959):45–56. For more details about the controversy at *Commentary* and *Dissent* concerning Arendt's essay, see Elisabeth Young-Bruehl, *Hannah Arendt: For the Love of the World* (1982; rpt., New Haven, CT: Yale University Press, 2004), 313–315. See also Norman Podhoretz, *Making It* (New York: Harper Colophon, 1967), 233; and Podhoretz, *Ex-Friends: Falling Out with Allen Ginsberg, Lionel and Diana Trilling, Lillian Hellman, Hannah Arendt, and Norman Mailer* (New York: Free Press, 1999), 146–147.

3. Hannah Arendt, "A Reply to Critics," *Dissent* 1(2) (Spring 1959):179–181. She is replying to David Spitz and Melvin Tumin.

4. Allen states, "Although Arendt thought she was writing about the photo of Elizabeth Eckford in Little Rock, Arkansas that appeared on the front page of the *New York Times* on September 5, 1957, the photo that she actually describes was the accompanying photo of Dorothy Counts in Charlotte, North Carolina" (*Talking to Strangers: Anxieties of Citizenship since Brown v. Board of Education* [Chicago: University of Chicago Press, 2004], 197). Allen continues, "It is the photo of Counts and not of Eckford that includes 'the white friend of her father' to whom Arendt refers" (ibid.). Actually, the newspaper photograph of Dorothy Counts shows her with Dr. Edwin Thompkins—a Black, not white, friend of her father.

5. The caption beneath the photograph reads, "LITTLE ROCK, ARK.: As a white student walks through the National Guard barrier at the left, 15-year-old Elizabeth Eckford is barred from entering Central High School."

6. Arendt describes the students as a "jeering and grimacing mob of youngsters" (RLR 236), while the *New York Times* describes them as "Jeering Whites" in the headline. The caption beneath the Counts photograph reads, "CHARLOTTE, N.C.: A crowd of students follows Dorothy Counts as she is escorted to Harding High School by Dr. Edwin Tomkins. She became the first Negro to attend [the] school" (note that Thompkins's name is misspelled in this caption, but spelled correctly in the accompanying article).

7. The Little Rock Nine were Carlotta Walls, Jefferson Thomas, and Gloria Ray, who previously attended Paul Laurence Dunbar Junior High School, and Ernest Green, Elizabeth Eckford, Thelma Mothershed, Terrence Roberts, Minnijean Brown, and Melba Pattillo, who previously attended Horace Mann High School.

8. Daisy Bates, *The Long Shadow of Little Rock: A Memoir of Daisy Bates* (1962; rpt., Fayetteville: University of Arkansas Press, 1984), 63.

9. Ibid., 66. Note that Benjamin Fine in "Arkansas Troops Bar Negro Pupils; Governor Defiant" (*New York Times*, September 5, 1957) states that four white ministers came with seven of the nine students.

10. Ibid., 75.

11. Ibid., 70.

12. Ibid., 71. Eckford's experience in this mob, coupled with Fine's experience after coming to her aid, is an example of white supremacist racism as both anti-Black and antisemitic.

There are multiple layers of racism, sexism, and antisemitism operating simultaneously in this scene.

13. Clarence Dean, "School Integration Begins in Charlotte with Near-Rioting," *New York Times*, September 5, 1957.

14. Ibid.

15. This even after seeing the black-and-white photo in which Dr. Thompkins appears darker in complexion than Dorothy (who is described elsewhere as "fair skinned") and the jeering white mob surrounding them.

16. Including an A.B. from the College of Liberal Arts at Johnson C. Smith University, a seminary degree from Johnson C. Smith Theological Seminary, an A.M. in religious education from McCormick Theological Seminary in Chicago, and a Ph.D. in religious education and philosophy from the University of Pittsburgh. Additionally, he did graduate work in French at Clark University in Atlanta. Biographical information from the program for "The Service of Installation for the Reverend Herman Lacoste Counts, Senior Pastor Elect: Bethpage and Cedar Grove United Presbyterian Churches," April 12, 1970. Available in the Digital Smith Collections at John C. Smith University Library. Identifier: 19b10f9e.

17. Frye Gaillard, *The Dream Long Deferred: The Landmark Struggle for Desegregation in Charlotte, North Carolina* (1998; rpt., Columbia: University of South Carolina Press, 2006), 5.

18. Tommy Tomilson, "Portrait of Pride, Prejudice: Students See Themselves through History's Lens," *Charlotte Observer* (September 2, 2007) (my emphasis).

19. Hannah Arendt, "Was bleibt? Es bleibt die Muttersprache," originally published in Günter Gaus, *Zur Person* (Munich, 1965), 17. Hyphenation and capitalization of "anti-Semitism" and "anti-Semitic" are as they appear in the interview as translated by Joan Stambaugh, "'What Remains? Language Remains': A Conversation with Günter Gaus," in *EU*. The terms "antisemitic" and "antisemitism" are neither hyphenated nor capitalized by Arendt in other texts, like *The Origins of Totalitarianism*.

20. Elisabeth Young-Bruehl, *Hannah Arendt: For the Love of the World* (1982; rpt., New Haven, CT: Yale University Press, 2004), 311 (hereafter, *HALW*).

21. Gaillard, *Dream Long Deferred*, 3. And while "Counts recognized that his was a view with political implications," he also understood that "somebody had to be first" (ibid.).

22. Tomilson, "Portrait of Pride, Prejudice."

23. Gaillard, *Dream Long Deferred*, 4.

24. Tomilson, "Portrait of Pride, Prejudice."

25. This question is problematized by Anne Norton in "Heart of Darkness: Africa and African Americans in the Writings of Hannah Arendt," in *Feminist Interpretations of Hannah Arendt*, edited by Bonnie Honig (University Park: Penn State University Press, 1995). Norton notes, "The strategy of moral metempsychosis is used to question the actions of the Negro mother. . . . Arendt inserts herself into the mind of the Negro mother, but she does not invite that woman into hers" (258).

26. This might mean that Arendt is acknowledging that segregated schools put Black students in a humiliating position insofar as she describes integrating a school as "more" humiliating.

27. Zora Neale Hurston, "Court Order Can't Make Races Mix," letter to the editor, *Orlando Sentinel*, August 11, 1955.

28. Kwame Ture and Charles V. Hamilton, *Black Power: The Politics of Liberation* (1967; rpt., New York: Vintage, 1992), 37.

29. The three who graduated were Ernest Green (the first Black student to graduate from Central High School, 1958), Jefferson Thomas (graduated in 1960), and Carlotta Walls (also graduated in 1960).

30. After attending Harding High School the first day, Dorothy Counts missed two days of school because of a fever and sore throat. She returned to school for three additional days before her parents withdrew her. Dorothy's father, Dr. Counts, issued the following statement:

> It is with compassion for our native land and love for our daughter Dorothy that we withdraw her as a student at Harding High School. As long as we felt she could be protected from bodily injury and insults within the school's walls and upon the school's premises, we were willing to grant her desire to study at Harding. . . . Contrary to this optimistic view, her experiences at school on Wednesday disillusioned our faith and left us no alternative. . . . We wish to express our most sincere gratitude to the many friends of democracy and Christianity in America and abroad, for their understanding and appreciation of our daughter's modest efforts to enjoy full citizenship in the country which we all love. (Gaillard, *Dream Long Deferred*, 6–7)

31. Ibid.

32. Ellison's comments on Arendt are in the interview transcribed in "Leadership from the Periphery," in Robert Penn Warren's *Who Speaks for the Negro?* (New York: Random House, 1965), 343. See also Ellison's "The World and the Jug," 108. James Patterson has cited Ellison's hopeful sentiments about the *Brown* decision expressed in a letter to a friend. Ellison writes, "The Court has found in our favor and recognized our human psychological complexity and citizenship and another battle of the Civil War has been won. The rest is up to us and I'm very glad. . . . What a wonderful world of possibilities are unfolded for the children" (quoted in Patterson, *Brown v. Board of Education: A Civil Rights Milestone and Its Troubled Legacy* [New York: Oxford University Press, 2002], xiv).

33. "Leadership from the Periphery," 344.

34. Ibid. Danielle Allen contrasts Arendt's position with Ellison's:

> Whereas Arendt developed a political theory that might protect children from politics, by transforming politics into an epic arena for full-grown warriors only, Ellison has a more tragic vision: rituals to solidify social order inevitably involve children in politics, however much one might wish the case otherwise. . . . For Ellison, as not for Arendt, the Little Rock parents were heroes. They were acting politically, even in Arendt's own terms, for, as Ellison describes them, they were illustrating ideas about how a democratic community might organize itself. (Allen, *Talking to Strangers*, 28, 30)

Ross Posnock describes the parents and children as engaging in political action: "Like natality and forgiveness, action on behalf of political ideals permits the possibility that those reduced to being pawns might overcome their sense of helpless oblivion and resentment in action's surge of freshness" (Posnock, "Meaning of Politics," 210).

35. James Bohman, "The Moral Costs of Political Pluralism: The Dilemmas of Difference and Equality in Arendt's 'Reflections on Little Rock,'" in *Hannah Arendt: Twenty Years Later*, edited by Larry May and Jerome Kohn (Cambridge, MA: MIT Press, 1996), 57.

36. *HALW* 317.

37. As Posnock notes, Ellison's critique of Arendt points to "her notorious misreading of black parents' attempts at integrating segregated grade schools as a parvanu [*sic*] effort at social climbing" ("Meaning of Politics," 201). Interestingly, Posnock goes on to consider the similarities between these two figures, "Reducing the Arendt/Ellison connection to this disagreement disguises the actual, surprising grounds of their affinity: an effort to revitalize politics as creative action in public, a commitment sustained while remining skeptical of political ideologies preaching radical social change" (202–203).

38. Again, Arendt is out of line with the facts. When school integration was pursued, the NAACP often intentionally selected Black students with stellar grades to integrate white

schools. Another factor was location. The students had to live in a neighborhood where the white school was actually their neighborhood school or was the school closer to their homes than the assigned Black school.

39. *HALW* 311. Like Arendt, Young-Bruehl is wrong about Counts's father being absent.

40. Seyla Benhabib, *Situating the Self: Gender, Community, and Postmodernism in Contemporary Ethics* (New York: Routledge, 1992), 94.

41. *Rahel Varnhagen: The Life of a Jewish Woman: First Complete Edition*, edited by Liliane Weissberg and translated by Richard Winston and Clara Winston (1957; rpt., Baltimore, MD: Johns Hopkins University Press, 1997). See especially the chapters "Assimilation," "Between Pariah and Parvenu," and "One Does Not Escape Jewishness." Arendt examines the consequences of attempting to escape the pariah status by choosing to be a parvenu. Presenting Varnhagen as an example, Arendt states, "As a Jew, Rahel always stood outside, had been a pariah, and discovered at last, most unwillingly and unhappily, that entrance into society was possible only at the price of lying, of a far more generalized lie than simple hypocrisy. She discovered that it was necessary for the parvenu—but him alone—to sacrifice every natural impulse, to conceal all truth, to misuse all love, not only to suppress all passion, but worse still, to convert it into a means for social climbing" (*RV* 244).

42. Additionally, Lazare was known for his involvement with and then separation from the Zionist movement. In a preface to Lazare's *Job's Dungheap*, Arendt writes, "What made him different and what raised his writings above the mere expression of the spirit of his time and milieu was his early recognition of the importance of the Jewish question and his consistent courage in making this recognition the central fact of his life" (Arendt, "Preface to Bernard Lazare, *Job's Dungheap*," reprinted in *Reflections on Literature and Culture*, edited by Susannah Young-ah Gottlieb [Stanford, CA: Stanford University Press, 2007], 143–144.) Arendt in "The Jew as Pariah" prominently features Lazare as one of four prototypical pariahs discussed.

43. Richard Bernstein, *Hannah Arendt and the Jewish Question* (Cambridge, MA: MIT Press, 1996), 17.

44. Ibid., 16–17.

45. Davidson M. Douglass, *Reading, Writing, and Race: The Desegregation of the Charlotte Schools* (Chapel Hill: University of North Carolina Press, 1995), 26. He adds, "During the same summer that the three urban school boards granted the twelve transfer requests, the requests of almost two hundred other African American students throughout the state, even those living in counties with no black schools, were denied" (45).

46. Hook, "Democracy and Desegregation," *New Leader* (April 21, 1958):14 (my emphasis).

47. PRB 64.

48. Ibid., 65.

49. Pie 71.

50. Hook, "Democracy and Desegregation," 7. One white parent who sought to enroll her child in a Black school is Grace Lorch, the woman who helped Elizabeth Eckford to the bus on the first day of school in Little Rock. Lorch, a former schoolteacher in New York, had just relocated to Little Rock from Nashville, Tennessee. While living in Nashville, she put in a request to have her daughter, Alice, attend a Black public school in her neighborhood. The request was denied and then her husband, Lee Lorch, was fired from his position as a math professor at Fisk (a historically Black university). It has been suggested that white board members at Fisk University orchestrated the firing. After moving to Little Rock, Grace Lorch made a verbal request followed up by a written request for Alice to be permitted to attend a Black school. The letter to Virgil Blossom, dated September 21, 1955, states in part, "We confirm in writing our request that our daughter, Alice, age 11, be allowed to attend the same school to which her immediate playmates go. . . . Although we have been in Little Rock only about two weeks, she has

already become very friendly with several girls her own age in our immediate neighborhood and would like to be in school with them." The request was denied. See the University of Arkansas Digital Collections, "Land of (Un)Equal Opportunity: Documenting the Civil Rights Struggle in Arkansas. Title: Letter to Virgil Blossom requesting permission for white student to attend black school."

51. bell hooks, *Teaching to Transgress* (New York: Routledge, 1994), 3.

52. Juan Williams, *Eyes on the Prize* (New York: Penguin, 1987), 2. Genna Rae McNeil also notes, "Early in the campaign, Houston made a film exposing racial discrimination in the rural schools of South Carolina and favored making more such films" (*Groundwork: Charles Hamilton Houston and the Struggle for Civil Rights* [Philadelphia: University of Pennsylvania Press, 1983], 140).

53. W. E. B. Du Bois, "Does the Negro Need Separate Schools?," *Journal of Negro Education* 4(3) (July 1935):328–335.

54. Du Bois describes the harms of white schools on Black children in this way: "I have repeatedly seen wise and loving parents take infinite pains to force their little children into schools where white children, white teachers, and white parents despised and resented the dark child, made mock of it, neglected or bullied it, and literally rendered its life a living hell. . . . For the kind of battle thus indicated, most children are under no circumstances suited. It is the refinement of cruelty to require it of them" (ibid., 330–331).

55. Ibid., 331.

56. Ibid., 328–329.

57. Ibid.

58. Concerning teachers, he states, "The proper education of any people includes sympathetic touch between teacher and pupil; knowledge on the part of the teacher, not simply of the individual taught, but of his surroundings and background, and the history of his class and group; such contact between pupils, and between teacher and pupil, on the basis of perfect social equality, as will increase this sympathy and knowledge; facilities for education in equipment and housing, and the promotion of such extra-curricular activities as will tend to induct the child into life" (ibid., 328).

59. Ibid., 330.

60. Ibid., 331.

61. W. E. B. Du Bois, "What Is the Meaning of 'All Deliberate Speed'?," *National Guardian* (November 4, 1957), reprinted in *W. E. B. Du Bois: A Reader*, edited by David Levering Lewis (New York: Holt, 1995) (hereafter, All Deliberate Speed). For more on Du Bois and the *Brown* decisions, see Stanley O. Gaines Jr., "W. E. B. Du Bois on *Brown v. Board of Education*," *Ethnic Studies Review* 27(1) (April 30, 2004):23–31, and Gaines, "Color-Line as Fault-Line: Teaching Interethnic Relations in California in the 21st Century," *Journal of Social Issues* 60 (2004):175–193. See also Patterson, *Brown v. Board of Education*; D. M. Scott, *Contempt and Pity: Social Policy and the Image of the Damaged Black Psyche, 1880–1996* (Chapel Hill: University of North Carolina Press, 1997). Gaines rejects what he calls Patterson's and Scott's "revisionist critiques" of Du Bois as taking a position against the NAACP and school integration.

62. All Deliberate Speed 422.

63. Ibid., 422–423.

64. Ibid., 422, 419.

65. Ibid., 423.

66. Derrick Bell, *Silent Covenants: Brown v. Board of Education and the Unfulfilled Hopes for Racial Reform* (Oxford: Oxford University Press, 2004), 5 (hereafter, *Silent Covenants*).

67. Ibid., 96.

68. During the Reagan era there were pointed attacks against civil rights legislation and

"color-conscious" policies, like the busing of minority students to predominately white schools and affirmative action programs, using three key principles and thinly coded (racialized) catchphrases: (1) color-blind justice (anti–affirmative action and anti-busing), (2) states' rights (limited federal government), and (3) welfare queens and young bucks (images of Black women and men abusing and manipulating the welfare system). For more on this topic, see Bernard Boxill, "Introductions: The Color-Blind Principle," in his *Blacks and Social Justice* (1984; rpt., Lanham, MD: Rowman and Littlefield, 1992); Kathryn T. Gines, "From Color-Blind to Post-Racial: *Blacks and Social Justice* in the Twenty-First Century," *Journal of Social and Political Philosophy* 41(3) (Fall 2010):370–384.

69. *Silent Covenants* 114.

70. Ibid., 115. Bell is noting that although school integration did not lead to the equal educational opportunities that were hoped for, this does not negate the fact that access to equal educational opportunities was the goal.

71. For more on the persistent educational inequalities in public schools, see Jonathan Kozol, *Savage Inequalities: Children in America's Schools* (New York: Crown, 1991); Kozol, *The Shame of a Nation: The Restoration of Apartheid Schooling in America* (New York: Crown, 2005); Charles T. Clotfelter, *After "Brown": The Rise and Retreat of School Desegregation* (Princeton, NJ: Princeton University Press, 2006); and Patterson, *Brown v. Board of Education*.

2. "The Most Outrageous Law of Southern States"

1. For more on *Dred Scott*, see Don E. Fehrenbacher, *The Dred Scott Case: Its Significance in American Law and Politics* (1978; rpt., New York: Oxford University Press, 2001); and Andrew Napolitano, *Dred Scott's Revenge: A Legal History of Race and Freedom in America* (Nashville, TN: Thomas Nelson, 2009). See also Derrick Bell, *Silent Covenants: Brown v. Board of Education and the Unfulfilled Hopes for Racial Reform* (Oxford: Oxford University Press, 2004), 36–39 (hereafter, *Silent Covenants*).

2. Section 1 of the Fourteenth Amendment states: "All persons born or naturalized in the United States, and subject to the jurisdiction thereof, are citizens of the United States and of the state wherein they reside. No state shall make or enforce any law which shall abridge the privileges or immunities of citizens of the United States; nor shall any state deprive any person of life, liberty, or property, without due process of law; nor deny to any person within its jurisdiction the equal protection of the laws."

3. On June 7, 1892, Homer Plessy (a man who was "seven-eighths Caucasian") was arrested for refusing to move from a whites-only rail car in Louisiana, a violation of that state's 1890 segregation law, An Act to Promote the Comfort of Passengers, which said that "the State, shall provide equal but separate accommodations for white, and colored, races." For more on *Plessy*, see Richard Kluger, *Simple Justice: The History of Brown v. Board of Education and Black America's Struggle for Equality* (New York: Vintage, 2004), 71–83 (hereafter, *Simple Justice*). See also Derrick Bell, "*Plessy*'s Long Shadow," in his *Silent Covenants* 11–14; and Michael Klarman, "The *Plessy* Era," in his *From Jim Crow to Civil Rights: The Supreme Court and the Struggle for Racial Equality* (Oxford: Oxford University Press, 2004), 8–60 (hereafter, *Jim Crow*).

4. Klarman notes that the single dissenting judge in the *Plessy* decision, John Marshall Harlan, was a "former slave owner and opponent of emancipation" (*Jim Crow* 22). He also asserts that although cases concerning segregation in public schools did not come before the Court during what he calls the *Plessy* era (1895–1910), "This Court almost certainly would have sustained public school segregation" (25).

5. Napolitano states, "Taken together, the Missouri Compromise and the *Dred Scott* case represent an unsuccessful effort first to compromise on slavery through legislation, and then to settle the issue permanently through the judiciary" (*Dred Scott's Revenge* 52). These compromises occurred long after those made by the founding fathers on the issue of slavery. Arendt does mention the *Dred Scott* decision in "Civil Disobedience" (*CR* 91).

6. *Jim Crow* 25 (my emphasis).

7. Ibid., 26–27. Even years after the *Brown* decisions (and long after Reconstruction), Derrick Bell underscores, Black parents took considerable risks to move forward with school desegregation litigation: "Before signing them on as plaintiffs, we carefully explained to parents the risks in challenging segregation. We knew that some whites, trying to curb the new militancy among blacks, were making physical threats and exerting economic pressures. In that climate, we urged parents to carefully consider the risks before making a final commitment to join in the litigation" (*Silent Covenants* 97).

8. Klarman states bluntly, "The temptation to 'rape the Negro school fund' was great and seldom resisted" (*Jim Crow* 45).

9. Houston committed his life to teaching African Americans their constitutional rights and decreasing the gap between rights as they existed on paper and rights as they existed in Black communities. He worked as a professor, vice dean, and then dean of Howard Law School. Under Houston's leadership the law school shifted from night classes to day classes, adopted stricter admissions requirements, and became accredited. For more on Houston's significance and contributions to Howard University Law School, see Genna Rae McNeil's "Developing Cadres: The Howard Years, 1924–1935," in her biography of Houston, *Groundwork: Charles Hamilton Houston and the Struggle for Civil Rights* (Philadelphia: University of Pennsylvania Press, 1983) (hereafter, *Groundwork*). See also Juan Williams's *Eyes on the Prize* (New York: Penguin, 1987), 7 (hereafter, *Eyes*).

10. The campaign was launched in 1922 to help give "the southern Negro his 'constitutional rights, his political and civil equality, and therewith a self-consciousness and self-respect'" with financing from Charles Garland (*Eyes* 9).

11. The Margold Report is named for Nathan Ross Margold, a white lawyer from Harvard University who was commissioned by a joint committee of the NAACP and the Garland Fund. The Garland Fund approved a $100,000 grant to the NAACP "for taxpayer suits to challenge the dual school systems in the South, for legal protection of blacks' civil liberties, for litigation seeking an end to segregation and jury exclusion, for attacking American imperialism in the western hemisphere, particularly Haiti and Nicaragua, and for propaganda in support of the legal campaign" (*Groundwork* 114). Margold produced a report titled "Preliminary Report for the Joint Committee Supervising the Expenditure of the 1930 Appropriation by the American Fund for Public Service to the NAACP." With the impact of the Depression, these funds were eventually reduced to $10,000 (116).

12. Ibid., 114.

13. The report continues, "We can transform into authoritative adjudication the principle of law, now only theoretically inferable from *Yick Wo v. Hopkins,* that segregation coupled with discrimination resulting from administrative action permitted but not required by state statutes, is just as much a denial of equal protection of the laws as is segregation coupled with discrimination required by express statutory enactment" (ibid., 115). Yick Wo was a Chinese immigrant with a laundry business in San Francisco. In 1880 the city passed an ordinance requiring a permit to operate laundries in wooden buildings. While white-owned laundries were rarely unable to obtain the required permit (only about one in eighty denied), Chinese laundry owners were altogether denied the required permit. Yick Wo continued to operate his business in

a wooden building, was fined, refused to pay the fine, and was arrested. In the *Yick Wo v. Hopkins* case, one of the main issues emphasized was not so much the law requiring the permit itself under the guise of safety, but the discrimination in administrating it—namely, the distribution of the permits and enforcement of the law. The Supreme Court determined that the discriminatory administration of the statute was a violation of the Fourteenth Amendment: "The rights of the petitioners, as affected by the proceedings of which they complain, are not less, because they are aliens and subjects of the Emperor of China. . . . The Fourteenth Amendment to the Constitution is not confined to the protection of citizens." And furthermore, "Though the law itself be fair on its face and impartial in appearance, yet, if it is applied and administered by public authority with an evil eye and an unequal hand, so as practically to make unjust and illegal discriminations between persons in similar circumstances, material to their rights, the denial of equal justice is still within the prohibition of the Constitution." See Abraham L. Davis and Barbara Luck Graham, *The Supreme Court, Race, and Civil Rights: From Marshall to Rehnquist* (London: Sage, 1995), 49. These are very different arguments and conclusions from those made in *Plessy*.

14. *Groundwork* 116–117. Limited resources made attacking discrimination through litigation in more than one area cost prohibitive. McNeil describes Houston's variation from Margold's strategy in this way: "Desiring to see black institutions and students receive more funds and secure enlarged educational opportunities even within the context of an objectionable and racially discriminatory system, Houston suggested that the attack against racial discrimination begin with the issue of *unequal apportionment of school funds* in the South, preparation of a model bill and brief seeking state grants-in-aid for black students legally barred from admission to state universities attended by whites and suits on behalf of teachers who were victims of discriminatory salary differentials" (116, my emphasis). Additionally, "Houston believed the step-by-step process" of trying strategic cases was more viable than an immediate and direct attack on the constitutionality of segregation "because it would take into account the lack of tradition for equality within the American system" (135). This strategy was also expected to help to "neutralize the poor white masses and persuade them of the logic and justice of the NAACP position" (ibid.). Williams notes, "Houston chose to start at the higher education level because there the injustice was most obvious and, to the public at large, change would not be as threatening" (*Eyes* 11).

15. *Groundwork* 117.

16. Ibid., 141. See also Charles Houston, "Educational Inequalities Must Go," *Crisis* 42 (October 1935):300.

17. Michael Klarman notes, "Thomas Hocutt brought the first university equalization suit in 1933 when the University of North Carolina School of Pharmacy denied him admission based on race. The court dismissed that suit because Hocutt's undergraduate school failed to provide the transcript required for admission" (*Jim Crow* 149). For more on the Hocutt case, see *Simple Justice* 155, 157–158. Kluger notes that Dr. James Shepard of North Carolina College for Negroes (Hocutt's undergraduate institution) "was not about to participate in an effort to desegregate the University of North Carolina" and refused to supply the transcript (*Simple Justice* 157). Another early case involved Donald Gaines Murray, who sought admission to the University of Maryland Law School. Lawyers petitioned on Murray's behalf to have his application to the law school considered and for the law school to admit him if he met the general admission standards. The judge in *Murray v. The University of Maryland* (1935) "directed the university to admit Murray—in accordance with his constitutional right—pending appeal" (*Groundwork* 139). See also *Jim Crow* 149; *Simple Justice* 185–196. The Maryland Court of Appeals affirmed the decision for Murray to be admitted. In a case in 1938 (*State ex rel. Gaines v. Canada*), Houston argued that "for the separate-but-equal doctrine to stand, the black and white schools had to

truly be equal" (*Eyes* 15). Of course, the segregated professional schools and law schools were not equal. The Supreme Court agreed with Houston's argument and rendered a decision that "made it clear that states had an obligation to provide equal education for their citizens, black and white" (ibid.). For more on segregation cases in higher education, see *Jim Crow* 204–212.

18. Houston died on April 22, 1950. For more on Houston, see *Groundwork* 211.

19. Nabrit graduated from Northwestern Law School, eventually joined the faculty at Howard Law School, and created the first civil rights law course in the United States (*Simple Justice* 127).

20. Ibid., 291. He also stated, "I am going to try these cases on the theory that segregation per se is unconstitutional" (*Eyes* 17–18). It has been noted that Marshall was initially more cautious than Nabrit on this point (*Simple Justice* 291–292). One might say that Nabrit returned to the initial position outlined in the Margold Report.

21. *Eyes* 18. Klarman notes, "*Sweatt* and *McLaurin*, inconsistent with legal sources that were generally considered binding by these justices, are best explained in terms of social and political change," including gradual desegregation in major league baseball and in the military (*Jim Crow* 209).

22. *Simple Justice* 291. Quoting Herbert Hill, Kluger continues, "There was lots of resistance in the branches because real progress toward equalization was now beginning to be made" (ibid.).

23. Kluger explains, "In short, the NAACP would argue that black public schools violated the Fourteenth Amendment because they were (1) demonstrably unequal to and (2) separate from the whites schools in the community" (ibid., 293).

24. *Silent Covenants* 115.

25. Later, in *On Revolution*, Arendt elaborates on the pursuit of happiness as public happiness and emphasizes the dual meaning of "public happiness" in the American context. Arendt explains that it used to have implications for both private welfare and public happiness (*OR* 127, 128, 132). But over time this double meaning has shifted from the idea of "a share in public affairs . . . to a guarantee that the pursuit of private happiness would be protected by public power" or "understood as the right of citizens to pursue their personal interests . . . to act according to the rules of private self-interest" (135). In spite of this shift, Arendt asserts, "the revolutionary notions of public happiness and political freedom have never altogether vanished from the American scene" (138).

26. Elisabeth Young-Bruehl, *Hannah Arendt: For the Love of the World* (1982; rpt., New Haven, CT: Yale University Press, 2004), 310 (hereafter, *HALW*).

27. According to Norman Podhoretz, "In Sidney's version of the incident, Hannah, upon receiving the galley proofs of his rejoinder, was so shaken by the power of the case he had made against her that she lost her nerve and therefore changed her mind about the simultaneous publication. In Hannah's version, as set forth in a letter to the editors at *Commentary*, the postponements to which the publication of her article had been subjected had caused her considerable harm" (*Ex-Friends: Falling Out with Allen Ginsberg, Lionel and Diana Trilling, Lillian Hellman, Hannah Arendt, and Norman Mailer* [New York: Free Press, 1999], 149–150). Sidney Hook presents his version of the events at *Commentary* in a published letter to the editors at *Dissent*. Hook criticizes Arendt for referencing the unpublished galleys and states, "I was shocked when informed that Miss Arendt had withdrawn her piece from publication after she saw the galleys of my critical reply" (*Dissent* 6(2) [Spring 1959]:203). Arendt responds: "Mr. Hook misrepresents the facts. It never occurred to me to withdraw my article because of his reply" (ibid.).

28. Although Arendt is not named in Hook's essay, it is obvious in many places that he is responding to the positions she takes in "Reflections on Little Rock." The publication date for "Democracy and Desegregation" in the *New Leader* is April 21, 1958—not April 13 as indicated in the "Preliminary Remarks" by Arendt and even in the letter to the editors at *Dissent* from

Sidney Hook (*Dissent* 6(2) [Spring 1959]:203). In a note that appears after Hook's letter, the editors at *Dissent* acknowledge, "The reference to the *New Leader* was inserted by the editors through a misunderstanding. We regret our error, and offer our apologies to Dr. Hook.—Eds" (ibid.). Numerous other sources have mistakenly cited the April 13 date.

29. It has been pointed out to me that there is a certain irony to Arendt's claim that oppressed minorities were never the best judges of the order of priorities insofar as she makes similar claims in *The Origins of Totalitarianism* about German Jews who prioritized social issues over political issues. She asserts that for assimilated Jews, "the Jewish question had lost, once and for all, all political significance; but it haunted their private lives and influenced their personal decisions all the more tyrannically" (*OT* 67). Arendt also raises the issue of mixed marriages: "The adage, 'man in the street and a Jew at home,' was bitterly realized: political problems were distorted to the point of pure perversion when Jews tried to solve them by means of inner experience and private emotions; private life was poisoned to the point of inhumanity—for example in the question of mixed marriages—when the heavy burden of unsolved problems of public significance was crammed into that private existence which is much better ruled by the unpredictable laws of passion than by considered policies" (ibid.).

30. Alfred Schutz, "Equality and the Meaning of the Structure of the World," in his *Collected Papers*, vol. 2 (The Hague: Martinus Nijhoff, 1964), 245.

31. Robert Bernasconi, "The Invisibility of Racial Minorities in the Public Realm of Appearances," in his *Race* (Malden, MA: Blackwell, 2001), examines Schutz's "Equality and the Meaning of the Structure of the World." Bernasconi explains, "Schutz appealed to Myrdal's account [in *An American Dilemma*] of how 'the white man's rank order of discriminations' was the inverse of 'the Negro's rank order'" (292). Bernasconi continues, "Myrdal had observed that whereas Whites in the United States tended to focus on laws against intermarriage and sexual intercourse involving white women as the most important type of discrimination to correct . . . Blacks were more concerned with discrimination in economic matters such as securing land, credit, jobs, and public relief, with discrimination in the law courts and the by the police next in the order of priority" (ibid.). See also Gunnar Myrdal's *An American Dilemma* (New York: Harper, 1944).

32. Myrdal, *An American Dilemma*, ch. 3, "Facets of the Negro Problem."

33. Ibid., 58.

34. Ibid., 60.

35. Ibid., 60–61.

36. Ibid., 591.

37. Ibid.

38. Ibid., 61.

39. Ibid.

40. Ibid.

41. *Eyes* 16–17.

42. The title of the Virginia law had been changed from A Bill to Preserve the Integrity of the White Race. The law prohibited marriage between whites and nonwhites, with the exception of allowing marriage between whites and those with one-sixteenth or less American Indian heritage. This exception was made for prominent white Virginians with bloodlines going back to the marriage between John Wolfe and Pocahontas. See Walter Wadlington, "The *Loving* Case: Virginia's Anti-Miscegenation Statute in Historical Perspective," *Virginia Law Review* 52 (1966):1189; and Paul A. Lombardo, "Miscegenation, Eugenics, and Racism: Historical Footnotes to *Loving v. Virginia*," *U.C. Davis Law Review* 21 (1987–1988):421. Another important earlier Virginia case is *Naim v. Naim* (1955). A Chinese man married a white woman in North Carolina to bypass the anti-miscegenation law in Virginia. Later, the white wife sought an an-

nulment under the anti-miscegenation law in Virginia, and the state granted the annulment although the husband argued it was unconstitutional. The Supreme Court upheld the annulment in an effort not to confirm suspicions that school desegregation would amount to invalidating anti-miscegenation laws (*Jim Crow* 321).

43. According to Klarman, "In 1883, the Court in *Pace v. Alabama*, with Harlan's acquiescence, had squarely rejected color blindness and unanimously sustained an Alabama statute that imposed heavier penalties on fornication when participating parties were of different races" (*Jim Crow* 21). He adds, "Analytically, *Plessy*'s endorsement of separate but equal was a straightforward application of *Pace*" (ibid.). Furthermore, after *Plessy* it could be argued that segregation qualified as "a reasonable police-power objective, because it advanced state interests in reducing inter-racial violence and preventing miscegenation" (24).

44. For example, I have argued elsewhere that it was problematic for white feminists to ignore the racism faced by women of color or to exclude women of color from the "women's movement" for the practical purpose of gaining support in the South for suffrage. See Kathryn T. Gines, "Sartre, Beauvoir, and the Race/Gender Analogy: A Case for Black Feminist Philosophy," in *Convergences: Black Feminism and Continental Philosophy*, edited by Maria Davidson, Kathryn T. Gines, and Donna Dale Marcano (Albany: State University of New York Press, 2010), 35–51. See also Gines, "Racism and Sexual Oppression in Anglo-America: A Genealogy (A Review)," *Symposium on Gender, Race, and Philosophy* 6(1) (Spring 2010):1–5.

45. *Miscegenation* (New York: H. Dexter, Hamilton, 1864). This pamphlet endorsing race mixing was first published anonymously in 1863 and has been described as "a hoax, written by two Democratic partisans to embarrass the Republican party" by William H. Tucker in *The Science and Politics of Racial Research* (Champaign: University of Illinois Press, 1994), 302n92. The authors were David Goodman Croly and George Wakeman, and their intention was to discredit Abraham Lincoln, who was running for presidential reelection. See also F. G. Wood, *Black Scare* (Berkeley: University of California Press, 1968); and Peggy Pascoe, *What Comes Naturally: Miscegenation Law and the Making of Race in America* (New York: Oxford University Press, 2009).

46. *Miscegenation* 1. In a list of "New Words Used in This Book," we find: "Miscegenation—from the Latin *Miscere*, to mix, and *Genus*, race, is used to denote the abstract idea of the mixture of two or more races" (2). Also, *"Reasons for coining these words—*(1.) There is, as yet, no word in the language which expresses exactly the idea they embody. (2.) Amalgamation is a poor word, since it properly refers to the union of metals with quicksilver, and was, in fact, only borrowed for an emergency, and should now be returned to its proper signification. (3.) The words used above [are] just the ones wanted, for they express the ideas with which we are dealing, and, what is as important, they express nothing else" (ibid.).

47. Winthrop Jordan, *White over Black: American Attitudes toward the Negro 1550–1812* (Chapel Hill: University of North Carolina Press, 1968), 139.

48. Edmund Morgan, *American Slavery, American Freedom* (New York: Norton, 2003), 333. Morgan notes that this case "could reflect religious rather than racial feeling that a Christian should not lie with a heathen" or "a case of sodomy rather than fornication" (ibid.).

49. Ibid.

50. Ibid., 335.

51. Ibid., 336.

52. Ibid.

53. Ibid., 337.

54. In *American Nightmare: The History of Jim Crow* (New York: St. Martin's, 2002), Jerrold Packard explains, "And *that* [the issue of anti-miscegenation], it was feared, would overshadow the issue of school integration, perhaps even pushing the South to armed resistance to the will

of the federal government, if not to another attempt at outright secession" (235). In *The Science and Politics of Racial Research* (Champaign: University of Illinois Press, 1996), William H. Tucker explains that in the aftermath of the *Brown* decision:

> The white segregationists would introduce another "scientific" concern that they insisted was the core of the controversy—the necessity to prevent miscegenation. To discourage the "unthinkable," the southern states had all enacted antimiscegenation laws, many of which imposed penalties of up to ten years' imprisonment. . . . Despite the existence of these punitive sanctions, the strict enforcement of segregation, especially among impressionable school children, was still considered an essential prophylactic, and when the *Brown* decision threatened to demolish the wall of racial separatism, horrified southern defenders envisioned widespread "amalgamation" rising from its ruins. (150–151)

And according to Klarman, Justice Felix Frankfurter explained, "One reason *Brown* was written as it was—emphasizing the importance of public education rather than condemning all racial classifications—was to avoid the miscegenation issue" (*Jim Crow* 321).

55. *Eyes* 34. Klarman notes that many framed the NAACP campaign for school desegregation as a covert attempt "to open the bedroom doors of our white women to the Negro men" and "to mongrelize the white race" (*Jim Crow* 321).

56. University of Arkansas, University Libraries, Digital Collections: Land of (Unequal) Opportunity, MC1364, box 8, file 1: Virgil Blossom, http://scipio.uark.edu/cdm/singleitem/collection/Civilrights/id/501/rec/1.

57. Henry Hampton and Steve Fayer, *Voices of Freedom: An Oral History of the Civil Rights Movement from the 1950s through the 1980s* (New York: Bantam, 1990), 51.

58. I have transcribed the quotes that follow from an audio CD of the radio broadcast, which is included with Herb Boyd's *We Shall Overcome* (Naperville, IL: Sourcebooks, Inc., 2004), CD 1, track 5. The Little Rock Nine representatives on the panel were Minnijean Brown, Melba Pattillo, and Ernest Green. The overtly racist white segregationists on the panel were Sammie Dean Parker and Kay Bacon, both of whom helped to organize the white student walkout at Central High School. The two white students on the panel in favor of integration were Robin Woods and Joe Fox. See Kekla Magoon, *Today the World Is Watching You: The Little Rock Nine and the Fight for School Integration, 1957* (Minneapolis, MN: Twenty-First Century Books, 2011), 101.

3. "The Three Realms of Human Life"

1. Elisabeth Young-Bruehl, *Hannah Arendt: For the Love of the World* (1982; rpt., New Haven, CT: Yale University Press, 2004), 310 (hereafter, *HALW*).

2. Ibid., 318.

3. It seems that on these grounds Arendt should have supported the *Brown* decision, which overturned the legal enforcement of segregation in public education. Arendt asserts, "Segregation is discrimination enforced by law, and desegregation can do no more than abolish the laws enforcing discrimination; it cannot abolish discrimination and force equality upon *society*, but it can, and indeed must, enforce equality within the body politic" (RLR 50). She adds, "While the government has no right to interfere with the prejudices and discriminatory practices of society, it has not only the right but the duty to make sure that these practices are not legally enforced" (53).

4. Hook, "Democracy and Desegregation," *New Leader* (April 21, 1958):4–5. He is rejecting Arendt's claim that public services, even if they are privately owned—like public transportation or hotels and restaurants that everyone needs to conduct business and lead his life—should

not be segregated (RLR 52). It is peculiar that public education does not fall into the realm of public services for Arendt.

5. Hook, "Democracy and Desegregation," 10.

6. Ibid., 6.

7. Ibid., 10. This goes against Arendt's claim, on the one hand, that "it is not the social custom of segregation that is unconstitutional, but its *legal enforcement*" (RLR 49, emphasis in original) and, on the other hand, "the moment social discrimination is legally abolished, the freedom of society is violated" (53).

8. Hook, "Democracy and Desegregation," 10. Hook is prioritizing the safeguarding of human freedom against discrimination while Arendt privileges the government's duty to "safeguard the rights of every person to do as he pleases within the four walls of his home" (RLR 53). Hook replies, "Even if the right to privacy were absolute, it would not carry with it the right to push out one's walls until they encompassed the public neighborhood, school, and factory" ("Democracy and Desegregation," 11).

9. Hook, "Democracy and Desegregation," 10 (emphasis in original). Young-Bruehl states, "She wrote out of moral anger at Negro parents who allowed their children to bear the burden of racial struggle" (*HALW* 308–309).

10. Hook, "Democracy and Desegregation," 10–11.

11. Ibid.

12. Ibid.

13. See Robert Bernasconi's "The Double Face of the Political and the Social: Hannah Arendt and America's Racial Divisions," *Research in Phenomenology* 26 (1996):18 (hereafter, DFPS).

14. George W. Cable, *The Negro Question* (1890; rpt., New York: Scribner's, 1898).

15. Ibid., 11.

16. Ibid., 39.

17. Ibid., 37–38. Bernasconi points out that both Cable and Arendt are attempting to assuage white fears and adds, "The problem is how far one needed to go to assuage those fears" (DFPS 19).

18. Cable, *The Negro Question*, 2.

19. Ibid., 3.

20. Ibid., 4.

21. Ibid. (emphasis in original).

22. Ibid., 5.

23. Ibid., 34.

24. Ibid., 39–40.

25. Ibid., 43.

26. Ibid., 43–44.

27. Ibid., 44.

28. Ibid., 45.

29. Ibid., 46.

30. Canovan describes the roles of labor, work, and action in Arendt's project as follows: "Labor is predictable because it is bound by necessity; work contains an element of freedom but once the process of making an object is embarked upon the activity is bound by the end at which it aims; action alone is free, for it consists above all in the capacity to initiate" (*Political Thought of Hannah Arendt* [New York: Harcourt Brace Jovanovich, 1977], 60). Each human being is "capable of doing the unexpected and acting in ways that no role-prescriptions can foresee" (59).

31. Seyla Benhabib describes Arendt's notion of "the rise of the social" well: "By 'the rise of the social' in this work, Arendt means the institutional differentiations of modern societies into

the narrowly political realm on the one hand and the economic market and the family on the other. As a result of these transformations, economic processes which had hitherto been confined to the 'shadowy realm of the household' emancipate themselves and become public matters" ("Models of Public Space," in her *Situating the Self: Gender, Community, and Postmodernism in Contemporary Ethics* [New York: Routledge, 1992], 90).

32. Hanna Pitkin explores Arendt's separation of action and behavior and makes the observation that for Arendt, "Behavior contrasts action. . . . it does not produce anything tangible . . . its product is normalized, rule-governed conduct" (Pitkin, "Conformism, Housekeeping, and the Attack of the Blob: The Origins of Hannah Arendt's Concept of the Social," in *Feminist Interpretations of Hannah Arendt*, edited by Bonnie Honig [University Park: Penn State University Press, 1995], 56). Benhabib makes a similar observation: "The political realm is being absorbed by the social resulting in individuals 'merely behaving' as economic producers, consumers, and urban city dwellers rather than acting" (*Situating the Self*, 90).

33. Pitkin summarizes Arendt's account of the social in this way: "the rise of the social, then, seems to mean the development of a complex economy . . . in which people are profoundly interdependent, yet no one is in charge. . . . it reaches beyond the supervision of any human head" ("Conformism," 54).

34. Canovan, *Political Thought of Hannah Arendt*, 11.

35. Margaret Canovan, *Hannah Arendt: A Reinterpretation of Her Political Thought* (New York: Cambridge University Press, 1992), 2.

36. Maurizio Passerin D'Entrèves, *The Political Philosophy of Hannah Arendt* (New York: Routledge, 1994), 5, 34.

37. Ibid., 48.

38. Richard Bernstein, *Hannah Arendt and the Jewish Question* (Cambridge, MA: MIT Press, 1996), 83. But even Bernstein has described Arendt's replies, when pressed on the social problem–political problem distinction, as "evasive and feeble" and tending to "obfuscate the issues." See Bernstein, "Rethinking the Social and the Political," in his *Philosophical Profiles: Essays in Pragmatic Mode* (Cambridge: Polity, 1986), 251. Bernstein discusses Albrecht Wellmer's claim that "social problems in our country are unavoidable political problems. . . . a distinction between the social and the political is impossible to draw." To this, Arendt replied with an example of housing: "The social problem is certainly adequate housing. But the question of whether this adequate housing means integration or not is certainly a political question" (ibid.). Bernstein is quoting from *Hannah Arendt: The Recovery of the Public World*, edited by Melvyn A. Hill (New York: St. Martin's, 1979), 317.

39. See Catharine MacKinnon, *Toward a Feminist Theory of the State* (Cambridge: Cambridge University Press, 1989); Susan Moller Okin, *Justice, Gender, and the Family* (New York: Basic, 1989); Jean Bethke Elshtain, *Public Man, Private Woman: Women in Social and Political Thought* (Princeton, NJ: Princeton University Press, 1981); Carole Pateman, "Feminist Critiques of the Public/Private Dichotomy," in *Public and Private in Social Life*, edited by Stanley Benn and G. F. Gauss (New York: St. Martin's, 1983); Pateman, *The Sexual Contract* (Cambridge: Polity, 1988); and Joan B. Landes, ed., *Feminism: The Public and the Private* (Oxford: Oxford University Press, 1998).

40. Benhabib, *Situating the Self*, 93.

41. Ibid.

42. Ibid., 91.

43. Ibid., 108. Contrary to Arendt's position, Benhabib emphasizes that fluidity between the public and private spheres has brought liberation. She asserts, "The rise of the social was accompanied by the emancipation of these groups [women, slaves, and so on] from the 'shadowy interior of the household' and by their entry into public life."

44. DFPS 6.

45. Norma Moruzzi, *Speaking through the Mask: Hannah Arendt and the Politics of Social Identity* (Ithaca, NY: Cornell University Press, 2000), 6.

46. Mary G. Dietz, *Turning Operations* (New York: Routledge, 2002), 107.

47. Ibid.

48. Raymond Geuss, *Public Goods, Private Goods* (Princeton, NJ: Princeton University Press, 2001), 106.

49. Ibid., 113. Earlier in the text Geuss examines the public-private distinction in the work of Benjamin Constant, Wilhelm von Humboldt, Augustine, John Stuart Mill, and John Dewey.

50. Benhabib, *Situating the Self*, 94.

51. Ibid.

52. DFPS 15.

53. It has been pointed out to me that Arendt herself admitted that her distinctions broke down on the matter of political thinking and action in the labor movement in nineteenth- and twentieth-century Europe, including Hungary. For example, see *HC* 212–217; the final chapter of *OR*; and the additions on Hungary in the 1958 edition of *OT*. It has also been suggested that Arendt's analysis of totalitarianism in Germany and Russia might be instructive for understanding Arendt's wariness of federal intervention in Little Rock. But it seems to me that Arendt's analysis of totalitarianism and terror is better applied to the governors, school administrators, and residents of the states, towns, and school districts using violence and terror to prevent school integration rather than to the federal government enforcing legal integration and attempting to protect Black students exercising their legal right to attend previously all-white schools.

4. "The End of Revolution Is the Foundation of Freedom"

1. For an extreme version of this charge, see Pitkin's claim: "Although the study sets out to contrast the success of the American Revolution to the failure of the French Revolution, it provides two conflicting explanations of the latter, eventually concedes that the American Revolution didn't succeed after all, offers three rival explanations of that, and finally claims that it makes no sense to speak of failure or success, a claim that makes mincemeat of the book's stated purpose" (*The Attack of the Blob: Hannah Arendt's Concept of the Social* [Chicago: University of Chicago Press, 1998], 219).

2. According to Arendt, "The word 'revolution' was originally an astronomical term which gained increasing importance in the natural sciences through Copernicus . . . designating the regular, lawfully revolving motion of the stars . . . characterized neither by newness or violence" (*OR* 42). The word also "indicates a recurring cyclical movement" (ibid.).

3. From this perspective, Arendt asserts that the aims of restoration in the French and American Revolutions was initially similar insofar as "[both] were played in their initial stages by men who were firmly convinced that they would do no more than restore an old order of things that had been disturbed and violated by the despotism of absolute monarchy or abuses of colonial government" (*OR* 44) These men pleaded to go back to an old order and time "when things had been as they ought to be" (ibid.). Nonetheless, Arendt also emphasizes the connections between revolution, freedom, and new beginnings in this text.

4. For an excellent analysis of natality in Arendt, see Peg Birmingham's *Hannah Arendt and Human Rights: The Predicament of Common Responsibility* (Bloomington: Indiana University Press, 2006).

5. But this problem is addressed through "the introduction of a beginner whose own beginnings are no longer subject to question because he is 'from eternity to eternity'" (*OR* 206). Arendt describes this eternity as an "absolute" of temporality sought by men in revolutions

who have been "influenced by age-old thought-customs of Western men, according to which each completely new beginning needs an absolute from which it springs and by which it is 'explained'" (ibid.). This attention to beginnings and foundations comes from Roman, rather than Greek, influences.

6. But if the "political" is simply that which occurs in public space, does that mean that bringing "private" and "social" issues (as Arendt defines them) into public space then makes them political issues?

7. Arendt asserts that Machiavelli is relevant for a history of revolution in this regard because "he was the first to think about the possibility of founding a permanent, lasting, enduring body politic" (*OR* 36). Machiavelli is "the spiritual father of revolution," who revived the spirit and institutions of Roman antiquity.

8. There are insightful commentaries on Arendt's assertion that compassion and pity have no place in politics. In particular, Shiraz Dossa has noted, "Arendt recognizes that pity for those who suffer from necessity and perennial poverty is a legitimate human feeling. But pity is too diffuse and limitless an emotion to serve as a platform of revolutionary action in politics, only because suffering is ubiquitous and protean in its manifestations" ("Hannah Arendt on Billy Budd and Robespierre: The Public Realm and the Private Self," *Philosophy and Social Criticism* 9 [1982]:312). Likewise, Canovan elucidates Arendt's claims about compassion not belonging in politics and explains, "Her argument is not concerned to deny the goodness of compassion, but only to consider what happens when it moves out of the sphere of direct, face-to-face personal relationships and becomes entangled in politics. For her claim is that compassion, like love and (as we shall see) like pure goodness, is an essentially unpolitical phenomenon" (*Hannah Arendt: A Reinterpretation of Her Political Thought* [New York: Cambridge University Press, 1992], 170). Ferenc Feher has taken a more critical position in "Freedom and the Social Question (Hannah Arendt's Theory of the French Revolution)," *Philosophy and Social Criticism* 12 (1987):1–30. According to Feher, Arendt takes this unsentimental solidarity to the extreme: "Since the separation of the 'social' from the 'political' is the guarantee of a 'spirit of freedom' in the intellect of the revolutionary, and since, further, compassion as absolute goodness regularly turns into radical evil, the true revolutionary has to be 'cold,' to the point of being unsympathetic towards suffering which is a household problem, and not one which should obtrude into political discussion" (21).

9. This description appears again in "Reply to Critics," when Arendt calls slavery "the original crime of this country's history" (Reply 181).

10. In "The Double Face of the Political and the Social: Hannah Arendt and America's Racial Divisions," *Research in Phenomenology* 26 (1996):3–24, Robert Bernasconi points out, "Although Arendt denied that the Founding Fathers were faced with a social question, she used the fact that Jefferson saw the problem posed by slavery as a political one to support her application of the distinction between the political and the social in the American Revolution" (13).

11. In his classic work *Slavery and Social Death: A Comparative Study* (Cambridge, MA: Harvard University Press, 1982), Orlando Patterson examines institutionalized slavery and its relationship to civilization and the very concept of freedom. Patterson states, "THERE IS NOTHING notably peculiar about the institution of slavery. . . . It was firmly established in all the great early centers of human civilization" (vii, emphasis in original). This was as true for the historical models of Greece and Rome preferred by Arendt as for other civilizations. He continues, "Ancient Greece and Rome were not simply slaveholding societies; they were what Sir Moses Finley calls 'genuine' slave societies, in that slavery was very solidly the base of their socioeconomic structures" (ibid.).

12. Toni Morrison, *Playing in the Dark: Whiteness and the Literary Imagination* (New York: Vintage, 1992), 38. I understand that Morrison's conception of freedom here (i.e., one is not en-

slaved) is not the same as Arendt's conception of freedom, but Morrison's point is still applicable to Arendt's analysis of freedom. On a different note, Ronald R. Sundstrom critiques Morrison's claim that "assimilation and integration into the United States happen upon the 'back of blacks'" (*The Browning of America and the Evasion of Social Justice* [Albany: State University of New York Press, 2008], 81). Sundstrom is criticizing the "Black-white Binary" as a historical claim about the "precedence of the African American experience as well as the relative severity of the conflict between African Americans and whites" (ibid.). For more on this binary and critiques of it, see *Critical Philosophy of Race* 1(1) (Spring 2013)—a special journal issue titled "Critical Philosophy of Race beyond the Black-White Binary."

13. Hannah Arendt, *The Burden of Our Time* (London: Secker and Warburg, 1951), 294. I quote from the first edition here because Arendt revised this part of the text in *Origins*. The revised version of the passage is on page 297 of *Origins*, where there is no longer a reference to concentration camps or to modern terror. Arendt also added several paragraphs to clarify her assertion and defend it against critics.

14. Having just mentioned Aristotle in this section, it is possible that Arendt has in mind the issue of slavery in general, or perhaps even ancient forms of slavery.

15. Thomas Jefferson, *Writings*, edited by Merrill D. Peterson (New York: Viking, 1984), 22.

16. Ibid., 18. For a closer analysis of Jefferson's writings on race, see K. Anthony Appiah and Amy Gutmann, *Color Conscious* (Princeton, NJ: Princeton University Press, 1996), 42–52.

17. It has also been argued that Jefferson had children with Sally Hemings, an enslaved woman he owned. See Annette Gordon Reed, *Thomas Jefferson and Sally Hemings: An American Controversy* (Charlottesville: University of Virginia Press, 1997), and Reed, *The Hemingses of Monticello: An American Family* (New York: Norton, 2008).

18. For more on the racial and economic motivations for slavery, see "Why Were Africans Enslaved?" by David Northrup, "Economics, Not Racism, as the Root of Slavery" by Eric Williams, and "The Simultaneous Invention of Slavery and Racism" by Winthrop Jordan—all in *The Atlantic Slave Trade*, edited by David Northrup (Boston: Wadsworth, 2010).

19. James Horton and Lois Horton, *Slavery in the Making of America* (Oxford: Oxford University Press, 2005), 29.

20. Ibid. Also see Winthrop Jordan's *White over Black: American Attitudes toward the Negro: 1550–1812* (Chapel Hill: University of North Carolina Press, 1968), 75; and Darlene Clark Hine, William Hine, and Stanley Harrold, *The African American Odyssey*, 3rd ed. (Upper Saddle River, NJ: Pearson Prentice Hall, 2003), 57.

21. Edmund Morgan, *American Slavery, American Freedom* (New York: Norton, 2003), 315.

22. Horton and Horton, *Slavery*, 30.

23. Ibid.

24. Ibid., 32.

25. Ibid., 30.

26. Frederick Douglass, *The Frederick Douglass Papers*, ser. 1, vol. 2: *1847–1854*, edited by John W. Blassingame (New Haven, CT: Yale University Press, 1982), 368. See Charles Mills's analysis of Douglass in "Whose Fourth of July?: Frederick Douglass and 'Original Intent,'" in his *Blackness Visible: Essays on Philosophy and Race* (Ithaca, NY: Cornell University Press, 1998).

27. Aside from the social question being central to the French Revolution, Arendt is also critical of the shift from action to spectatorship. With the French Revolution, the term "irresistibility" became associated with revolution (in addition to novelty, beginning, and violence) (*OR* 47–48). A problem with this irresistibility of the revolution came the consequence that "none of its actors could control the course of events" (51). Revolution began to be seen as a continuation of a movement, a permanent revolution, or "the notion that 'there never has been such a thing as several revolutions, that there is only one revolution, self-same and perpetual'" (ibid.).

Related to this is the notion of the force of history and historical necessity: "Theoretically, the most far-reaching consequence of the French Revolution was the birth of the modern concept of history in Hegel's philosophy" (ibid.). Arendt describes Hegel's notion of historical motion, which "is at once dialectical and driven by necessity" or "the famous dialectics of freedom and necessity in which both eventually coincide," as "perhaps the most terrible and, humanly speaking, least bearable paradox in the whole body of modern thought" (54). Thus eighteenth-century revolutions, particularly the French Revolution, ushered in the philosophy of history, but politically, the fallacy of this philosophy is that "it consists in describing and understanding the whole realm of human action, not in terms of the actor and the agent, but from the standpoint of the spectator who watches the spectacle" (52).

28. Hanna Pitkin has noted that Arendt offers different accounts of where the blame lies for the failure of the French Revolution. One is that the poor, driven by necessity, were at fault. Another is that it was the leaders of the French Revolution who were at fault. Finally, Pitkin asserts, "Arendt, then, is unclear as to whether it was the biologically driven poor or the sentiment driven leaders who ruined the Revolution. . . . Sometimes Arendt blames those she thinks driven by biological necessity, sometimes those overwhelmed by pity for the suffering of others; sometimes both; and sometimes no one" (Pitkin, *The Attack of the Blob: Hannah Arendt's Concept of the Social* [Chicago: University of Chicago Press, 1998], 221).

29. Failing to recognize poverty as a way of experiencing oppression or, more important, as a political issue, demonstrates the limitations of Arendt's notion of the political. When conceived in this way, the political realm excludes the poor and denies them the political agency to confront poverty as a political issue.

30. Perhaps this does not mean that oppression as such is not political, but rather that oppression of the poor is not political.

31. Margaret Canovan, "The Contradictions of Hannah Arendt's Political Thought," *Political Theory* 6(1) (February 1978):15.

32. Ibid., 16. She also writes in a footnote that Arendt seems more sympathetic to the poor in other texts, such as the *Partisan Review* article "The Cold War and the West" (ibid., 25n34).

33. Richard Bernstein, "Rethinking the Social and the Political," in his *Philosophical Profiles: Essays in Pragmatic Mode* (Cambridge: Polity, 1986), 243.

34. Ibid., 246.

35. Ibid., 255.

36. Feher, "Freedom," 23. Alternatively, Feher suggests, "A free republic would be able to address the social problem by creating the requisite institutionalized channels through which, eventually, this problem might be solved, even if only in a relative sense" (ibid.).

37. See *OT* 290–302. Jacques Rancière critiques Arendt's position on the Declaration of the Rights of Man in *Origins* in "Who Is the Subject of the Rights of Man?," *South Atlantic Quarterly* 103(2.3) (Spring–Summer 2004):297–310. Anthony Court defends Arendt in "Recovery of the Public Realm," in his *Hannah Arendt's Response to the Crisis of Her Times* (Amsterdam: Rozenberg/UNISA, 2008).

38. Arendt states, "The practical outcome of this contradiction was that from then on human rights were protected and enforced only as national rights and that the very institution of a state, whose supreme task was to protect and guarantee man his rights as man, as citizen and as national, lost its legal, rational appearance and could be interpreted by the romantics as the nebulous representative of a 'national soul' which through the very fact of its existence was supposed to be beyond or above the law" (*OT* 230–231).

39. See Laurent Dubois, *A Colony of Citizens: Revolution and Slave Emancipation in the French Caribbean, 1787–1804* (Chapel Hill: University of North Carolina Press, 2004).

40. See Sue Peabody's *"There Are No Slaves in France": The Political Culture of Race and Slavery in the Ancien Régime* (Oxford: Oxford University Press, 1996). See also Valerie Quinney, "Decisions on Slavery, the Slave Trade and Civil Rights for Negroes in the Early French Revolution," *Journal of Negro History* 55(2) (April 1970):117–130. Quinney examines how the early French revolutionaries compromised their stated ideals in order to preserve slavery and the triangular trade in slaves and other goods between France, Africa, and the French West Indies.

41. This group has been described as an intermediate category between enslaved people and free whites (Dubois, *Colony of Citizens*, 54–55). Dubois notes that *gens de couleur* included men of African descent, but often also with European ancestry.

42. Ibid., 68. Dubois is clear that the code offered no process for gaining one's freedom. Furthermore, there was other legislation that dismantled the rights of the *gens de couleur* (including poll taxes, restrictions on mixed marriages, limits on professions, and even the possibility of re-enslavement).

43. This is an example of citizenship rights being granted in writing but denied in practice—a case in which one might be a citizen of a state and yet be unprotected as if stateless. See Charles O. Hardy, *The Negro Question in the French Revolution* (Menasha, WI: George Banta, 1919); and Anna Julia Cooper, *Slavery and the French and Haitian Revolutionists*, edited and translated by Francis Richardson Keller (New York: Rowman and Littlefield, 2006).

44. Louis Sala-Molins, *Dark Side of the Light: Slavery and the French Enlightenment*, translated by John Conteh-Morgan (French edition 1992; Minneapolis: University of Minnesota Press, 2006), 59.

45. Ibid., 61.

46. Ibid., 16. Recall Arendt's critiques of the Enlightenment on the basis of its antisemitism. For Arendt, the Jewish question, especially as it relates to pressures to assimilate, is situated in the age of the Enlightenment (OA 22). She asserts, "The modern Jewish Question dates from the Enlightenment; it was the Enlightenment—that is, the non-Jewish world—that posed it. Its formulations and its answers have defined the behavior and assimilation of Jews" (EJQ 3). Richard Bernstein asserts, "The dark underside of the Enlightenment conception of a human being as someone who possesses rights simply by virtue of being an 'abstract human being' is to leave human beings completely defenseless and powerless in the face of totalitarian terror" (*Hannah Arendt and the Jewish Question* [Cambridge, MA: MIT Press, 1996], 85).

47. For example, while the colonists abroad fought with French merchants over the slave trade and general trade regulation issues (the colonists wanted to be able to trade with countries other than France while French merchants demanded a monopoly on trade in slaves and goods with the French colonies), they shared a mutual interest in the continuation of the slave trade and the institution of slavery.

48. For an insightful counternarrative to Arendt's emphasis on the French and American Revolutions to the exclusion of the Haitian Revolution, see Nick Nesbitt, *Universal Emancipation: The Haitian Revolution and the Radical Enlightenment* (Charlottesville: University of Virginia Press, 2008). Nesbitt asserts, "If the French and American revolutions had first articulated an abstract recognition of universal human rights, the Haitian Revolution brought to bear a simple truth denied by these earlier political sequences: the freedom of the few cannot be predicated upon the enslavement of the many" (12).

49. Sibylle Fischer, *Modernity Disavowed: Haiti and the Cultures of Slavery in the Age of Revolution* (Durham, NC: Duke University Press, 2004), ix.

50. Ibid., 7.

51. Ibid., 9. Fischer considers the ways that prominent philosophical figures like Hegel and

Arendt have erased this revolution: "In an astonishing convergence, both Hegel and Hannah Arendt (whose theory was explicitly anti-Hegelian) make revolutionary slaves vanish. In the case of Arendt, slaves disappear first in the disavowal attributed to European travelers and American revolutionaries, who did not 'see' the slaves that labored in the fields, and then again, conceptually, in the abyss between the social and the political" (32).

52. Ibid., 9.

53. See C. L. R. James, *The Black Jacobins: Toussaint L'Ouverture and the San Domingo Revolution* (New York: Vintage, 1963).

54. David Scott, *Conscripts of Modernity* (Durham, NC: Duke University Press, 2004), 217.

55. Ibid., 218.

56. Ibid., 220. Scott says that C. L. R. James presents Louverture "in the incomparable role of a political statesman and strategist, the embodiment of the *vita activa*, stepping into the political realm and acting with brilliant and eloquent decision" (ibid., 219.)

57. Fischer, *Modernity Disavowed*, 9.

5. "A Preparatory Stage for the Coming Catastrophes"

1. See Elisabeth Young-Bruehl, *Hannah Arendt: For the Love of the World* (1982; rpt., New Haven, CT: Yale University Press, 2004), 200 (hereafter, *HALW*); and Richard King, *Race, Culture, and the Intellectuals: 1940–1970* (Baltimore, MD: Johns Hopkins University Press, 2004), 96, 98. Young-Bruehl also notes that Arendt referred to the book as *The Three Pillars of Hell* and as *A History of Totalitarianism*.

2. *HALW* 159. Young-Bruehl notes that Arendt and Blücher went to Lisbon in January 1941 and then sailed to New York three months later. Martha Arendt was able to join them in New York after her visa arrived in May 1941 (ibid.).

3. *HALW* 201.

4. Michael Rothberg, *Multidirectional Memory: Remembering the Holocaust in the Age of Decolonization* (Stanford, CA: Stanford University Press, 2009), 37.

5. Arendt does acknowledge that Africans, in particular the (former) slaves of South Africa, were "well on their way to becoming workers, a normal part of human civilization" at the time she was writing *Origins*. This may suggest that by becoming workers (as Arendt understands the term) these South Africans became humanized rather than naturalized. See *OT* 195.

6. Arendt notes that it was not the intent of European colonizers to extend the rights of citizenship to the colonized in Africa. But she describes this as a refusal to "impose" their laws on a foreign territory.

7. Colin Palmer, "Rethinking American Slavery," in *The African Diaspora*, edited by Alusine Jalloh and Stephen E. Maizlish (College Station: Texas A&M University Press, 1996), 75. Palmer cites several sources on the issue of Iberians' attitudes of superiority toward Africans, including A. J. R. Russell-Wood, "Iberian Expansion and the Issue of Black Slavery: Changing Portuguese Attitudes, 1440–1770," *American Historical Review* 85(1) (January 1978):16–42; and David Eltis, "Europeans and the Rise and Fall of African Slavery in the Americas: An Interpretation," *American Historical Review* 98(1) (January 1993):1399–1423.

8. I am not dismissing contemporary race theorists and historians who situate biological race thinking in the eighteenth century; rather, I want to interrogate theoretical frameworks that minimize questions of "difference" (religious, cultural, or racial) and yet are used to describe categories and events that have come to shape our understanding of slavery and genocide during the colonial era. One might adopt the term "proto-racism," as Robert Bernasconi

does in his essay "Proto-Racism: Carolina in Locke's Mind," in *Racism and Modernity*, edited by Iris Wigger and Sabine Ritter (Berlin: LIT, 2011), 68–82.

9. King, *Race, Culture, and the Intellectuals*, 112–113. See also Richard King, "On Race and Culture: Arendt and Her Contemporaries," in *Politics in Dark Times: Encounters with Hannah Arendt*, edited by Seyla Benhabib (New York: Cambridge University Press, 2012).

10. Charles Mills, *The Racial Contract* (Ithaca, NY: Cornell University Press, 1997), 102–104.

11. Ibid., 102.

12. W. E. B. Du Bois, *The World and Africa: An Inquiry into the Part Which Africa Has Played in World History* (New York: International, 1946), 23. This passage by Du Bois is also quoted in King, *Race, Culture, and the Intellectuals*, 47. King notes, "Although one can quarrel with details of Du Bois' statement here, it clearly anticipates Arendt's thesis that what Europeans learned in ruling their colonies 'blew back' into Europe and helped degrade the political thought, culture, and practice of Europe" (ibid.).

13. Du Bois, *The World and Africa*, 23. He goes on to connect this idea of a superior race in Europe and America to economics or "the astonishing ideal of wealth and luxury." Du Bois also makes connections between Nazism and apartheid in South Africa, citing at length the Declaration to the Nations of the World issued by the Non-European United Committee, Cape Town, South Africa, in 1945 (ibid., 39–41).

14. Aimé Césaire, *Discourse on Colonialism*, translated by Joan Pinkham (New York: Monthly Review Press, 2000), 31. Throughout, Césaire criticizes colonialism in terms of race and economics. He offers an explicitly racial and socialist critique.

15. Ibid., 36.

16. Dana Villa, ed., *The Cambridge Companion to Hannah Arendt* (Cambridge: Cambridge University Press, 2000), 3.

17. King, *Race, Culture, and the Intellectuals*, 100. King later states, "I would suggest that Arendt is best read as arguing not for strong causality but for historical prefiguration or foreshadowing. What happened in Africa, she seems to say, created an ethos in which total domination and mass extermination might more easily take hold in Europe" (107). But in the end King argues that Arendt "under- rather than over-stated the pervasive impact of the colonial experience on the cultural life of Western Europe, North America, and the Antipodes" (108).

18. Shiraz Dossa, "Human Status and Politics: Hannah Arendt on the Holocaust," *Canadian Journal of Politics/Revue canadienne de science politiques* 13(2) (June 1980):317.

19. Ibid. Dossa notes that, for Arendt, Nazi totalitarianism eliminated spontaneity and difference, violated human plurality through mass murder, and undermined the human status of man. But Arendt is also already aware of genocides going back to antiquity. He goes on to argue that her understanding of the uniqueness of the totalitarian Holocaust is based on her own ethnocentrism.

20. See A. Dirk Moses, "Hannah Arendt, Imperialisms, and the Holocaust," in *German Colonialism: Race, the Holocaust, and Postwar Germany*, edited by Volker Langbehn and Mohammad Salama (New York: Columbia University Press, 2011), 73 (emphasis in original). Moses cites Dan Diner's *Genläufige Gedächtnisse* as a "conscious defense of the Arendtian thesis against comparative genocide studies and postcolonial memory" (84).

21. Rothberg, *Multidirectional Memory*, 42.

22. Ibid., 73. He notes, "A dialectical encounter between Arendt and Césaire demonstrates how intersecting memories of colonialism, slavery, and genocide lead to unprecedented insights in their work but also sometimes cloud the clarity of their vision" (107).

23. Ibid., 114.

24. W. E. B. Du Bois, "The Negro in the Warsaw Ghetto," *Jewish Life* (May 1952):15.

25. Ibid.; also cited in Rothberg, *Multidirectional Memory*, 116.

26. And it is on these terms that Jewish behavior was separated from others: "During the long period of mere social anti-Semitism, which produced and prepared the discovery of Jew-hating as a political weapon, it was the lack of 'innate personality,' the lack of tact . . . etc. which separated the behavior of his [the German's] Jewish colleague" (*OT* 169). Arendt maintains that *antisemitism* (a social phenomenon) must be distinguished from *Jew hatred* (a political phenomenon), but she notes that the former paved the way for the latter. The discovery of Jew hatred was prompted by racism as a tool against Blacks and as a justification for slavery and colonialism. Jews just happened to fit into racial ideologies that had been developed by anti-Black racism. Arendt criticizes conceptions of race based on blood ties and familial characteristics because this is a notion that became problematic for Jews when antisemitism turned to Jew hatred. A consequence of a notion of race based on blood and family ties was that "when, for reasons which had nothing to do with the Jewish question, race problems came to the foreground of the political scene, the Jews at once fitted all ideologies and doctrines which defined a people by blood ties and family characteristics" (28). Arendt notes that the family played a major role in the preservation of the Jewish people and that this became a stereotype that antisemites would use against them: "Family ties were among the most potent and stubborn elements with which the Jewish people resisted assimilation and dissolution" (ibid.). And then she writes, "The anti-Semitic picture of the Jewish people as a family closely knit by blood ties had something in common with the Jews' own picture of themselves" (ibid.).

27. It is significant that Arendt credits Gobineau with the invention of racism, since his essays were published between 1853 and 1855, about thirty years before what Arendt describes as the age of imperialism.

28. Arendt may have been unaware that Gobineau's popularity in the United States probably resulted more from his translators than from Gobineau himself. Robert Bernasconi explains in *The Idea of Race* that the first two essays of *The Inequality of Human Races* were published in 1853, and three years later Josiah Nott and Henry Hotz translated the book into English. Bernasconi asserts, "The result was a seriously doctored text" (Robert Bernasconi and Tommy Lott, *The Idea of Race* [Indianapolis, IN: Hackett, 2000], 45).

29. Arendt expands on her analysis of ideologies in relationship to totalitarianism later in *Origins*, when she asserts that ideologies have three totalitarian elements: (1) ideologies have a tendency to explain not what is, but what becomes, (2) ideologies become independent of all experience, from which they cannot learn anything new, and (3) since ideologies have no power to transform reality, they achieve this emancipation of thought from experience through certain methods of demonstration (*OT* 470–471). When facts that contradict ideologies are presented, the facts are rejected while the ideas behind the ideologies are embraced.

30. For more on race in South Africa, see Saul Dubow, *Scientific Racism in Modern South Africa* (Cambridge: Cambridge University Press, 1995). Dubow examines the "collective amnesia" that has "obscured the centrality of intellectual racism in Western thought during the early part of the twentieth century" (1). He notes that while the trauma of the Holocaust alerted many to the horrors of politicized racism, "the horrors perpetuated by Nazism have also had the effect of disguising the extent to which similar racial ideas were current in European and American thought in the pre-war generation" (1–2).

31. Okon Edet Uya, "Prelude to Disaster: An Analysis of the Racial Policies of Boer and British Settlers in Africa before 1910," in *Africa and the Afro American Experience*, edited by Lorraine Williams (Washington, DC: Howard University Press, 1977), 114.

32. The argument that slavery domesticates or civilizes an animalistic slave population has frequently been used to defend and justify slavery in the United States as well as the imperialist projects in Africa, Asia, and other parts of the globe. The violent oppression of entire popu-

lations has been justified by claims that the oppressors were spreading "civilization," Christianity, or (more recently) "democracy and freedom."

33. Gail Presby, "Critic of Boers or Africans?: Arendt's Treatment of South Africa in *The Origins of Totalitarianism*," in *Postcolonial African Philosophy: A Critical Reader*, edited by Emmanuel Chukwudi Eze (Oxford: Blackwell, 1996), 167.

34. Ibid., 168. Moses makes a similar claim that, for Arendt, "it was understandable, if not admirable, that the Boers became racists" ("Arendt, Imperialisms, and the Holocaust," 78).

35. For a more exhaustive analysis of economics and the political in Arendt's work, see Robert Bernasconi's "The Double Face of the Political and the Social: Hannah Arendt and America's Racial Divisions," *Research in Phenomenology* 26 (1996):3–24.

36. Presby, "Critic of Boers or Africans?," 166.

37. Seyla Benhabib, "Arendt's *Eichmann in Jerusalem*," in *The Cambridge Companion to Hannah Arendt*, edited by Dana Villa (Cambridge: Cambridge University Press, 2000), 65. Benhabib and others argue that this controversy results in large part from a misinterpretation of Arendt's work. See Bernard Bergen, *The Banality of Evil: Hannah Arendt and "The Final Solution"* (New York: Rowman and Littlefield, 1998); Richard Bernstein, "From Radical Evil to the Banality of Evil: From Superfluousness to Thoughtlessness," in *Hannah Arendt and the Jewish Question* (Cambridge, MA: MIT Press, 1996); and Dana Villa, "Conscience, the Banality of Evil, and the Idea of a Representative Perpetrator," in his *Politics, Philosophy, Terror: Essays on the Thought of Hannah Arendt* (Princeton, NJ: Princeton University Press, 1999).

38. Presby, "Critic of Boers or Africans?," 166–167.

39. Or, as King states, "Though she is reporting on the reactions of the European settlers to the otherness of Africa, Arendt seems at the same time to share their shock of nonrecognition" (*Race, Culture, and the Intellectuals*, 116).

40. Villa, *Cambridge Companion*, 4. See also George Kateb, *Hannah Arendt: Politics, Conscience, Evil* (Totowa, NJ: Rowman and Allanheld, 1984), 61–63.

41. Anne Norton, "Heart of Darkness: Africa and African Americans in the Writings of Hannah Arendt," in *Feminist Interpretations of Hannah Arendt*, edited by Bonnie Honig (University Park: Penn State University Press, 1995), 253.

42. Ibid.

43. Conrad's *Heart of Darkness* is often debated among scholars. In "An Image of Africa," Chinua Achebe asserts that Conrad is a racist and *Heart of Darkness* represents white racist attitudes toward Africa that have become such a normal way of thinking that they frequently go unnoticed. See Achebe, "An Image of Africa," *Massachusetts Review* 18(4) (Winter 1977):788. Peter E. Firchow defends *Heart of Darkness* in *Envisioning Africa: Racism and Imperialism in Conrad's Heart of Darkness* (Lexington: University Press of Kentucky, 2000). According to King, "Indeed, at times *Origins* sounds like a rewrite of *Heart of Darkness* in the negative as well as positive sense" (*Race, Culture, and the Intellectuals*, 117). For him, "Arendt's characterization of African culture does not discredit her work as such, but it does, however, shed fresh light on several fundamental characteristics of her thought" (ibid.). Dossa asserts that, for Arendt, Conrad's *Heart of Darkness* is "a literary tale [that] becomes the vehicle for making serious philosophical arguments" ("Human Status and Politics," 319). See also Jimmy Casas Klausen's "Hannah Arendt's Antiprimitivism," *Political Theory* 38(3) (2010):397; and Rothberg, *Multidirectional Memory*, 55–58, 82–85.

44. Moses connects this point back to the uniqueness-of-the-Holocaust position. Looking at the genocide in the Belgian Congo, he problematizes the way Arendt "literally consign[s] to a footnote the apparently atypical case of the Belgian Congo, which she knew cost tens of millions of lives, and excus[es] the large-scale massacres as instrumentally limited actions" (78). He continues, "Far from trying to link European colonialism in Africa to Nazism and the Ho-

locaust, then, the purpose of *The Origins of Totalitarianism* and her oeuvre in this respect was to disentangle them and distinguish the Holocaust from previous genocides" ("Arendt, Imperialisms, and the Holocaust," 78).

45. See Robert Bernasconi's "When the Real Crime Began: Hannah Arendt's *The Origins of Totalitarianism* and the Dignity of the Western Philosophical Tradition," in *Hannah Arendt and the Uses of History: Imperialsm, Nation, Race, and Genocide,* edited by Richard King and Dan Stone (New York: Berghahn, 2007).

46. W. E. B. Du Bois, *The World and Africa: An Inquiry into the Part Which Africa Has Played in World History* (New York: International, 1946), 23. Citations are from the enlarged edition with new writings on Africa by Du Bois from 1955 to 1961 (New York: International, 2003).

47. Aimé Césaire, *Discourse on Colonialism,* translated by Joan Pinkham (New York: Monthly Review Press, 2000), 36.

48. Kateb, *Hannah Arendt: Politics, Conscience, Evil,* 61.

49. King, *Race, Culture, and the Intellectuals,* 116–117.

50. Dossa, "Human Status and Politics," 320. Dossa explains, "These sentiments [in *Origins* and in *On Violence*] are ethnocentric in the precise sense that they are judgments made from an intellectually and culturally European point of view, and in the sense that they presuppose the truth and validity of this point of view. More crucially, these sentiments assume the 'inhumanity' of blacks as self-evident. . . . they treat the matter as if it were settled" (321).

51. Norma Moruzzi, *Speaking through the Mask: Hannah Arendt and the Politics of Social Identity* (Ithaca, NY: Cornell University Press, 2000), 97.

52. Klausen, "Hannah Arendt's Antiprimitivism," 396 (emphasis in original). He later adds, "*If* there is a racist aspect to *Imperialism's* antiprimitivism, then, it is not confined simply to judgments associated with epidermal schema but also has to do with differential judgments about capacity for moral responsibility as correlative with cultural development" (405). See also Ayten Güdogdu, "Arendt on Culture and Imperialism: A Reply to Klausen," *Political Theory* 39(5) (2011):661–667; and Klausen, "Reply to Güdogdu," *Political Theory* 39(5) (2011):668–673.

53. Charles Johnson disagrees with me on this point and argues that Arendt espouses anti-Black racism in "Reading between the Lines: Kathryn Gines on Hannah Arendt and Antiblack Racism," *Southern Journal of Philosophy* 47 (2009):77–83.

6. "Only Violence and Rule over Others Could Make Some Men Free"

1. Patricia Owens, *Between War and Politics: International Relations and the Thought of Hannah Arendt* (Oxford: Oxford University Press, 2007), 1. Peg Birmingham examines Arendt's analysis of violence and war in "Arendt and Hobbes: Glory, Sacrificial Violence, and the Political Imagination," *Research in Phenomenology* 41 (2011):1–22, and "On Violence, Politics, and the Law," *Journal of Speculative Philosophy,* n.s., 24(1) (2010):1–20. See also Arendt's "Introduction into Politics," the last section of which is "The Question of War," in *The Promise of Politics,* edited by Jerome Kohn (New York: Schocken, 2005).

2. Although Arendt clearly distinguishes colonialism from imperialism, I use the terms interchangeably here because what Arendt labels "imperialism," Sartre and Fanon refer to as "colonialism."

3. As Young-Bruehl points out, the distinction between power and violence is central to *On Revolution.* See *Hannah Arendt: For the Love of the World* (1982; rpt., New Haven, CT: Yale University Press, 2004), 413.

4. As Moruzzi explains, "The internal and external limits of the strictly political life of the

city are demarcated by the abrupt restrictions on the possibility of violence. The space of the political is enclosed by the violence outside the city walls; within those walls, violence is privately present but publically [*sic*] mute, legitimately existing within the domestic confines of the household" (Norma Moruzzi, *Speaking through the Mask: Hannah Arendt and the Politics of Social Identity* [Ithaca, NY: Cornell University Press, 2000], 138). She continues, "For Arendt, the codification of violence into something other than the public—whether that be domestic or barbarian, and either way barbarous, stammering, deprived of speech—is absolutely necessary for her political schema" (139).

5. Arendt elaborates on the violent conditions for slaves in the private realm and their exclusion from the public realm. She notes not only their poverty, but also their subjugation to necessity and to "man-made violence" (*HC* 31). Arendt describes the multilayered oppression of slavery as a "twofold and doubled 'unhappiness'" (ibid.). This "unhappiness" is contrasted with the Greek *eudaimonia,* which connotes happiness that is dependent on freedom, wealth, and health, among other conditions (ibid.).

6. Arendt contrasts the prepolitical force (i.e., the aforementioned "man-made violence" that the head of household uses to rule over his family and slaves) with the violence depicted by Hobbes as the "war of all against all" in the state of nature (*HC* 32). To be clear, it is the household master's violence that is described as justified for political freedom rather than any violent resistance among those enslaved in the private realm.

7. Dossa has described Arendt's representation of the animal laborans in *The Human Condition* as an example of the ethnocentrism implicit in her normative political theory: "it is true and legitimate to say that her political theory entails an ethnocentric strain. . . . There is no escaping this conclusion: the parallels between her view of the blacks and her depiction of the animal laborans are too strident to be accidental" ("Human Status and Politics," 323).

8. Arendt notes that this is at least a public space, even if it is not a "political realm, properly speaking" (*HC* 160).

9. In "Introduction into Politics," Arendt extends this analysis of violence against nature for the purpose of fabrication, or building our world, to the violence of war (154).

10. Margaret Canovan takes this quote as her focal point in "Terrible Truths: Hannah Arendt on Politics, Contingency and Evil," *Revue Internationale de Philosophie* 53(208) (1999):173–189. Canovan explains, "When she points out that freedom and civilization have historically been founded on violence and injustice, she says (and means) that this is a 'terrible truth.' Nonetheless, it is a truth, and modern humanitarian sentiment does not make it any less true" (176). For Canovan, this position shows that "Arendt did not believe in progress, and it is this that makes her thought so hard for many readers to understand and sympathize with" (177). According to Canovan, "Looking back at the costs of civilization—that of the Greeks, for example— we cannot make moral sense of them. We are horrified by the price of civilization, paid by the slaves who sustained it. To quote [Walter] Benjamin again, 'There is no document of civilization which is not at the same time a document of barbarism'" (186). Here, perhaps, Canovan misses the significance of Benjamin's insights. What Benjamin expresses in this quote is the point that civilization has gone hand and hand with barbarism. Acknowledging this fact does not mean that we should cease to be critical of it. The very concept of civilization needs to be interrogated. And such an interrogation should not be reduced to over-optimism or a longing for a perfect society, as it is by Canovan. Naming and interrogating these "terrible truths" provides a space to respond to one of the central problems of Western civilization, namely, that it denies its own barbarity and savagery (and attempts to project it onto "others"). This is one of the key arguments concerning Europe in *Discourse on Colonialism*. Having described Nazism as the barbarism that sums up all barbarisms, Césaire asserts, "To go further, I make no

secret of my opinion that at the present time the barbarism of Western Europe has reached an incredibly high level, being only surpassed—far surpassed, it is true—by the barbarism of the United States" (47).

11. See Bruce Levine, *Half-Slave and Half-Free: The Roots of Civil War*, rev. ed. (New York: Hill and Wang, 2005), 20–21.

12. Jean-Paul Sartre, "Colonialism Is a System," in his *Colonialism and Neocolonialism*, translated by Azzedine Haddour, Steve Brewer, and Terry McWilliams (New York: Routledge, 2001), 39.

13. Arendt states: "A Jewish army is not utopian if the Jews of all countries demand it and are prepared to volunteer for it. But what is utopian is the notion that we could profit in some way from Hitler's defeat, if we do not also contribute to it" (*JW* 137). She later adds: "We can do battle against antisemitism only if we battle Hitler with weapons in our hands" (143, December 26, 1941).

14. This connection is repeated when Arendt argues: "During this war there is for us only one single goal in our program that must be achieved if all Jewish politics is not to fail: full participation in the war with full and equal rights, that is, a Jewish army" (*JW* 178, October 22, 1942).

15. Peg Birmingham has written insightfully about this and argues, "Arendt's early thinking on glory and its political link to sovereign, sacrificial violence is much closer to Hobbes than is normally thought to be the case. Only later, and I speculate this is in large part due to the declaration of the state of Israel and to the development of nuclear weapons, does Arendt change her mind, calling for a transformed notion of glory, no longer rooted in sovereign, sacrificial violence, but instead, in a conception of political responsibility charged with the task of bearing the world" ("Arendt and Hobbes," 12). Elsewhere, Birmingham has noted, "Arendt's call for a Jewish army is not simply a call for self-defense; instead, she argues that the constitution of a people depends on its ability to manifest itself through action. . . . In her call for a Jewish army, Arendt is calling for active resistance against what could be seen as one's destiny and fate" ("On Violence, Politics, and the Law," 9).

16. See Césaire's *Discourse on Colonialism*.

17. The settlers are constantly distinguished from the natives and are thought to represent everything the colonized are not and can never be. The colonized are characterized as the quintessence of evil, as insensible to ethics, and as both the absence and the negation of values. The colonized are perceived as ugly and immoral; they are a collection of wicked powers and the instruments of blind forces.

18. Frantz Fanon, *The Wretched of the Earth* (New York: Grove, 1963), 39. The quotes and page numbers provided are from the English translation by Constance Farrington. There is a 2004 English translation by Richard Philcox (also published by Grove Press).

19. Ibid., 53.

20. Ibid., 51.

21. Ibid., 94.

22. Georges Sorel authored *Reflections on Violence*, translated by T. E. Hulme (London: Allen and Unwin, 1916), and Vilfredo Pareto was an economic and social theorist. Arendt notes that Fanon used Sorel's categories even when his own experiences spoke against them (*CR* 168).

23. Fanon reveals, "This is the period when the niggers beat each other up, and the police and magistrates do not know which way to turn when faced with the astonishing waves of crime in North Africa" (*Wretched of the Earth*, 14).

24. Ibid., 52.

25. Ibid., 54. Since the colonized are not yet able to see a way out of the colonial system, they display patterns of avoidance: "It is as if plunging into a fraternal bloodbath allowed them to ig-

nore the obstacle, and to put off until later the choice, nevertheless inevitable, which opens up the question of armed resistance to colonialism" (ibid.). Self-destruction through intragroup violence is only the first stage of violence; it is followed by violence that organizes the colonized against the colonizers.

26. Ibid., 70.

27. Ibid., 36–37. Let us consider these claims by Fanon alongside Arendt's claims about the battles in the Warsaw ghetto: "At the end of August [1942] a group of workers and intellectuals realized that ultimately armed resistance was the only moral and political way out. . . . From the Jewish side this war was a *levée en masse*: everyone had worked together fortifying streets and buildings, everyone had a weapon, everyone had a specified task. Everyone knew that the coming war could only end in military defeat and would lead to physical annihilation. Everyone knew . . . 'that the passive death of Jews had created no new values; it had been meaningless; but that death with weapons in hand can bring new values into the life of the Jewish people'" (*JW* 216–217, July 28, 1944).

28. Ibid., 130. Like Arendt in her arguments for a Jewish army, Fanon is connecting the struggle for liberation to nationhood (that is, he is making a political argument).

29. Ibid., 129.

30. Ibid., 69.

31. Jean-Paul Sartre, preface to *The Wretched of the Earth* (New York: Grove, 1963), 14, quoted in Arendt, *On Violence*, 114.

32. Sartre, preface, 21, quoted in Arendt, *On Violence*, 114.

33. Sartre, preface, 17, quoted in Arendt, *On Violence*, 114.

34. This is discussed at length in Sartre's *Critique of Dialectical Reason*, vol. 1, translated by Alan Sheridan-Smith (New York: Verso, 1991).

35. Sartre, preface, 22, quoted in Arendt, *On Violence*, 115.

36. R. D. Laing and D. G. Cooper, *Reason and Violence: A Decade of Sartre's Philosophy 1950–1960* (New York: Humanities Press, 1964), 9.

37. Ibid., 114, quoted in Arendt, *On Violence*, 186.

38. Sartre, *Critique of Dialectical Reason*, 133.

39. Laing and Cooper, *Reason and Violence*, 114, quoted in Arendt, *On Violence*, 186.

40. Sartre, *Critique of Dialectical Reason*, 133.

41. Ibid.

42. Ibid., 111.

43. Ibid.

44. Laing and Cooper, *Reason and Violence*, 114, quoted in Arendt, *On Violence*, 186.

45. Sartre, *Critique of Dialectical Reason*, 133.

46. Laing and Cooper, *Reason and Violence*, 121, quoted in Arendt, *On Violence*, 186.

47. Laing and Cooper, *Reason and Violence*, 122, quoted in Arendt, *On Violence*, 186.

48. Sartre, *Critique of Dialectical Reason*, 260.

49. Ibid.

50. Ibid., 264.

51. Fanon, *Wretched of the Earth*, 84.

52. Ibid., 84.

53. Ibid., 70. This dynamic also operated in the U.S. context. For example, King and his non-violent philosophy became more appealing when juxtaposed with Malcolm X or the Black Panther Party.

54. Ibid., 41. The colonized come to realize that "colonialism only loosens its hold when the knife is at its throat," and they do not find these terms too violent (61). This phrase appeared on a famous leaflet distributed by the FLN (Front de Libération Nationale or National Liberation

Front) in 1956. Fanon posits that these terms of decolonization "only expressed what every Algerian felt in his heart: colonialism is not a thinking machine, nor a body endowed with reasoning faculties. It is violence in its natural state and it will only yield when confronted with greater violence."

55. Ibid., 35.

56. Ibid., 36.

57. Ibid., 89. According to Fanon, "Terror, counter-terror, violence, counter-violence: that is what observers bitterly record when they describe the circle of hate, which is so tenacious and so evident in Algeria" (ibid.). In a footnote he explains in more detail the tenacity of the violence launched against the colonized rebels (90). While the United Nations asked for a peaceful and democratic solution, Robert Lacoste set out to organize European militias in Algeria to "lighten" the load of the French military there. The army was given civil powers, and civilians were given military powers. Every European was armed and instructed to open fire on any person who seemed suspect to him. Every Frenchman was authorized and encouraged to use his weapons. When the UN asked him to stop the bloodshed, Lacoste replied that the best way to do that was to make sure there remained no blood to be shed (ibid.).

58. Ibid., 79.

59. Sartre, "Colonialism Is a System," 31.

60. Ibid., 47.

61. Ibid.

62. Sartre, *Critique of Dialectical Reason*, 733.

63. Ibid., 718.

64. Ibid.

65. I am aware of the debate about whether Sartre's preface distorts Fanon's purpose in *The Wretched of the Earth*. Although I think Sartre's aim in the preface and Fanon's aim in the book are not one and the same, Sartre's comments do not undermine Fanon's overall project.

66. Arendt gives the example of "Billy Budd sticking the witness who bore false witness against him" (*CR* 161).

67. Fanon, *Wretched of the Earth*, 149–150.

68. Ibid., 154–155.

69. Ibid., 194.

70. Ibid., 200.

71. Ibid., 193.

72. Dossa, "Human Status and Politics," 313. Dossa adds, "More significantly she is far from condemning the exercise of violence per se: the human necessity for violence and domination emerges as one of the central *motifs* of her vision of true politics developed at length in *The Human Condition*" (ibid.).

7. "A Much Greater Threat to Our Institutions of Higher Learning than the Student Riots"

1. To *On Violence*, we should add her comments in "Civil Disobedience" and "Thoughts on Politics and Revolution." A notable exception to the lack of focus on Arendt's comments in *On Violence* is Anne Norton's "Heart of Darkness: Africa and African Americans in the Writings of Hannah Arendt," in *Feminist Interpretations of Hannah Arendt*, edited by Bonnie Honig (University Park: Penn State University Press, 1995).

2. *Between Friends: The Correspondence of Hannah Arendt and Mary McCarthy* (London: Secker and Warburg, 1996), 229.

3. Ibid.

4. Ibid., 230.

5. Norton, "Heart of Darkness," 249.

6. Concerning the description of Swahili as a "no language," Norton retorts, "By this standard, English cannot escape censure, and Arendt's regard for Yiddish and modern Hebrew becomes almost inexplicable" (ibid., 252).

7. See David Halberstam, *The Children* (New York: Fawcett, 1998), 450; and Peter Ackerman and Jack Duvall, *A Force More Powerful: A Century of Nonviolent Conflict* (New York: Palgrave, 200), 310–311.

8. Halberstam, *The Children*, 528. Martin Luther King Jr. sheds some light on the events that unfolded at this rally (where Carmichael called for "Black Power" rather than "Freedom Now") in his essay "Black Power," reprinted in *A Testament of Hope: The Essential Writings and Speeches of Martin Luther King, Jr.*, edited by James Washington (San Francisco: HarperSanFrancisco, 1986).

9. It is ironic that Arendt upholds Rustin's position as praiseworthy here, since in the context of her discussions of school integration Rustin's civil rights work would likely be subject to the same critiques she launches against Black parents and the NAACP.

10. *HALW* 419.

11. See Robin Wilson, "Past Their Prime: After 35 Years on Campuses, Black Studies Programs Struggle to Survive," *Chronicle of Higher Education* 51(33) (April 22, 2005):A9, http://chronicle.com/weekly/v51/i33/33a00901.htm. Rooks also mentions the 2002 remarks made by Harvard president Larry Summers, objecting to Cornel West's activism and scholarship. At the time the House majority leader, Dick Armey, "called African American programs 'pure junk' and labeled them all 'crib courses.'" See Rooks, *White Money/Black Power: The Surprising History of African American Studies and the Crisis of Race and Higher Education* (Boston: Beacon, 2006), 11.

12. I am borrowing this phrase from Benjamin Quarles, *The Negro in the Making of America*, 3rd ed. (New York: Touchstone, 1996), which explores the plights and contributions of Black people in America from 1619 through the 1980s.

13. Norton, "Heart of Darkness," 252.

14. Ibid., 248.

15. Judith Butler, "I Merely Belong to Them," *London Review of Books* 29(9) (May 10, 2007):26–28, http://www.lrb.co.uk/v29/n09/judith-butler/i-merely-belong-to-them.

16. Rooks, *White Money/Black Power*, 13. Of course, we should also note Ira Katznelson's *When Affirmative Action Was White: An Untold History of Racial Inequality in Twentieth Century America* (New York: Norton, 2005).

17. Rooks, *White Money/Black Power*, 14.

18. Ibid., 15.

19. Fabio Rojas, *From Black Power to Black Studies: How a Radical Social Movement Became an Academic Discipline* (Baltimore: Johns Hopkins University Press, 2007), 22.

20. Martin Luther King Jr., "The Social Organization of Nonviolence" (1959), in *A Testament of Hope*.

21. King, *Where Do We Go from Here: Chaos or Community?* in *A Testament of Hope*, 569. In this essay King highlights the patterns of systematic violence against Black Americans in the United States. He explains that in a meeting of the Southern Christian Leadership Conference in Atlanta in the aftermath of the Meredith shooting, the executive staff agreed that "the march [initiated by Meredith] should continue in order to demonstrate to the nation and the world that Negroes would never again be intimidated by the *terror of extremist white violence*" (ibid., emphasis added). The evidence of the devaluation of Black life is buttressed by the killing of unarmed young Black men, like Trayvon Martin in 2012.

22. Rooks, *White Money/Black Power*, 24–25.

23. Ibid. See also Rojas, *From Black Power to Black Studies*, 24.

24. Rojas, *From Black Power to Black Studies*, 34. Rojas continues, "Despite these disagreements, a critical mass of students and intellectuals felt that black studies was worth fighting for" (ibid.).

25. *HALW* 415–416.

26. Ibid., 416.

27. Ibid., 417.

28. Rooks, *White Money/Black Power*, 20.

29. Ibid., 8

30. Ibid.

31. Arendt ignores or is unaware of the fact that the Black-white dichotomy was constructed and is still maintained by whites; it is not a Black invention.

32. This point is important because Arendt is acknowledging that there are "real grievances." She even goes so far as to assert (following Fogelson), "The riots are 'articulate protests against genuine grievances'" (*CR* 173–174). See Robert M. Fogelson, "Violence as Protest," in *Urban Riots: Violence and Social Change*, edited by Robert H. Connery (New York: Vintage, 1968).

33. For more on racism and ideology in Arendt, see "Race-Thinking before Racism" and "Ideology and Terror" in *The Origins of Totalitarianism* (New York: Harcourt Brace, 1966).

34. Arendt quotes from *To Establish Justice, to Insure Domestic Tranquility*, the final report of the National Commission on the Causes and Prevention of Violence (December 1969), page 99: "If the decision to break the law really turned on individual conscience, it is hard to see in the law how Dr. King is better off than Governor Ross Barnett, of Mississippi, who also believed deeply in his cause and was willing to go to jail" (*CR* 64).

35. In "Civil Disobedience" Arendt also argues that laws cannot bring social change: "The law can indeed stabilize and legalize change once it has occurred, but the change itself is always the result of extralegal action" (*CR* 80). She offers the example of the Fourteenth Amendment: "It was meant to translate into constitutional terms the change that had come about as a result of the Civil War. This change was not accepted by the Southern states, with the result that the provisions for racial equality were not enforced for roughly a hundred years" (81). This is an important recognition of the racial inequality in the United States that persisted long after the abolition of slavery. But the point Arendt is reinforcing is that social changes cannot be legislated, so she offers the example of the Fourteenth Amendment: "it was finally enforced by legal action of the Supreme Court, *but . . .* the plain fact is that the court chose to do so *only* when civil-rights movements that, as far as Southern laws were concerned, were clearly movements of civil disobedience had brought about a drastic change in [the] attitudes of both black and white citizens" (ibid., emphases added). Arendt's argument is that although the Supreme Court did enforce legal action, "not the law, but civil disobedience brought into [the] open the 'American dilemma' and, perhaps for the first time, forced upon the nation the recognition of the enormity of the crime, not just of slavery, but of chattel slavery—'unique among all such systems known to civilization'—the responsibility of which the people have inherited, together with so many blessings, from their forefathers" (ibid.; the internal quotation is from Stanley M. Elkins, *Slavery* [New York, 1959]).

Conclusion

1. Richard Bernstein has identified contradictions in Arendt's description of judgment in "Judging the Actor and the Spectator," in his *Philosophical Profiles: Essays in Pragmatic Mode* (Cambridge: Polity, 1986), 221–237. Meili Steele offers a comparative analysis of Arendt and El-

lison on the issue of judgment and language in "Arendt versus Ellison on Little Rock: The Role of Language in Political Judgment," *Constellations* 9(2) (2002):184–206.

2. Arendt discusses communication (or communicability) in relationship to critical thinking in *Lectures on Kant's Political Philosophy,* edited by Ronald Beiner (Chicago: University of Chicago Press, 1992): "Now communicability obviously implies a community of men who can be addressed and who are listening and can be listened to" (*LKPP* 40).

3. Arendt also states, "Judging is one, if not the most important activity in which sharing-the-world-with-others comes to pass" (*BPF* 221).

4. Arendt connects judgment to impartiality in the Kant lectures: "You see that impartiality is obtained by taking the viewpoints of others into account; impartiality is not the result of some higher standpoint that would then actually settle the dispute by being altogether above the melée [*sic*]" (*LKPP* 42).

5. In the Kant lectures Arendt states, "The 'enlargement of the mind' plays a crucial role in the *Critique of Judgment.* It is accomplished by comparing our judgment with the possible rather than the actual judgments of others, and by putting ourselves in the place of any other man" (ibid., 43). The ability to make present that which is absent, or the faculty of having present what is absent, is imagination (65, 79).

6. Again, there is elaboration in the Kant lectures where Arendt discusses judgment in relationship to critical thinking and impartiality: "The trick of critical thinking does not consist in an enormously enlarged empathy through which one can know what actually goes on in the mind of all others" (ibid., 43). Enlarged thought is about disregarding private interest and self-interest, which are limiting (ibid.).

7. Using the notion of "misrecognition" rather than misrepresentation, Melissa V. Harris-Perry argues, "To be fair, a system must offer equal opportunities for public recognition, and groups cannot systematically suffer from misrecognition in the form of stereotype and stigma" (*Sister Citizen: Shame, Stereotypes, and Black Women in America: For Colored Girls Who've Considered Politics when Being Strong Isn't Enough* [New Haven, CT: Yale University Press, 2011], 37). Moving from social contract theory to an explicit examination of Arendt's public-private analysis, Harris-Perry goes on to argue:

> The problem for marginal and stigmatized group members should be obvious. These citizens face fundamental and continuing threats to their opportunity for accurate recognition. Individuals denied access to the public realm or whose group membership limits their social possibilities cannot be accurately recognized. An individual who is seen primarily as a part of a despised group loses the opportunity to experience the public recognition for which the human self strives. Further, if the group itself is misunderstood, then to the extent that one is seen as part of that group, that 'seeing' is inaccurate. Inaccurate recognition is painful not only to the psyche but also to the political self, the citizen self. (38)

8. Anne Norton, "Heart of Darkness: Africa and African Americans in the Writings of Hannah Arendt," in *Feminist Interpretations of Hannah Arendt,* edited by Bonnie Honig (University Park: Penn State University Press, 1995), 248. Likewise, Robert Bernasconi states, "Arendt's expression of 'sympathy for the cause of the Negroes, as for all oppressed or underprivileged peoples' (RLR 46) was, *on her own terms,* of no value, because as is clear from *On Revolution,* she regarded such feelings as politically irrelevant and any intervention of them into politics as almost certainly disastrous" ("The Double Face of the Political and the Social: Hannah Arendt and America's Racial Divisions," *Research in Phenomenology* 26 [1996]:16).

Index

KATHRYN T. GINES is Assistant Professor of Philosophy at Pennsylvania State University and is founding Director of the Collegium of Black Women Philosophers and Director of Cultivating Underrepresented Students in Philosophy. She is a founding editor of the new journal *Critical Philosophy of Race* and she is editor (with Maria del Guadalupe Davidson and Donna-Dale L. Marcano) of *Convergences: Black Feminism and Continental Philosophy.*

CPSIA information can be obtained at www.ICGtesting.com
Printed in the USA
LVOW12s2258060414

380585LV00001B/250/P